THE MISGUIDED SEARCH FOR THE POLITICAL

For Maisie (again), Freddie and Solomon

THE MISGUIDED SEARCH FOR THE POLITICAL

Social Weightlessness in
Radical Democratic Theory

Lois McNay

polity

Copyright © Lois McNay 2014

The right of Lois McNay to be identified as Author of this Work has been asserted in accordance with the UK Copyright, Designs and Patents Act 1988.

First published in 2014 by Polity Press

Polity Press
65 Bridge Street
Cambridge CB2 1UR, UK

Polity Press
350 Main Street
Malden, MA 02148, USA

All rights reserved. Except for the quotation of short passages for the purpose of criticism and review, no part of this publication may be reproduced, stored in a retrieval system, or transmitted, in any form or by any means, electronic, mechanical, photocopying, recording or otherwise, without the prior permission of the publisher.

ISBN-13: 978-0-7456-6262-6
ISBN-13: 978-0-7456-6263-3 (pb)

A catalogue record for this book is available from the British Library.

Typeset in 10.5 on 12 pt Palatino by
Servis Filmsetting Ltd, Stockport, Cheshire
Printed and bound in Great Britain by
T.J. International Ltd, Padstow, Cornwall

Every effort has been made to trace all copyright holders, but if any have been inadvertently overlooked the publisher will be pleased to include any necessary credits in any subsequent reprint or edition.

For further information on Polity, visit our website: www.politybooks.com

Contents

Acknowledgements		vi
	Introduction	1
1	Suffering and Social Weightlessness	28
2	The Unbearable Lightness of Theory: Mouffe's Dissociative Agonism	67
3	Freedom beyond the Subject: Feminism, Agency and Agonism	98
4	All or Nothing: Rancière's Ruptural Agonism	132
5	Pluralism and Practice: The Existential Agonism of Connolly and Tully	168
	Conclusion: Political Theory as Critique: Reconsidering the Negative	207
Notes		220
References		226
Index		241

Acknowledgements

A shorter version of chapter 2 first appeared as 'The Unbearable Lightness of Theory: Social Weightlessness in Mouffe's Radical Democracy', in Sumi Madhok, Anne Phillips and Kalpana Wilson (eds) *Gender, Agency and Coercion* (London: Palgrave Macmillan, 2013). A shorter version of chapter 3 first appeared as 'Feminism and Post-Identity Politics: The Problem of Agency', *Constellations* 17 (4) (2010), 512–25.

I am extremely grateful to Michael Freeden and Mark Philp for taking the time to read and comment on sections of the manuscript. I would also like to thank Mark Philp and Marc Stears for the snatched conversations, in and around our co-teaching of the M.Phil. Political Theory class in the Department of Politics at Oxford University, that proved to be both stimulating and valuable in clarifying my thoughts on various matters. John Thompson first identified the potential for this book in a paper I gave at a symposium in Cambridge in 2011, encouraged me to write it and came up with the title – for this I am most appreciative. The copyeditor, Justin Dyer, introduced greater lucidity into my prose with his helpful suggestions. I am grateful to Frances Corner for the enthusiastic interest she has shown in the project, especially when mine was sometimes waning. I would like to thank Michael McNay for his advice on various cover options. Above all, I am indebted, as ever, to Marian McNay and Murray Hunt, without whose support I could not have managed.

Introduction

If Benjamin said that history had hitherto been written from the standpoint of the victor, and needed to be written from that of the vanquished, we might add that knowledge must indeed present the fatally rectilinear succession of victory and defeat, but should also address itself to those things which were not embraced by this dynamic, which fell by the wayside – what might be called the waste products and blind spots that have escaped the dialectic. It is in the nature of the defeated to appear, in their impotence, irrelevant, eccentric, derisory. ... Theory must needs deal with cross-grained, opaque, unassimilated material, which as such admittedly has an anachronistic quality, but is not wholly obsolete since it has outwitted the historical dynamic.

(Adorno 2005: 151)

THE RISE OF THE POLITICAL

Since at least the 1990s, normative theory, of all stripes, has taken a distinctly abstract turn in so far as it has been very much concerned with identifying the quintessential principles that shape political life and, on that basis, formulating abstract models of democracy. The present moment abounds with diverse and competing models of democracy: there are the numerous accounts of deliberative and cosmopolitan democracy derived from the work of John Rawls and Jürgen Habermas, the various ideas of agonist democracy taken from Hannah Arendt, Carl Schmitt and Michel Foucault, left Heideggerian theories of democracy-to-come and Deleuzian accounts of democracy as becoming, to name but a few. This preoccupation with purified political dynamics and democratic principles might appear on the face of it to be unremarkable, for what else should the task of theory be but to sketch out, in the abstract, the outline of more desirable forms of social organization? While this might capture the ends of democratic theory in the most general sense, there is, nonetheless, something distinctive about the contemporary mode of thinking about the political which relates to its peculiarly abstract and free-floating nature. Its transcendental cast becomes evident if it is compared, say, to political theory in the 1960s, 1970s and 1980s, which was more closely tied to a social scientific agenda and whose theoretical concerns were driven by debates on issues such as the decline of class, the rise of pluralism, state legitimacy, and so on. Political theory nowadays has pulled away from the social sciences and has established itself as a separate, even ascendant, form of inquiry, namely a philosophy of politics whose fundamental task is, in the first instance, to isolate and capture the very essence of political being. It is this interest, then, in conceptualizing the political as an autonomous realm with its own intrinsic logic that constitutes the distinctiveness of the current moment in democratic theory. By thinking about the political in isolation from other areas of social life, and by identifying its inherent features – those all-encompassing qualities that are capable of transforming any given thing from a 'mere thing' to a 'political thing' – theorists hold that the democratic imagination can be renewed and transformed: 'Political imagination ... could be restored to its former power and dignity by an authentic political philosophy which would present, or rather discover, the sole and all-embracing concept of the political' (Heller 1991: 330).

There are a variety of reasons for this resurgent interest in the autonomous dynamics of political life. In terms of intellectual influences, the ideas of Rawls, Arendt and Schmitt have been notable catalysts in the disengagement of political theory from a social scientific agenda and in engendering a certain transcendental way of thinking about the constitutive features of democratic existence. The influence of Rawls' notion of justice as fairness on egalitarian liberal theory can hardly be over-estimated: ours is a moment where the majority of political theorists are engaged in producing some kind of comprehensive account of a just society either with or against Rawls. The resurgent interest in the work of Arendt and Schmitt has also been influential in the rise of ideas of the political, especially for a certain type of radical democratic theory. Their basic idea that, in so far as it represents the essence of human freedom and sociality, an autonomous sphere of the political must be kept apart from the mundane, instrumental concerns of social life has resonated with contemporary worries about widespread depoliticization. Asserting the primacy and all-encompassing nature of the political is seen as part of an effective response to the depoliticizing social tendencies that have been unleashed by a resurgent, globalized capitalism and that are best dealt with from within a more universal democratic frame. It is also seen as the most compelling way of moving beyond the limiting preoccupation of a previous phase of democratic theory with pluralism and the politics of identity, issues which are often held to terminate in the dead-end of ethical relativism. The 'new' recuperative spirit of neoliberal capitalism has forced democratic theorists to reconsider the thrust of categories and ideas that they had previously considered to be progressive but, in fact, now regard as complicit with the pernicious dynamics of increasingly marketized social relations (e.g. Boltanski and Chiapello 2007; Fraser 2009). The capacity of neoliberal capitalism to neutralize challenging activities by transforming them into opportunities for consumerism has necessitated a wholesale rethinking of the political and associated forms of democratic collective agency. In short, the 'obsession with the exclusively political' is bound up with a more general historical and paradigmatic crisis, where old conceptual frameworks are held to be in need of radical rethinking in the light of rapidly changing social contexts (Heller 1991: 336). To quote Philippe Lacoue-Labarthe and Jean-Luc Nancy: 'With the collapse of certainties, with the deterioration of their foundations and the effacement of their horizons, it became possible – even necessary and urgent – to resume the question of what had been called "the essence of the political"' (1997: 144).

It goes without saying that underlying this common concern with identifying the essence of the political, there is little agreement amongst democratic theorists about the best way of going about this task, about what might constitute the most convincing methods, approaches and ideas. Despite such divergences, what they share nonetheless is the catalysing insight that some kind of withdrawal from the complexities and messiness of the social realm is vital in order to reflect properly on the independent political dynamics that form the grounds of a robust theory of democracy. The political realm does not take its essential shape from underlying social dynamics and interests which it relatively passively reflects and transmits into the democratic arena. Rather, the political is accorded its own distinct logic that not only renders it autonomous but also gives it primacy over other social realms. The rise of the political can be said therefore to be accompanied by a corresponding retreat from the social, although this retreat is not intended to be permanent; it is not, as Ian Shapiro (2007) would have it, a one-way 'flight from reality' into abstraction. Instead, it is meant to be a strategic theoretical manoeuvre, a temporary bracketing of social life, that enables the clearer identification of constant political dynamics and principles within the flux of daily existence, and consequently of possibilities for progressive democratic change.

There is no doubt that this transcendental mode of reflection on the political has breathed new life into democratic theory. Agnes Heller goes so far as to claim that it came to the rescue of political philosophy and saved it 'after it had fallen victim to too much science, too much compromise, too much realism' (1991: 336). But it also has some troubling entailments for democratic theory, and the central argument of this book is that, in some cases, it is a misguided move tending towards what Pierre Bourdieu (2000) has called a 'socially weightless' mode of thought. Bourdieu uses the term 'social weightlessness' to denote an abstract way of thinking about the world that is so far removed from the actual practices and dynamics of everyday life that, ultimately, its own analytical relevance and normative validity are thrown into question. To be clear, this is not an argument against abstraction per se. It is an inescapable and crucial element of political theorizing to 'abstract' from the complexities and flux of ordinary life in order to highlight generalities and tendencies that can be used to underpin the formulation of democratic principles and procedures. There are, however, different ways of going about this task of abstraction, and I argue that some are more plausible than others, and that, in some cases, abstraction goes awry and what was originally intended as a strategic and temporary retreat from the social becomes a more lasting withdrawal into a reified and self-referential model of the political. Abstraction might be unavoidable but, in the context of democratic theory, it must somehow or another be linked to thought about what can be changed in our collective ways of being if it is not to become what Sheldon Wolin (2000) has termed a 'theoretic theory' rather than a genuinely political one. If thought is to be politically effective, in other words, it must be conducted in the same directions as the tendencies of the world, not at a great remove from them (Bourdieu 2000). It is my claim that some types of democratic theory have become so enmeshed in a style of abstract and closed reasoning about the political that their relevance to the phenomenal social world and to the logic of embodied action is cast into doubt along with, ultimately, their purportedly progressive political implications. For such democratic theories, it might be more productive to relinquish the misguided desire to rescue purified models of the political from what Arendt (1999) famously called the 'social question' and, instead, to do more or less the opposite, namely situate ideas of the political more securely within an account of the social world that subtends it.

ABSTRACTION, IDEALIZATION, ONTOLOGY

From what has been said so far, it might seem that an obvious target for the criticism of social weightlessness is the analytical liberalism, associated with the work of Rawls and others, that is currently so dominant in the discipline of political theory. On the face of it, a critique such as mine concerned above all with the troubling entailments of abstraction for democratic theory seems to fall clearly on one side of the burgeoning debate on ideal versus real theory. But, in fact, so-called 'ideal theory' is not the focus of this book's discussion. A reason why this is so is the straightforward one that there are already many discussions about the merits and limitations of an approach that begins with the premise of the fact independence of moral principles and understands its primary task as supplying, in as rigorous and detailed a manner as possible, the normative content of democratic orders. Another reason why I do not focus on this type of democratic theory is that, although it might initially appear to be vulnerable to the criticism of social weightlessness given the counterfactual nature of much of its reasoning, this is not in fact the case. The postulation by analytical democrats of the necessarily free-standing nature of normative thought (although they differ considerably over the nature and extent of this fact independence) pre-empts the criticism of social weightlessness, rendering it, in a sense, redundant. On their view, reflection on democratic moral principles should indeed be without social weight in as much as it expresses a logic that is as objective as possible, that is, unclouded by the concerns of daily social existence. Whatever one may think about the intellectual plausibility of such a method, the kind of issues raised in the critique of social weightlessness about the actual tendencies of the world, about power and asymmetrical social relations, leave many analytical liberals relatively untroubled because they do not regard these as pertaining to the realm of the ideal thought in the first place. Instead they belong to the realm of the 'real', which is, in their view, the proper concern of sociologists, politicians and policy makers but not of political philosophers (e.g. Swift and White 2008). In short, given the intellectual terms in which ideal theorists operate, it is not possible to conduct the type of immanent critique that I am interested in pursuing here with the notion of social weightlessness. To criticize thinkers of ignoring hierarchical relations of power and domination when they explicitly state that they are not interested in such issues in the first instance is, at least from their perspective, no criticism at all.

The focus of my discussion of social weightlessness is instead radical democratic theory and, in particular, those types that could be loosely classified as agonist in nature. Unlike analytical theorists, thinkers of radical democracy (and others) do not subscribe to such a clear-cut separation of the real from the ideal; indeed, many would regard it as a false antithesis that simplifies the complex, dialogic relationship between normative political thought and the social world it addresses. Radical democrats maintain, in one way or another, that thought about emancipatory norms cannot be disconnected from an account of existing social inequalities, either with regard to the kind of presuppositions upon which it rests or with regard to its potential political entailments. One of the distinguishing features of this dialectical way of thinking is that it pushes against the formal models of democracy that ensue from the severing of political ideals from the underlying context of power. From this perspective, what are presented as impartial procedures and universal norms often turn out to be unexamined generalizations of the interests and *modus vivendi* of dominant groups. Formal models of democracy lead too easily to what Bourdieu has described as 'a fictitious universalism' where 'to grant "humanity" to all, but in a purely formal way, is to exclude from it, under an appearance of humanism, all those who are deprived of the means of realizing it' (2000: 65). Thus, for radical democrats, an essential feature of political theorizing is not so much its internal logical rigour but the extent to which it is tied to and furthers a critique of power.

What is meant, though, by the critique of power varies according to what type of radical democratic theory is in question. Radical realist thinkers, such as Raymond Geuss, for instance, would emphasize above all the institutional circumstances that form the inevitable context of political activity. Such a perspective results in a vision of politics as the instrumental pursuit of power, as involving conflict and struggle and as the imposition of authority using a variety of means, some more legitimate than others. Democratic theory that does not take into account the ineluctable context of power is, on this view, at best naïve and, at worst, dangerous in its disregard of the actuality of political life. In contrast, the critique of power in a post-Habermasian tradition of Critical Theory stresses that political theory should constantly scrutinize and reformulate its presuppositions and proposals in the light of what existing inequalities and political struggles may tell us about their progressive potential, or lack of it. On this view, political theorizing forms part of a larger interdisciplinary project where dialogue with other types of inquiry – such as social and cultural theory – engenders an enlarged understanding of the world and also a heightened awareness of one's own theoretical and methodological presuppositions. Other types of democratic theory, for example Chantal Mouffe's idea of agonism, maintain that the relational logic around which democratic identities are created and maintained necessarily involves the exclusion of certain groups as the political enemy or Other. It is the job of the radical democrat to challenge this exclusionary logic, in so far as it reinforces unjustifiable social hierarchies, and to suggest instead other egalitarian forms of collective identity around which citizen loyalty can be focused. Finally, for proponents of the genealogical approach to politics, such as James Tully, the critique of power entails an awareness of the act of theorizing itself as a practical intervention on the part of the oppressed in their struggles for freedom. The democratic theorist does not stand above citizen struggle reflecting dispassionately on its outcomes, but participates directly in it. It behoves her, therefore, to be as mindful as possible of the strategic outcomes of her partisan intervention within the field. In one way or another, then, despite significant variation in their understanding of the nature of politics, radical democrats emphasize the intrinsic connection that exists between the theoretical enterprise and the critique of power.

Differently put, radical democratic theory must build into itself, in some way or another, a responsiveness to the asymmetrical social relations from which it arises and which form the basis of many of its presuppositions as well as its normative proposals. Nancy Fraser's description of the guiding principle of Critical Theory can stand, *ceteris paribus*, as the distinguishing feature of radical democratic theory more generally, namely to produce an account of society that has the practical aim of unmasking domination and, in doing so, revealing possible paths to emancipation: 'to conceptualize society in a way that [makes] visible its historical fault lines, revealing the contradictions and emancipatory potentials that mark a given time and place' (Fraser and Naple 2004: 1107). Ironically, however, it is precisely this claim about its intrinsic connection to the critique of power that renders radical democratic theory vulnerable to the criticism of social weightlessness. To accuse analytical liberals of social weightlessness is, in some sense, to talk past them, given that their concern is explicitly not with examining social inequalities but rather with producing logically robust normative proposals. Radical democrats do not subscribe to the free-standing nature of normative political thought, and that is why the criticism of social weightlessness has critical bite in relation to their work. To make such a criticism is to imply that they are failing to realize their own stated aim of challenging settled political orthodoxies in the name of excluded and oppressed groups and are instead falling back into precisely the type of political formalism that it appears they explicitly reject.

If the charge of social weightlessness refers to the dangers of excessively abstract modes of thought with regard to an account of power, then more needs to be said about the nature of the problem given that abstraction is an inescapable, indeed constitutive, feature of political theory. To do this, it is helpful to turn in the first instance to Onora O'Neill's criticism of the deployment of idealized abstractions in normative political theory. O'Neill observes that the difficulty with so-called 'ideal' political theory is not that it abstracts away from the underlying social context, with the consequence, as ethical particularists maintain, that it substitutes simplified universal norms for the more complex reality of situated moral practices. Abstraction in a straightforward sense is not where the problem lies because it involves the bracketing, but crucially not the denying, of predicates that are true of the matter under discussion. In this respect, abstraction is a fundamental aspect of most forms of reasoning, including even the most contextually sensitive ethical thought, which itself necessarily highlights certain features of moral practice at the expense of others in order to ground its claims. The merit of abstraction in this strict sense is that it 'never arbitrarily augments a given starting point, so will not lead one validly from a truth to a falsehood' (O'Neill 1996: 40). The real problem with ideal theory, in O'Neill's view, is the way in which its abstractions are tacitly idealized, or augmented in such a manner that they deny certain predicates and, as a consequence, may easily lead to falsehood: 'An assumption, and derivatively a theory, idealizes when it ascribes predicates – often seen as enhanced, "ideal" predicates – that are false of the case in hand, and so denies predicates that are true of that case' (O'Neill 1996: 41). For example, the assumption that individuals have the capacity for rational choice, or self-sufficiency or independence from others, is an idealized abstraction with potentially misleading consequences when it is evident that many or even most individuals do not display such attributes in their daily lives. Theories of justice that start from such unvindicated idealizations of personhood are problematic because, in denying the non-rational, vulnerable and dependent aspects of personhood, they finish in principles that are inapplicable to most cases 'where they are not satisified' (O'Neill 1996: 41). Similar difficulties have been identified with the idealizing assumptions of full compliance and the lexical ordering of principles (e.g. Farrelly 2007).

Extrapolating from O'Neill's discussion, Charles W. Mills argues that it is important to distinguish between different types of ideal theorizing. There is ideal theory in the sense of a schematized model of the essential features or workings of an actual thing and there is ideal theory in a second sense of creating idealized models of how something should or ought to work. The first type is reconstructive in nature, a descriptive model that resembles Weber's notion of the ideal type, based on simplifying assumptions that highlight certain essential features of the phenomenon under consideration. Like O'Neill's idea of straightforward abstraction, Mills regards such reconstructive ideals as a constitutive element of systematic reasoning. The difficulties lie for Mills with the second type of ideal theory, based in an idealizing mode of reasoning, because, in its preoccupation with how things ought to be, it disregards the systematic workings of how things are in actuality. When the actual is not some straightforward, predictable mechanical problem (like a vacuum cleaner that is not working in the way it should) but the complex and changeable realm of human action, then the separation of idealized forms from their actual instantiation becomes potentially problematic. The central flaw of so-called 'ideal' political theory is not its use of ideals per se, since 'non-ideal' theory will also invoke ideals and norms, although the structure of this normativity will vary. Rather, the problem lies for Mills with its downgrading of the actual vis-à-vis idealized constructions: 'What distinguishes ideal theory is the reliance on idealization to the exclusion, or at least marginalization, of the actual' (2005: 168). Ideal theory is underpinned by a disregard for the given either in as much as it thinks that the latter is not worth theorizing in its own right or because it thinks that the best way of understanding democratic change is through idealized assumptions. Thus, for instance, it abstracts away from structural relations of domination, oppression and exploitation that are a constitutive feature of many individuals' lives and instead relies on an idealized social ontology – the formal, undifferentiated equality of atomized individuals typical of the contract model. In treating oppression as a deviation from the norm rather than as intrinsic to capitalist social relations, its lived reality is downgraded and effectively ignored. A corollary of idealized social ontology is the attribution to persons of idealized capacities, both psychological and cognitive (rationality, autonomy, etc.). This, too, compounds the neglect of actuality in so far as there is a failure to appreciate the effects of oppression upon embodied being, the way in which inequalities shape, hinder and distort the realization of certain capacities and dispositions often in line with an agent's social location. As Mills puts it, 'A general social transparency will be presumed, with cognitive obstacles minimized as limited to biases of self-interest or the intrinsic difficulties of understanding the world, and little or no attention paid to the distinctive role of hegemonic ideologies and group-specific experience in distorting our perceptions and conceptions of the social order' (2005: 169).

The central problem, then, with ideal theory is not abstraction per se, but rather its reliance on idealized abstractions that treat inequality, domination, and so forth, as anomalies or deviations from a hypothetical norm. Such sanitized abstractions are therefore deficient, a 'distortional complex of ideas, values, norms, and beliefs' (Mills 2005: 172) that ignores the constitutive significance of asymmetrical power relations in determining social reality. Ideal theory, from this view, is an ideology which, like many ideologies, tacitly universalizes the world-view and experience of a privileged group and marginalizes the perspective of other groups which, *inter alia*, might reveal different aspects of reality. Clearly, ideal theory is ideological not in a conspiratorial sense, but rather in an unintentional, unreflective sense, namely that it fails to scrutinize sufficiently the extent to which its premises are in fact extrapolations from 'a non-representative phenomenological life-world (mis)taken for *the* world', and reinforced by 'the absence of any countervailing group interest that would motivate dissatisfaction with dominant paradigms and a resulting search for better alternatives' (Mills 2005: 172). Mills concludes that starting with idealized premises is a wrong-headed way of going about the job of normative political theorizing because, in abstracting away from crucial realities of the world, it terminates in principles that have little purchase on existing injustices and major inequalities of gender, race and class. Indeed, so-called 'non-ideal' theorists, such as feminists and race theorists, have always been sceptical of idealized assertions of political equality, and so forth, on the grounds that, despite the formal universality, their neglect of crucial underlying social realities results in tacit conceptual biases and exclusions:

> If it were obvious that women were equal moral persons, meant to be fully included in the variable 'men,' then why was it not obvious to virtually every male political philosopher and ethicist up to a few decades ago? Why has liberalism, supposedly committed to normative equality and a foundational opposition to ascriptive hierarchy, found it so easy to exclude women and nonwhites from its egalitarian promise? (Mills 2005: 178)

In the first instance, then, for Mills, the task of normative theorizing would be better served not through the strategy of idealization but through abstractions grounded in a reconstruction of the fundamental inequalities that structure social existence.

Clearly, idealization is not the cause of social weightlessness in radical democratic theory. Radical democrats would agree with sceptical assessments of the value of idealizing abstraction as a method for emancipatory thought and would strongly endorse the idea that political norms should be linked more securely to an examination of the crucial social reality of inequality. The problem in their case, then, is one of ontology. The over-reliance by radical democrats on a certain ontological way of thinking about the political results in a not dissimilar disregard of the actual to the one described above and that undercuts their purported central concern with the critique of power. In the final analysis, the failure to attend sufficiently to certain crucial features of social reality, particularly the lived experience of inequality, has troubling implications for the emancipatory import of their theories. The ontological turn taken by radical democrats has been widely noted and described in various terms as weak versus strong ontologies, ontologies of abundance versus ontologies of lack, negative versus positive ontologies, and so on (e.g. Connolly and Strathausen 2009; Tønder and Thomassen 2006a; White 2000). At the most general level, the ontological turn represents the leftist version of the widespread preoccupation amongst democratic theorists with capturing the essence of political being, defining its sovereign and autonomous logic and, on that basis, formulating comprehensive models of democracy. For radical democrats, the use of political ontologies is seen as a promising way of thinking about transformative political change beyond the problematic alternatives of prioritarian reasoning, on the one side, and uncritical ethical relativism, on the other. Indeed, in their view, it is precisely the failure to understand the political in its ontological dimension that is the root cause of what is seen as a widespread inability to think about politics in a genuinely radical way (Mouffe 2006: 8). To this end, many radical democrats frequently deploy some kind of distinction between the 'ontological' and the 'ontic' or the 'political' and 'politics', to expand our understanding of the world and the way it may be changed. The problem, however, with this theoretical strategy is that there is frequently a kind of ontological reduction upwards where social being is interpreted exclusively through certain supposedly foundational political dynamics and thereby denied specificity and autonomous significance. Clearly, to some degree or another, ontological reflection is an unavoidable aspect of political thinking in so far as the latter is always grounded, explicitly or implicitly, in certain presuppositions about fundamental features of social reality and human agency. Without such suppositions, 'democratic theory would simply fail to sustain critical reflection about its core commitments and would remain unguarded against the various attempts at entrenching or reviving the spectre of an essentially closed world' (Kioupkiolis 2011: 692). The problem is that radical democrats frequently fail then to make the next theoretical move, namely to think through how these ontological political dynamics are played out in the social realm and, in particular, in asymmetrical relations of power. The ideas of emancipatory action that are derived from this style of reasoning are conceptually lopsided – in so far as they fail to go beyond a persistent reiteration of supposedly essential political dynamics and consequently have little sense of how these connect to embodied social existence and to issues of oppression and disempowerment that supposedly lie at the heart of the radical democratic agenda.

For a number of radical democrats, the thought of Arendt and Schmitt has been extremely influential in developing these political ontologies. It hardly needs restating that, for both thinkers, the assertion of an autonomous realm of political action that is sovereign over other social realms is inseparable from the critique of liberal democracy. Schmitt's depiction of political being in terms of a warrior ethic of struggle and the assertion of power emerges from his scorn for the pusillanimity of inter-war liberal democracy, which, in his view, dissipated strong and decisive leadership in favour of endless deliberation. Famously, Arendt's understanding of the political as the paramount site of creative collective action was an attempt to rescue democracy from the depoliticized administration of social affairs into which it had descended in modernity and to reinvest it with the egalitarian potential that it had, in her view, for the Ancients. For both Arendt and Schmitt, reflection on the political reveals what it means to be human: that is, the capacity to act autonomously and to shape the world according to one's ends.

As such, the sphere of the political expresses the core of human freedom and has primacy over all other spheres of social action.

It is this insight of Arendt and Schmitt into the fundamentally open-ended and creative nature of political freedom that radical democrats generalize as the key feature of their political ontologies, namely a thorough-going anti-foundationalism. Reflection on the essential dynamics of the political does not reveal certain or determining principles; rather, it exposes the fundamental groundlessness of social existence and the potentially limitless ways in which it may be shaped. Social being has no necessary form; it is only through numerous endless political endeavours to shape the world in one way or another that it acquires stability and significance. But it is also in the political realm, in virtue of it being the site of struggle and contestation, that stability and meaning are undone and reconstituted along new lines. Reflection on the nature of the political reveals the radical contingency of social existence and this, in turn, opens up accounts of democracy to the ever-present possibility of challenge and change, that things could always be otherwise. Just as it did for Arendt and Schmitt, political ontology seems to offer radical democrats a powerful way of questioning the orthodoxies and apparent inevitabilities of a given social order and of imagining the radical reshaping of the world. Schmitt, of course, was interested not in revealing new possibilities for democracy but rather in restoring authoritarian state power. Whilst Arendt's idea of natality offers a renewed sense of the inaugural potential of collective action, it is strictly demarcated from the domain of social necessity that she regards as, by its very nature, unamenable to political transformation. The political ontologies of contemporary theory differ in that they explicitly deconstruct fixed boundaries between the social and the political in order to uncover unnoticed types of inequality and domination and consequently to open up new avenues of transformative democratic change. Such a questioning of the given is crucial to going beyond settled ways of thinking about the world and to the exploration of new grounds for radical democratic practice. This deconstruction of the given means, for instance, that, unlike other normative theorists, radical democrats don't have to ground their theories of democracy by appeals to pre-given interests or inevitable dynamics of human nature (e.g. rational individualism) but instead can conjure a more radical vision of how the world could be if it were reconstructed along more egalitarian lines.

It is in the light of this concern with emancipatory social change that radical democrats claim that their political ontologies are not free-floating abstractions untethered from any understanding of social reality but are, in fact, tightly bound to the critique of power. They are not pure abstractions which definitively bracket off the real because the political is represented as emerging from a necessary but impossible relation between the empirical and the trans-historical, the concrete and the universal. This relation is fundamentally circular in as much as the transcendental dynamics of the political are only ever realized in contingent, historical constellations, but these determinate historical circumstances can never give full access to the principle of radical contingency that the political represents (see Marchart 2007: 30–1). The attempt to access the essence of the political is viewed, therefore, not as a retreat from concrete issues of power and inequality into pure abstraction but rather as its opposite. The moment of transcendence is intended to sharpen an attentiveness to the often obscured injustices that underpin any democratic order and to heighten awareness of the repressed potential in daily existence for other, potentially more emancipated ways of living. In sum, these leftist formulations of the political are not frozen abstractions but characterized by a circular movement away from power in order to better understand power and to challenge its existing, unjust forms.

I argue, however, that, despite their assertions otherwise, radical democrats often fail to sustain their claim about the fundamental connection between ontology and the critique of power and, as a result, offer accounts of the political so rarefied that they close off the very issues of inequality and domination that are purportedly their central concern. In the end, this neglect of certain crucial social realities has troubling consequences for the emancipatory import of their ideas of action, which are mostly construed in terms of democratic agonism. The radical contingency revealed through reflection on the political leads to a privileging of a certain cluster of ideas to do with indeterminacy, flux, becoming, contestation, plurality, and so forth, which are then, in turn, used in a rather one-sided fashion to interpret social existence. Nonetheless, it does not follow from the claim of foundational contingency that social existence is straightforwardly amenable to challenge and transformation in the way that some of these accounts of agonist democracy suggest. Many aspects of social existence, particularly those related to structurally generated inequalities of class, race and gender, are deeply entrenched and systematically reproduced in a relatively predictable fashion. Many individuals, particularly those belonging to disempowered groups, do not experience their lives as an active process of becoming, nor do they regard their conditions of existence as open to struggle and transformation. The routinized, inert and experientially negative quality of subordination within these hierarchical social relations is too easily passed over by a radical democratic emphasis on the political as the site of indeterminacy, contestation, and becoming. Social relations of power are granted little specificity or significance other than as watered-down, empirical manifestations of foundational political dynamics, which produces the socially weightless thinking of radical democrats. It results ultimately in a deep discontinuity between the ideas of agonist democratic change that they promulgate and the social conditions of existence of the very individuals that these transformative theories supposedly address.

The tendency to conceptualize political dynamics in isolation from social ones ultimately results in a tacit hierarchy of the former over the latter. The aim of radical democratic theorizing is, of course, to identify certain distinct properties of the political that form the grounds of a renewed account of democratic bonds and practices. At the same time, these political ontologies are not intended to be purified abstractions since radical democrats acknowledge that their logic only ever manifests itself in concrete social practices. The problem is that insufficient thought is given to the ways in which this quasi-transcendental logic is imbricated within concrete existence and this tacitly transforms what is supposed to be a circular relation between the social and political realms into a conceptual hierarchy where the latter is accorded an unexplained and unjustified priority over the former. The detachment of the realm of the political from its social conditions of possibility empties it of much content and vitiates its relevance to the everyday practices that sustain and renew it. It leaves radical democrats unable to address a series of issues about empowerment and participation that are crucial to their theory, such as how to mobilize individuals in the first place or why the 'political' should be the principal focus of citizen loyalty rather than any of the many other constitutive attachments and bonds of social life. In its disregard of social relations, this stark 'politicism' fails to do justice to the complexity of structural causation in capitalism and cannot therefore conceptualize 'dialectically entwined sources of power asymmetry in contemporary society' (Fraser 2008: 343). The correlate to this unvindicated primacy of the political is that the social realm comes to be regarded implicitly as an inert positivity, a realm devoid of intrinsic complexity or significance that Arendt famously described as 'the dark background of mere givenness' (quoted in Rancière 2004: 299). On this view, an apodictic radical force is held to reside inherently within abstract dynamics of undecidability and indeterminacy rather than being understood as a property of the interventions of embodied individuals in the world.

AGENCY

To overcome tendencies to social weightlessness, radical democratic theorists need to attend more carefully to the social conditions that may be necessary to render their ideas of political action feasible. There are, of course, many ways in which such a concern with underlying power relations could be elaborated, from issues of institutional design to practices of good governance and widening democratic participation (see Bader and Engelen 2003; Fung 2007; Shapiro 2007). The discussion of power in this book concentrates on the issue of embodied agency and adopts a general approach that the Critical Theorist Axel Honneth (2004) has described as social theoretical negativism and is linked to the view that normative claims should be advanced through a critique of existing social inequalities. Accordingly, my discussion of embodied agency is narrowly focused on negative experiences of subordination within hierarchical relations and the repercussions that these have on the capacity of individuals to act as autonomous political agents. For many individuals, a consequence of the lived reality of oppression is that they may acquire a deep-seated dispositional reluctance to act as agents of their own interests. The disempowering effects of prolonged inequality may mean that individuals do not feel able to shape their lives in ways that might overturn some of its more intolerable aspects. Often, it may be felt that the only option is to endure, to make the best of a bad situation. This is not to reduce individuals to passive victims without any agency, but it is to say that the kind of second-order agency implied in democratic theory, namely the ability autonomously to shape one's conditions of existence, is far from a straightforward issue. When asymmetrical relations of power are internalized, they may be realized as subjective feelings of powerlessness, despair or resignation. This transformation of objective structures of subordination into subjective dispositions is a much-noted feature of disempowerment and domination and is attested to in a wide range of studies that correlate levels of political participation with access to material and symbolic resources. Yet, although the connection between depoliticization and inequality is widely acknowledged, radical democratic theory often gives scant attention to the entailments this might have for its ideas of political action. In short it tends to presume political agency as an unproblematic given and as a result proffers rarefied ideas of action that, in some cases, have a tenuous connection with the lives of those on whose behalf it claims to speak.

Obviously, it is a necessary and fundamental starting point of any non-elitist democratic theory to presume the capacity for equal and universal agency. The irony is, however, that in presuming such equality, too often the result is that many of the barriers to political participation that face marginalized and powerless groups are not considered in sufficient depth. A number of thinkers have commented on this 'paradox of participation', namely that it promotes equal agency while simultaneously marginalizing the people it is designed to help. This paradox is, by definition, never fully surmountable; it is impossible to predict, from the perspective of a general theory of agency, all the possible barriers that prevent individuals acting as agents in their own interests. Nonetheless, this should not pre-empt the attempt to explore enduring, entrenched and therefore relatively predictable obstacles to political mobilization. Nor should this concern with political agency be viewed as a second-order question that pertains only to sociological issues of power and mobilization but does not really belong in first-order normative political thought. After all, democratic theory should be action-guiding in some way, as Raymond Guess points out: 'Political philosophy must recognise that politics is in the first instance about action and the contexts of action, not about mere beliefs or propositions' (2008: 11). If radical democratic theory is to take seriously this relevance to action and, by implication, progressive social transformation, then it inevitably throws into question the viability of reasoning through ontological claims. The initial focus on political ontology seems to be a misguided first step that sets theorists off on a path of socially weightless reflection from which it is difficult to return. Too often they do not even begin to address the social conditions necessary for effective agency and instead simply assume the existence of ready-made political subjects.

This failure to pursue issues of disempowerment and agency is related partly to the understandable desire to avoid being pulled back into a problematic discourse of suffering and victimhood which often seems to accompany studies of oppression. Consequently, to break with the politics of the wound, there has been a kind of anti-experiential turn on the part of some theorists, who encourage subjects to set aside their particularistic identity concerns in order to participate in a broader, political conversation oriented towards ideas of solidarity and the common good. Accordingly, the ideas that prevail focus less on oppression, inequality and barriers to participation and more on abstract notions of political community and action where individuals are assumed to be more or less equal and political participation is assured. The cost of this is that certain issues related to the lived experience of inequality are perhaps not addressed as directly as they should be. Equality is assumed as an 'unthematized condition of possibility' of political debate rather than being thought more exhaustively in terms of the effort required to 'realize equality in conditions of social inequality' (Deranty and Renaut 2008: 44). In short, political agency cannot, in my view, be assumed as an unproblematic given in the way that it currently is by so many democratic theorists. To move towards the broader concerns of a radical democratic politics in the first place, it is not enough to simply urge individuals to lay aside a politics of personal injustice without inquiring first into how the experience of inequality and suffering might impose deeply felt constraints upon their willingness to act politically

well, duh!

Ideas of language play a significant role in this move away from power because linguistic dynamics are seen as a particularly fruitful way of modelling foundational political relations. It is easy to see the attraction of language for thinking through progressive models of democracy: it provides an inclusive and universal framework for political participation whilst being sufficiently 'thin' to accommodate problems of deep difference. The difficulty is, however, that the modelling of democratic relations as linguistic ones may result in an occlusion of certain forms of power and inequality that do not conform to the logic of signification. Thus, a major cause of socially weightless thinking in radical democratic theory is what might be called, following Bourdieu (2000), the tendency to linguistic universalism, where the more entrenched and pathological effects of social asymmetries are neglected by being assimilated to relations of meaning. Agonist formulations of democratic agency, for instance, often take their cue from a relational linguistic perspective and are construed around open-ended dynamics of indeterminacy, contestation and becoming. There is a mismatch between this valorization of agency as an open and mutable demeanour towards the world and others and a demeanour, say, of vulnerability and entrapment that might accompany the experience of chronic deprivation. It is not clear how the former speaks to the latter; indeed, such an agonistic ethos may be profoundly alienating for those disempowered individuals who do not necessarily have the material and symbolic resources to negotiate such a *modus operandi* with confidence. It is not of course that there is no value to agonistic accounts of agency, but in order for them to sustain their avowed concern with the unmasking of domination, they need to be accompanied by a fuller understanding of certain crucial dynamics of oppression and inequality.

Another type of socially weightless thought emanates not from the attempt to conceptualize political relations through a linguistic paradigm but rather from the deployment of ontologies of plenitude and abundance to think through the limitless plurality and dynamism of social existence. On this view, the countless, unremarked-upon practices and 'games of freedom' that make up the daily lives of ordinary citizens provide the grounds for thinking about radical democratic agency. In principle, such a bottom-up approach pays more attention to the diverse and 'thick' logic of embodied existence, in both its negative and positive aspects, than the etiolated and determinist linguistic constructivism that characterizes other types of democratic agonism. Yet, ultimately because the foundational notion of social plurality and flux is not sufficiently anchored within an account of structural inequality, it also results in a one-sided, glamorized account of mobile agency that downplays the fixity and stultification – both objective and dispositional – that may accompany persistent deprivation and inequality.

To overcome such tendencies to social weightlessness, agency needs to be understood according to a logic of embodiment and power, and I draw primarily on Bourdieu's notion of habitus to do this. Bourdieu shares with radical democratic theory the insight that the unmasking and challenging of arbitrary social hierarchies is the fundamental task of progressive critique. He would reject, however, the abstraction of much of this theory as a form of scholastic naïvety that retreats from an examination of the way in which power hierarchies are inscribed upon the bodies of individuals and lived as a multiplicity of 'ordinary' violences that distort social existence. The idea of habitus offers, above all, a powerful account of the depoliticizing effects of symbolic violence, understood as the internalization of domination in such a way that individuals may feel that their suffering is inevitable or unavoidable and that nothing can be done to change it. In this respect, Bourdieu's work stands as a challenge to the pressure-cooker or 'big bang' models of agency that often tacitly inform radical democratic theory and where the assumption is that if repression is strong enough, the oppressed will eventually resist (e.g. Lazzeri 2012). From a Bourdieusian perspective, resistance is far from inevitable. The internalization of domination may affect the ability of individuals to construe their problems as political in the first place and, even when they do, their willingness to participate in corrective political action is far from assured. There are significant differences between recognizing injustice, identifying systemic domination and common interests, devising strategies for action and finally feeling able to mobilize and act collectively. One does not follow inevitably from another. Consequently, a phenomenological interrogation of embodied agency – or lack of agency – should include, *inter alia*, an interpretative element: it must explore individuals' own understanding of their situation in the world and hence their reasons for acting or not acting in the way that they do. Focusing on the embodied register of social experience in this way potentially highlights mundane types of social injustice and domination that have significance for the individual but are often overlooked by political theorists. A focus on embodied experience sheds light not only on the said, but also on the unsaid, on negative social experiences which may remain unarticulated as a distinct claim about injustice even though their pathological effects may be widespread. In short, an interpretative perspective may deliver a deeper understanding of the reasons why individuals might be unwilling or unable to participate politically in the manner that radical democratic theorists prescribe for them. These arguments are intended not as a wholesale refusal of theories of radical democracy, but rather as a way of extending and deepening some of their important, but conceptually under-developed insights. They do undoubtedly question, however, whether the turn to ontology is the most conducive way of thinking about transformative agency and change and suggest instead that a phenomenally oriented disclosing critique might be a more fruitful approach.

NEGATIVE EXPERIENCE AND CRITIQUE

The intertwinement of body and power that informs Bourdieu's notion of habitus allows him to formulate an account of negative social experience or 'social suffering' that avoids psychological reduction. Along with the work of Axel Honneth in this area, I take up the idea of social suffering in order to exemplify the kind of insights that may be delivered by social theoretical critique. A key feature of all Bourdieu's phenomenological categories, including that of social suffering, is that embodied experience is profoundly shaped by social location. It is this immanent connection between embodied being and social position that rescues the Bourdieusian idea of suffering from the problems of subjectivism and moralism that thinkers such as Nancy Fraser find so troubling about other 'free-floating' formulations of injurious social experience. Social suffering is not a general existential or psychological category, for Bourdieu, but a socio-centric one that foregrounds the work of power. It is undoubtedly the case that all individuals suffer by virtue of their essential vulnerability and the finitude of the human condition, but social suffering is not something that afflicts all individuals equally. Social suffering is a politicized category in so far as it highlights the intrinsic connection between experiences of misery and deprivation and structural inequality. Of particular interest is the causal connection Bourdieu posits between the emergence of a distinctive new type of suffering and changing conditions of existence in neoliberal societies. Tendencies towards individualization and fragmentation that have been unleashed by a marketization of societal relations have created, in his view, pernicious new forms of social precariousness and marginality as well as intensifying existing inequalities of wealth. Social suffering denotes a phenomenal substrate of misery that, because it is largely unarticulated, falls below the register of democratic theorizing but is central to an explanation of widespread dynamics of uncertainty, disempowerment and injustice in contemporary societies. In other words, the focus on the lived reality of new forms of social precariousness adds another dimension to the issue of agency and why it is that so many disempowered individuals feel unable to do anything other than endure the often intolerable conditions of their daily lives. Throughout the book, I draw on Bourdieusian and other studies of suffering to illustrate my arguments about the tendencies to social weightlessness in radical democratic theory.

A common response to the idea of social suffering, and, more generally, to a one-sided focus on domination, is that it falls into a determinist miserabilism that over-predicts the powerlessness of oppressed individuals. I deal with this criticism in detail at several points in the book, and I conclude that it is misplaced. The charge is that emphasis on disempowerment and domination is itself tantamount to a denial of agency, a refusal to acknowledge the capacity of oppressed groups to engage in effective forms of political resistance and opposition. It thus compounds the domination that it observes. It is undoubtedly a vital task for radical democrats to affirm the agency of subaltern groups by drawing attention to new forms of collective action and popular protest, and there is indeed an important and growing literature in this area (e.g. Day 2005). One of the central premises of radical democracy is, after all, that political legitimacy flows from the everyday practices of ordinary citizens and not from just institutional arrangements and a priori principles. There is a further need for theorists to be attentive to these everyday forms of political agency in order to prevent their models of democracy becoming closed totalities governed by a formal rather than practical logic. Receptivity to agency from below means that democrats should be prepared to revise or even abandon certain theoretical tenets and presumptions if they seem to be only tenuously related to the dynamics of concrete struggle. Despite the undoubted importance of attesting to counter-hegemonic agency, it is not the particular concern of this book, but, nonetheless, the emphasis here on social suffering is envisaged as a complement to this constructive project rather than a negation of it. It is an avowedly narrow focus but, in my view, is necessary above all to keep in mind the plight of the most powerless groups in society. Arguably, this task is, if anything, even more pressing in the context of neoliberal forms of social control where deepening inequalities and widespread social precariousness are obscured under the distorting myth of individual choice and self-responsibility. Radical democratic theory claims to do precisely this, to speak for the most powerless groups in society, but in so far as it has become trapped within certain empty theoretical formulas – what E.P. Thompson (1996) famously denounced as an 'orrery' – it has become distanced from this aim. It seems to forget that there is no 'naturally articulate' subject of oppression, that there are groups who cannot easily speak or act for themselves, or if they do are simply not heard or recognized (Spivak 1987). Negative social critique, or what Adorno calls an 'unalleviated consciousness of negativity' (2005: 25), is not, then, a simple miserabilism that denies the agency of the oppressed but is essential to keeping issues of oppression and disempowerment within the purview of democratic theory.

Not all models of the political are devoid of a perspective on the negative dynamics of social life, but, in the hands of some radical democrats, an abstract negativism prevails that does not relate to embodied social existence. Ideas of the negative currently abound in radical democratic theory in ontologies of lack and associated notions of non-identity, undecidability, indeterminacy, and so forth. On the whole, however, they are conceptualized in isolation from the parameters of phenomenal existence as freestanding abstract categories – 'estranging enigmas of thought' – often invested with some kind of messianic, emancipatory promise of 'democracy to come' (Adorno 2005: 52). This abstract negativism underpins many of the one-dimensional models of action proffered by radical democrats and these socially weightless formulations speak more to impersonal, theoretical dynamics than they do to the capacities of embodied persons to control their lives. Indeed, in so far as this abstract negativism comes to be associated with the logic of the political *qua* undecidability, contingency, and so forth, it also stands at the root of a persistent downgrading of social experience as the merely empirical, the inert, the given, something without intrinsic significance. But, as Jay Bernstein claims, a political theory that is bound to exposing injustice must inevitably create space for sociality. Positive ideals of justice are always dependent on a second negative, emphatic sense of justice as the unmasking of concrete injustices and inequalities, 'justice as a fiery sword' (Bernstein 2005: 303). If this negative moment of repressed particularity is not kept in view, there is the risk that positive ideas of justice lapse into purely contemplative ideals, that abstractions become reified. For this reason, abstract negativism needs to be bound more closely to a social theoretical negativism that places emphasis on the lived reality of oppression and domination. This is intended not as a moralistic fetishization of experience, nor as providing us with the 'truth' of social injustice; rather, it is a way of keeping political theory open and responsive to what Adorno describes in our opening quotation as the 'cross-grained, opaque, unassimilated material' of social life (2005: 151).

Differently put, negative social critique is necessary to work against the theoretical closure that leads to socially weightless ideas of the political. The emphasis on social suffering is not just a way of providing phenomenal depth to otherwise formal models of democracy. Nor, more generally, does it undermine the theoretical enterprise of normatively informed and constructive generalization by confining the theorist to a descriptive mapping of hidden forms of suffering. But it undoubtedly suggests a different way of going about the job of theorizing other than trying to capture a purified political logic from the opaque flux of social existence. In the end, the primacy given to ontological reflection by radical democrats sets them off on a misguided theoretical path that ends in the effective detachment of political dynamics from social relations of power. A more fruitful approach, on my account, would be one that is dialogical (works within the intertwinement of fact and norm), interdisciplinary (especially between political and social theory), problem- rather than model-centred and, in a consideration of agency, includes phenomenological and interpretative elements. The overall aim of radical political theory in this sense would not be the delineation of a definitive model of political being but would be more aptly conceived as a contribution to the ongoing project of challenging oppression and sketching out of pathways of social empowerment. More will be said about political theory as critique in the conclusion.

CHAPTER OUTLINE

The structure and argument of the book are as follows. The aim of the first chapter is to set out this book's central thematic concern with socially negative thinking through a discussion of the idea of social suffering and the implications it has for political theory. It focuses on Bourdieu's influential formulation of the idea of social suffering and his use of it to counter tendencies towards 'social weightlessness' in academic inquiry. Although Bourdieu's work on social suffering has had considerable influence in a variety of disciplines, it has had limited impact in political theory. I show how Honneth's early work on disclosing critique helps to draw out the relevance of the idea of social suffering for political thinking. Honneth uses it to reveal the limitations in Habermas's rationalist formulation of deliberation that presumes that significant forms of social injustice and inequality can be articulated as formal justice claims. Honneth argues that some types of inequality will not be revealed through discursive reconstruction because they take the form of social pathologies whose distorting effects are realized in embodied existence in an indirect fashion. In short, the idea of social suffering shows how certain types of oppression are rendered politically invisible by being internalized as corporeal dispositions. Despite the critical potential opened up by Honneth's discussion of social suffering as part of disclosing critique, I conclude that it is never fully realized because of his increasing reliance upon a reductive social theory of recognition. The ultimate aim of my discussion of Bourdieu and Honneth on social suffering is to lay out aspects of the social theoretical negativism that I regard as crucial to countering the social weightlessness that prevails in certain types of radical democratic theory.

The second chapter examines Mouffe's idea of democratic agonism, which represents one of the main alternatives to theories of deliberation. From the agonist perspective, ideas of deliberation are profoundly anti-political because the stress they place on consensus obscures the constitutive role of power struggles in social life and consequently misrecognizes what is really at stake in politics.

Given the centrality of struggle to social life, it follows, for agonists, that the essence of a vibrant democracy resides not in the supersession of conflict but in the flourishing of disagreement and contestation within a stable institutional framework. Furthermore, if it is to be truly radical, agonist conflict should always be conducted in a manner that prioritizes the interests of marginalized and excluded groups. Despite this claim, Mouffe's agonism leads to the most rarefied form of social weightlessness that is unable to address the interests of the oppressed or associated issues of disempowerment and depoliticization. There is fundamental discontinuity between, on the one side, her repeated allusions to a substrate of concrete practice that is held up as the source of democratic renewal and, on the other, her reliance on a rigid anti-essentialism that regards such practices as an uninteresting social positivity. The formulaic anti-essentialism that governs Mouffe's agonist paradigm means that the intrinsic connection that is held to exist between the ontological and the ontic, the political and the social, turns out in fact to be a hierarchy of the former over the latter. The absolute priority granted to the supposedly necessary logic of the political over the inert realm of the social closes off issues of empowerment that are crucial to an emancipatory account of agency.

The third chapter focuses on social weightlessness in feminist political theory. Over the last few years, influential feminists have argued that feminism should shift its central focus from issues of gender identity to a more general set of 'post-identity' concerns. The claim is that the preoccupation with gender identity has enmeshed feminism in a parochial politics of recognition whose limited aims constrain its political imagination and prevent it from engaging in broader democratic debates. These post-identity arguments have much justifiable force, but I argue that they are weakened because they explicitly or implicitly raise questions about political agency that they cannot answer. I illustrate my arguments by focusing on the work of Wendy Brown and Linda Zerilli, both of whom have made influential interventions into the post-identity debate. I examine how the anti-subjectivist tendencies of their work are expressed in formulations of the idea of radical political agency through tropes of indeterminacy. This allows them to express the idea that radical political practice consists in a turning away from the experiential certainties of the self to take the form of a ceaseless contestation of boundaries and exploration of unforeseen modes of being. Although this is undoubtedly a valuable democratic ethos, the idea of radical agency as indeterminacy lacks phenomenological relevance and, as a result, fails to advance thought about the social conditions necessary for the emergence of effective political agency.

In the fourth chapter, I focus on the work of Jacques Rancière. On the face of it, Rancière appears to share the same concern as other radical democratic thinkers, namely the attempt to capture the essence of the political. The apparent similarity is misleading, however, for although Rancière thinks that political dynamics are radically distinct from social ones, he does not think they can be accorded any kind of essence, ontological or otherwise. In his view, the quest to define an autonomous political sphere is fundamentally misguided because what are identified as transcendental universal procedures are in fact generalizations of particular types of social being. The political resides only in the moment of radical disagreement where, by asserting their equality, 'the poor' undermine the legitimacy of the established political community and bring into being a new order. The political is, then, by definition evanescent; its emergence is unpredictable, its existence unsustainable and its occurrence rare. Despite its extreme social weightlessness, Rancière's idea of the political offers a renewed account of the discourses of recognition and rights that frees them from a certain kind of reductive ontological baggage and accords them a renewed centrality in emancipatory political struggle. It also points towards a notion of political theory as disclosing critique rather than as the production of models of democracy. Ultimately, however, the social weightlessness of Rancière's notion of the political prevents him from realizing what he believes is the central task of the theorist, namely the verification of the agency of the oppressed. In the context of his evanescent notion of the political, this verification turns out to be a naïve statement of faith that romanticizes the perpetual marginality of the poor and ultimately comes close to replicating the depoliticized analysis that he regards as so problematic in other thinkers.

The final chapter considers the ideas of radical pluralism developed by William Connolly and James Tully. In place of the movement from the abstract to the concrete that characterizes much democratic theory, they begin with a focus on everyday struggles and practice and work outwards towards a more general understanding of the political. By taking this bottom-up approach, emphasis falls on the dynamism and heterogeneity of the practices of ordinary citizens rather than on the principles and procedures that frame democratic agonism. On the face of it, then, both Connolly and Tully go some way to overcoming tendencies towards social weightlessness in radical democratic theory and offer an expanded account of possibilities for political agency. Despite this, I argue that their thought is also limited by a kind of social weightlessness that flows from a reliance on a model of social pluralism that is insufficiently integrated with an account of structural inequality. Their accounts of agency exaggerate the pluri-potentiality of social life by being skewed towards citizens already engaged in vibrant counter-hegemonic practice whilst disregarding those whose conditions of existence render them unable to do so. Despite the stress that both writers place on the ineluctably embodied and situated nature of agency, they pay scant regard to the lived reality of deprivation and marginality that may lead to dispositional reluctances on the part of disempowered individuals to participate in political activity. Ultimately they result in naïvely celebratory accounts of agonist contestation that pass over negative social experiences. What matters for both thinkers in the end seems to be the plurality of struggles per se rather than a consideration of how some struggles may go further than others in challenging deep seated asymmetries of power.

The book concludes with a consideration of some of the methodological implications that a phenomenology of social suffering has for radical democratic theory. I maintain that an approach based on disclosing critique is, in the end, more productive in the unmasking and analysis of inequality than one focused on ontology. Such an approach would be dialogical (works within the intertwinement of fact and norm), interdisciplinary (especially between political and social theory), problem- rather than model-centred and, in a consideration of agency, must include an interpretative element. Furthermore, its fundamentally 'negative' nature does not mean that it lacks a constructive or normative element. The aim of radical political theory in this sense would not be to delineate a definitive model of the political or univocal logic for democratic action, but rather to contribute to the ongoing project of challenging oppression and exploring pathways to empowerment.

1
Suffering and Social Weightlessness

INTRODUCTION

The aim of this chapter is to set out the idea of disclosing critique and its perspective on socially negative experience that will inform my discussion in the rest of the book. To do this, I focus on the idea of social suffering – as an exemplar of negative experience – and the implications it has for political theory. There is considerable scepticism on the part of democratic theorists of all stripes about the idea of suffering in so far as it seems to lead to a reductive and psychologically manipulative politics of pity. I argue in this chapter that the idea of social suffering can in fact be instructive for political theorists if it is conceptualized not as a free-floating existential category but as intrinsically linked to power and inequality. To illustrate what this might mean, I discuss Pierre Bourdieu's work on social suffering, which encapsulates a foundational complicity of body and world: that is, that embodied experience is profoundly shaped by the power relations particular to a given social position. This complicity is given powerful expression in Bourdieu's claim that there is a connection between the emergence of distinctive new types of social misery and the spread of neoliberal forms of social control. Above all, the idea of social suffering highlights the depoliticizing effects of domination: that when objective inequalities are taken into the body and naturalized as subjective dispositions, the capacity for political agency can be subtly eroded and undermined. Bourdieu's idea of social suffering stands as counter to what he describes as 'social weightlessness' in academic inquiry, by which he means an abstract way of thinking about the world that is so far removed from ordinary practices and everyday realities that its critical and normative relevance is thrown into question. This critique of social weightlessness can be extended to political theory in so far as it can be said to be overly preoccupied with formulating abstract models of democratic community where the ability and willingness of subjects to participate politically are taken as more or less given. This presumption of agency is problematic in so far as insufficient attention is paid to underlying questions of empowerment and the social conditions necessary to realize effective agency on the part of subordinated subjects.

A familiar response to a Bourdieusian focus on social suffering is that it falls into a rigid determinism that over-predicts the powerlessness of oppressed groups and is unduly pessimistic about the possibility of emancipatory social change. In fact, Bourdieu regards his critique as potentially empowering in so far as the disclosure of the impersonal causes of personal experiences may go some way to dismantling the latter's seeming psychological inevitability. In this respect, social suffering forms part of a wider project of disclosing critique or political thinking, which to be effective, in Bourdieu's view, should be conducted in the same direction as the tendencies of the world rather than at one remove from them. Bourdieu is not particularly concerned, however, to develop the more constructive entailments of his work for political theory, and in order to make these more explicit it is helpful to turn to the early work of Axel Honneth on disclosing critique. Here, Honneth draws on Bourdieu's idea of suffering to expose limitations in Jürgen Habermas's communicative ethics, where the presumption is that significant forms of social injury and inequality can be articulated as formal justice claims. Honneth maintains, against this, that some kinds of injustice cannot be revealed through such a process of rational reconstruction because they often take the form of diffuse social pathologies whose effects are realized in the insidious distortion of embodied existence. The somatization of social injustice as dispositions of disempowerment, as negative feelings of shame, boredom, hopelessness, for instance, often renders it difficult to put such experiences into words and therefore may undermine the capacity of individuals to act as agents of their own interests. In effect, certain types of structural oppression are rendered politically invisible by being internalized as corporeal dispositions, and, to combat this, political theory needs to have an interpretative element – a phenomenology of injustice – that is explicitly attuned to the ordinary violences of everyday life.

Although Honneth's formulation of political theory as disclosing critique is potentially significant, I conclude that he never fully realizes its full import because of his increasing reliance, in his subsequent work, upon a reductive ontology of recognition. This ontology engenders a simplified social theory where power relations are conceived as extrapolations from a primary dyad of recognition and mystifies a pre-social relation of care as a potentially emancipatory form of interaction. In this regard, Honneth's romanticized ontology diverges sharply from the primacy accorded to power in Bourdieu's ontology of body and world and which would rule out the possibility of retrieving an untrammelled mutuality as an antidote to reified social relations. These problems notwithstanding, the general aim of my discussion of Bourdieu and Honneth on suffering is to lay out aspects of the social theoretical negativism that I regard as crucial to countering the social weightlessness that prevails in certain types of radical democratic theory. Too often, radical democratic thinkers pass over these issues of power and agency as secondary matters that pertain to sociological and other forms of empirical inquiry but not to political theory. I argue on the contrary that social theoretical negativism should be understood as a way of opening up new problems – methodological and substantive – for political inquiry rather than simply, as some claim, a miserabilism that denies the oppressed the capacity for resistance.

SOCIAL SUFFERING AND DISEMPOWERMENT

In an edition of the journal *Daedalus* (Winter 1996) dedicated to the theme of *social suffering*, a number of the contributors remark upon the discrepancy that exists between methods of social scientific inquiry and the lived experience of suffering. They claim that the social scientific bias towards formal and rationalist methods overlooks a crucial feature of social reality, notably experiences of pain and misery, which, although widespread and intense, are often inchoate and unarticulated. Indeed, the failure to address such experiences serves to compound and intensify them in so far as ignoring their phenomenal significance buries them deeper under a carapace of technical analysis. Several contributors to the volume note that the adoption of interpretative methods represents a crucial move in overcoming this disconnection between formal methods and the lived reality of suffering, although they concede that it is by no means a straightforward matter. Certain experiences of pain and misery are, by their very nature, deeply internalized, have isolating effects on the individual and, consequently, may be incommunicable to others. Suffering presents a further challenge to social science in so far as it seems to require not only more interpretative depth, but also a type of interdisciplinary analysis that cuts across specialization within bounded fields of inquiry and unsettles a discrete disciplinary focus on single issues of poverty, crime, violence, disease, prejudice, and so forth. As Arthur Kleinman and his co-editors put it: 'The most interesting questions for theory and practice concerning social suffering are in the cracks between our categories and in the discursive processes that traverse our disciplines' (Kleinman et al. 1996: xiii). Despite these methodological challenges, it nonetheless behoves the social scientist to respond in some way to suffering, for the failure to do so attests to a lapse in ethical sensibility. Somehow or another, social scientists must strive to develop a 'felt thoughtfulness' in their work, understood as the capacity to acknowledge the pain of others and recognize its central existential significance for certain groups (Wilkinson 2011).

Since the clarion call of this special issue, there has been a growing body of work across various disciplines exploring aspects of social suffering. Despite this burgeoning interest, political theorists have, with a few exceptions, not engaged extensively with the idea, although some claim that it is a notion that 'politics cannot do without today' (Renault 2010: 221). There are several reasons for this reluctance, central amongst which is that the experiential orientation of the idea of social suffering is out of step with the current concern of many political theorists to reflect in a systematic fashion on the core principles and procedures necessary to secure democratic order. From this schematic perspective, the discourse of suffering seems to belong to a past phase of identity politics associated with troubling tendencies towards parochialism, subjectivism and political balkanization. Political theorists of all stripes therefore have an understandable resistance to the idea of suffering lest it pull them back into the politics of pity and its moralistic discourse of victimhood that pits groups against each other and loses sight of uniting democratic aims and an inclusive vision of social change (see chapter 3). As a result, political theory has taken what can be called an anti-experiential turn where it concentrates not so much on the discourse of suffering and what that might tell us about oppression but more on formulating models of democratic community and distributive principles necessary to deliver justice and equality.

Whilst the suspicion of the discourse of suffering is not unwarranted, it is, in my view, often exaggerated and carries with it some underappreciated theoretical costs. With the move towards procedural, impersonal formulations of democracy, political theory risks losing its grounding in a phenomenology of everyday experience and consequently its ability to identify and respond adequately to certain central social problems of our day. Without wishing to engage in an uncritical 'suffer-mongering', it is nonetheless the case that the experiences of marginal and oppressed groups give access to realities that might otherwise remain tangential or even invisible to an established or mainstream theoretical perspective (Brown and Halley 2002). It is possible to objectively identify types of subordination but still fail to appreciate its full ramifications without also the effort to comprehend its subjective reality. Feminists and theorists of race, for example, have demonstrated in many different ways how the particular experiences of women and black people undermine the supposed neutrality and inclusiveness of principles that are held by mainstream theorists to guarantee democratic community. It is not a question of simply asserting the incontestable authenticity of such experiences or of replacing an empty universalism with an equally troubling particularism of group experience. Rather, it is an issue of appreciating how the experience of subordinated social groups can yield a fuller theoretical knowledge of oppression and inequality whose phenomenal significance is either not immediately understood from the outside or not recognized at all. The concepts of patriarchy and white supremacy, for instance, were derived in the first place to explain the experiences of underrepresented groups and need not result in an uncritical subjectivism but may instead lead to revised theories of power and social relations: 'These terms are abstractions that *do* reflect the specificity of group experiences, thereby potentially generating categories and principles that illuminate rather than obfuscate the reality of different kinds of subordination' (Mills 2005: 173). It is crucial, then, not to treat experience as the site of self-evident truths but to develop the category in conjunction with an analysis of power. In this way, a focus on experience can engender a renewed understanding of social relations, a new 'cartography of the social' (Mills 2005: 175) that in turn may have significant implications for political thinking. Social suffering is one possible way of accessing this experiential substrate and therefore of acquiring insight into the lived consequences of oppression. In so far as such an experiential perspective is missing from democratic theory, the latter is in danger of becoming stranded in an abstract logic removed from the daily reality of those subjects on whose part it is supposed to speak.

Bourdieu's work on social suffering has particular significance because, in so far as it goes further than the work of any other thinker in conceptualizing the idea through an account of power and oppression, it potentially allays the concerns of political theorists about the reductive entailments of the category. By establishing an intrinsic connection between suffering and power, Bourdieu politicizes the former. Suffering for him is not a general, existential type of experience but a social one, connected to the asymmetrical distribution of power and the exercise of forms of social control. Above all, he regards the emergence of an unprecedented type of widespread social misery as ineluctably bound to the rise and spread of neoliberal modes of governance. Along with other commentators, Bourdieu maintains that the reorganization of practices and institutions around market principles has the effect of fragmenting social relations and intensifying fundamental inequalities. Given the indirect nature of neoliberal governance – what Foucault (1991) famously describes as the 'conduct of conduct' – its destructive social effects are not always immediately apparent since it seems, on the face of it, to promote individual autonomy and freedom rather than suppress it. On Bourdieu's account, it is in the phenomenal realm of ordinary daily existence that the insidious and diffuse nature of its effects become most apparent; in particular, what emerges is a central structuring paradox, namely that an overall increase in levels of affluence has been accompanied by elevated levels of social misery. There is, in Bourdieu's words, a 'whole side of the suffering characteristic of a social order which, although it has undoubtedly reduced poverty overall ... has also multiplied the social spaces ... and set up the conditions for an unprecedented development of all kinds of social suffering' (Bourdieu et al. 1999: 4–5). This growth in social misery is bound up, in particular, with the individualizing techniques of neoliberalism that, on one level, fragment and divide the poor and disempowered whilst, on another, they reinforce structural inequalities. The stress on an economized notion of 'self-responsibility' compels individuals, in the name of free choice, to try to manage states of affairs that they cannot possibly control, placing them under greater stress and ultimately eroding collective solutions to social problems. As a multitude of empirical data on poverty attests, these individualizing techniques have the effect of compounding rather than dislodging persistent economic and social inequalities and also of creating new forms of social vulnerability (e.g. Standing 2011).

Bourdieu develops his idea of social suffering mainly in the co-authored volume *The Weight of the World* (1999) – an extensive ethnographic study of deprivation that focuses on the daily lives of ordinary citizens inhabiting areas of 'urban relegation' (housing projects, sink estates, ghettos, *banlieues*, etc.) that are a ubiquitous feature of European and North American cities. A distinctive feature of these areas is that, unlike more traditional forms of urban working-class life, they are internally divided and fragmented. Under the double pressure of 'precarization and deproletarianization' the urban poor tend not to be unified by any type of shared collective identity. They are made up of a range of groups who although they share a common situation do not necessarily share a common trajectory or purpose: ageing industrial labourers and low-level clerks who have lost their jobs, precarious and temporary workers who drop in and out of employment, long-term recipients of welfare, the poor elderly, immigrants, the homeless, ex-criminals, beggars, and so forth (Wacquant 2008). For instance, the contemporary 'hyper-ghetto' is distinguished from its historical precedents, such as the black American ghetto, in so far as it is a 'denuded space . . . no longer a shared resource that African Americans can mobilize and deploy to shelter from white domination . . . on the contrary, it has become a vector of intra-communal division and an instrument for the virtual imprisonment of the black urban subproletariat' (Wacquant 2008: 242). In the light of structural tendencies to fragmentation, the crucial question for the sociologist is, as Bourdieu puts it, 'to understand what happens in . . . places which bring together people who have nothing in common and force them to live together, either in mutual ignorance and incomprehension or else in latent or open conflict – with all the suffering this entails' (Bourdieu et al. 1999: 3). Life in these areas is often accompanied by elevated levels of suffering, and it is evident that Bourdieu has a quite specific experiential typology in mind when he uses the term. It denotes primarily a register of mundane, daily suffering (*petites misères*) rather than a more traumatic register (*grandes misères*) arising from sudden and catastrophic misfortunes. The quotidian inflection Bourdieu gives to the idea of social suffering stands in contrast to the way other theorists use the term to examine extreme forms of political and social violence and harm: for example, Langer's work on the experience of Holocaust survivors or Wei-ming's work on the oppression of Chinese intellectuals (Langer 1996; Wei-ming 1996). For Bourdieu, the mundane nature of suffering means that it takes the form not so much of an identifiable event or specific injury but rather of a diffuse and persistent background state of affairs.

Another feature of social suffering is that, although it has its roots in 'real' material poverty, it is not concerned with the objective aspects of deprivation as much as its subjective or emotional ones: the feelings of unworthiness, shame, lack of dignity, indignation, and so forth, that make up the lived experience of social structures of oppression. It pertains, in other words, more to collective psychological dispositions, what Raymond Williams (1977) terms 'structures of feeling', rather than to the distribution of material goods. The very diffuseness of these feelings is indicative of a further aspect of social suffering, namely its relative social invisibility. For a variety of reasons, individuals often find it difficult to give expression to the feelings of dishonour, anger or resignation that accompany routinized deprivation. Suffering is often internalized as a deep-seated reluctance or even inability to speak about one's experience lest it further compound feelings of shame and the perceptions, held by others, of personal weakness and the failure to cope. This internalization may in turn intensify suffering, giving rise to what some theorists have termed 'double suffering': that is, the detachment of suffering from its social structural causes and its naturalization as embodied dispositions. By being incorporated in this manner, the social origins of suffering are obscured and are experienced instead as the fault of the individual. There are other reasons for the invisibility of social suffering: routinized types of misery often fall below the threshold of public attention and political interest and are, to a great extent, unarticulated as part of any formal agenda for action. Such experiences often only come to the fore through an interpretative perspective that attempts to go beyond publicly articulated forms of social injustice to disclose submerged forms of oppression. Social suffering refers to 'malaises' that are often 'unexpressed and often inexpressible', often only visible through a phenomenological perspective which focuses on the 'diffuse expectations and hopes which, because they often touch on the ideas that people have about their own identity and self-respect, seem to be a private affair and therefore legitimately excluded from public debate' (Bourdieu et al. 1999: 627). Finally, for Bourdieu, social suffering is a collective not an individual category. It refers not to the singular experiences of individual biographies but rather to certain generic types of subjective experience associated with class and other systemic inequalities. Suffering is, of course, a ubiquitous feature of human existence, marking the lives of all individuals at some point or another, but social suffering is what Bourdieu terms 'positional' rather than existential. It arises from the normalized structural violence that is routinely perpetuated by unequal social orders. Suffering in this positional sense is not evenly distributed around society because of the link with material inequality. Indeed, the reason why Bourdieu uses the epithet *social* is precisely to highlight these collective, systemic aspects of the experience and what that may tell us about the nature of inequality and domination.

This positional formulation of social suffering clearly derives its conceptual coherence from the idea of habitus, with which it is inextricably intertwined. Habitus is Bourdieu's well-known account of the intrinsic connection between embodied being and power, the way in which the impersonal tendencies and structures of the world are taken into the body and naturalized as physical and psychological dispositions. To quote Bourdieu, 'The most personal is the most impersonal ... many of the most intimate dramas, the deepest malaises, the most singular suffering that women and men can experience find their roots in the objective contradictions, constraints and double binds inscribed in the structures of the labour and housing markets' (Bourdieu and Wacquant 1992: 201; see also Renault 2008). It is this ontology of complicity or mutual possession between body and the world that is the cornerstone of hierarchical social relations: 'The analysis of the doxic acceptance of the world, due to the immediate agreement of objective structures and cognitive structures, is the true foundation of a realistic theory of domination and politics. Of all the forms of "hidden persuasion," the most implacable is the one exerted, quite simply, by the *order of things*' (Bourdieu and Wacquant 1992: 168). A necessary entailment of this ontological complicity is that embodied being is always necessarily marked by its social location; it is circumscribed, to a greater or lesser extent, by the relations of power that infuse a particular social space. It is such a notion that is central to the idea of social suffering that tracks the intrinsic but often latent connection between generic subjective experiences and unequal social relations. It is also crucial to its de-essentialization for, in the Bourdieusian account, suffering is no longer a vague, 'free-floating' category that leads to a psychological reductive account of politics but is connected to the way in which inequalities are materialized in the body and lived as deep-seated dispositions. *Social* suffering denotes the collective, generic aspects of incorporated experience (habitus) and what that might tell us about the nature of domination, understood as the 'presence of otherness at the very heart of subjectivity' (Bourdieu and Wacquant 1992: 201).

What, then, is the immediate relevance of Bourdieu's idea of social suffering for political theory? Of its various entailments, a key one is that it raises the issue of power and agency or, more precisely, the social conditions that facilitate or hinder its emergence. Social suffering draws attention to the way in which the internalization of objective structures of oppression into embodied being may undermine the capacity for agency in so far as individuals are unwilling or unable to act as agents of their own interests. This is Bourdieu's definition of symbolic violence, a type of internalized domination that renders individuals complicit with their own oppression – 'a somatised social relationship, a social law converted into an embodied law' (2001: 39). Some obstacles to political participation do not take the form of easily identifiable external barriers and sanctions against certain groups but instead operate through the inculcation of certain generic dispositions, feelings of powerlessness, resignation, and so forth, that mean that individuals accept, albeit unwillingly, rather than resist their condition of dispossession. Marginalization is not simply an explicit violation of equality but it also deprives individuals themselves of the capacity to demand inclusion. In Kevin Olson's words: 'Such people become politically invisible, trapped in a political black hole from which no information can escape. [This] is not merely a failure to treat others as peers in interaction. . . . It is more profoundly a self-perpetuating trap for people and political information' (2008: 262). Chronic experiences of marginalization and dispossession can engender in individuals a deep sense of disempowerment, a feeling that their suffering is inevitable or unavoidable and that very little can be done to change it (e.g. Charlesworth 2000; Wacquant 2008). It may prevent them from construing their problems as political in the first place, and, even when they do have a critical understanding of their situation, their willingness to participate in corrective political action is far from assured and their legitimacy as political subjects often not recognized. As Jane Mansbridge puts it: 'Subordinate groups sometimes cannot find the right voice or words to express their thoughts, and when they do, they discover they are not heard . . . [they] . . . are silenced, encouraged to keep their wants inchoate, and heard to say "yes" when what they have said is "no"' (1991: 127). It is important to note that disempowered individuals of course have agency in an immediate, first-order sense of surviving and coping; they engage with the world and interact with others in a daily and often routine fashion. But the type of agency that they could be said to lack is what might be called a 'second-order', politicized form, understood as the capacity to autonomously shape or change an individual or collective way of life (Frost and Hoggett 2008: 442). Given that it is a not uncommon feature of oppression, this lack of political agency or 'quiescence' should, according to John Gaventa, be one of the central issues of political theory; to explain not why individuals rebel but why, in situations of unjustifiable inequality, they do not:

> Why, in a social relationship involving the domination of a nonelite by an elite, does challenge to that domination not occur? What is there in certain situations of social deprivation that prevents issues from arising, grievances from being voiced, or interests from being recognized? Why, in an oppressed community where one might intuitively expect upheaval, does one instead find, or appear to find, quiescence? (1982: 3)

Quiescence is another way of expressing the kernel of the idea of social suffering: why and how those without power endure their conditions of oppression and the emotional costs that this imposes upon them.

As part of its task of overcoming inequality and injustice, normative political theory needs to cultivate, to some extent, an attentiveness to the experiences of individuals in the pre-political sphere where domination and political exclusion have their roots. Yet it is precisely such an attentiveness to social suffering and other subjective experiences of disempowerment that is missing from much political theory because of its general anti-experiential orientation. In the numerous models of democracy that currently abound, the ideas that prevail focus less on oppression, inequality and barriers to participation and more on abstract notions of political community and the nature of public reason, where individuals are assumed to be more or less equal and political participation is assured. Equality amongst agents is perhaps too swiftly assumed as an unproblematic condition of possibility of political debate rather than being thought through more carefully as something that has to be realized in the context of social inequality. Clearly, the idea of universal agency has to be one of the fundamental normative presuppositions of any non-elite theory of democracy, but, ironically, in making such a presupposition, the result too often is that many of the barriers to political participation that face marginalized and powerless groups are not considered in sufficient depth. This is what Olson has called the paradox of enablement: namely that the assumption of participatory parity promotes equal agency while simultaneously marginalizing the people it is designed to help (2008: 261–3). This paradox is, by definition, never fully surmountable; it is impossible to predict, from the perspective of a general theory of agency, all the possible empirical barriers that prevent individuals acting as agents in their own interests. Nonetheless, this should not pre-empt the attempt to explore certain enduring, entrenched and, in many cases, relatively predictable obstacles to political mobilization and agency. What is more, a concern with political agency should not be viewed as a second-order, sociological issue of power and mobilization that does not have a place in political theory for, in Raymond Guess's words: 'An "ideal theory" without contact to reality, is . . . no guide to action. . . . A theoretical approach with no place for a theory of power is not merely deeply deficient but actively pernicious because mystifying' (2008: 93–4). For the radical democrat, in particular, the ultimate source of democratic legitimacy emanates from the practices and claims of ordinary citizens. It follows that a fundamental task is to make heard the voices of those oppressed and disadvantaged groups whose formal inclusion in liberal democratic structures belies the actuality of their marginalization and exclusion. The assumption of equal agency is therefore necessary but insufficient to thought about democracy, for, as Bourdieu puts it, 'purely theoretical universalization leads to a fictitious universalism so long as it is not accompanied by any reminder of the repressed economic and social conditions of access to the universal or by any (political) action aimed at universalizing these conditions in practice' (2000: 65). Too often, however, radical democratic theory does not even begin to address possible causes of disempowerment; instead, as I go on to argue, it assumes the existence of ready-made political subjects and consequently proffers models of political action that are so rarefied they have little relation to the conditions of oppression they supposedly address.

Bourdieu uses the term 'social weightlessness' to describe such tendencies to rarefaction and, in the next section, I consider what he means by this term, what, in his view, may be done to counter it and what its implications are for political theory. The charge of social weightlessness insists that an attentiveness to the power dynamics that shape everyday being needs to be incorporated more fully into theoretical accounts of social and political relations. For political theory, it implies that formal equality should be thought through more carefully in relation to existing inequalities, and it also casts doubt on the preoccupation with formulating definitive, universally applicable models of democracy. For Bourdieu (2000), the attempt to isolate essential principles of democratic action may lead to an 'imperialism of the universal' that subordinates the concrete logic of practice to the reified logic of the model. Bourdieu's remarks are directed primarily against Habermas's idea of deliberative democracy, but, in my view, its implications can be extended to certain types of radical democratic theory. What Bourdieu intimates, but does not elaborate, is that, given its concern with challenging inequality, radical democratic theory might be better off eschewing an approach that prioritizes formal models of democracy and instead adopting a method closer to that of disclosing critique.

SOCIAL WEIGHTLESSNESS

The idea of social suffering can be viewed as a counter-weight to what Bourdieu regards as a widespread and problematic tendency in academic thinking and that he identifies as social weightlessness (2000: 13–14). Socially weightless thought is a type of scholastic reasoning that is so far removed from the practical mundanities and urgencies of the world that ultimately its own descriptive and normative relevance is thrown into question.[1] If it aspires to move beyond simple description of the world, then academic inquiry must necessarily break, in some way, with immediate appearances in order to discern structural tendencies and regularities that may not be evident in the present moment. Whilst abstraction is therefore fundamental to scholastic inquiry, the problem of social weightlessness arises when it takes the form of an over-rigid separation or ontological break between reflection and the world of ordinary practices.

In *Pascalian Meditations* (2000), Bourdieu examines how this discontinuity between the worlds of theory and practice is sustained by a series of fallacies or 'epistemic doxa' that commonly inform academic thought. The first of these fallacies is that of 'scholastic epistemocentrism', which cancels out the specificity of everyday practice by either assimilating it to theoretical knowledge or consigning it to the category of radical otherness, non-existence or, in Kant's phrase, 'barbarous taste'.[2] In other words, a rigid and hierarchical boundary is maintained between the scholastic and practical worlds where the active agent of applied knowledge is substituted with the reflecting subject of theoretical knowledge. This projection of the theoretical self into the practical other is related to a second fallacy, namely the privileging of the atemporal perspective of the 'lector' over the dynamic perspective of the 'auctor'. The fuzzy and creative logic of practical understanding is replaced with an abstract process of self-decipherment characteristic of scholastic interpretation. The subordination of the open and diachronic nature of praxis to synchronic analysis hypostatizes action, depriving it of temporal specificity and unyoking it from the specific social relations and tacit dynamics of power in which it is ineluctably embedded.[3]

The annexation of the social actor's perspective to that of the scholar leads to a third structuring fallacy of socially weightless thought, namely linguistic (or aesthetic) universalism. This refers to the widespread tendency amongst theorists, since the linguistic turn, to model social and political relations according to the formal dynamics of language. The difficulty here is that by assimilating social relations to linguistic ones, an account of power is replaced by a one-dimensional theory of signification that fails to grasp the enduring and insidious nature of many types of inequality and domination.[4] Ultimately, then, Bourdieu maintains that socially weightless thinking is a form *par excellence* of symbolic violence perpetuated by seemingly enlightened elites upon the practical activities of social actors. The totalizing dynamic of socially weightless thought sanctions the arbitrary and ahistorical distinction between intellectual reason and common sense, between scholar and actor, the latter of whom, 'being the dominated products of an order dominated by forces armed with reason ... cannot but give their acquiescence to the arbitrariness of rationalized force' (Bourdieu 2000: 83).

It is the last structuring fallacy of linguistic universalism that is the most frequent cause of social weightlessness in political theory, and Bourdieu discerns it at work in a range of different thinkers from Rawls, through Habermas to Butler. It is in relation to Habermas that Bourdieu undertakes his most extended discussion of its shortcomings with regard to an understanding of power. His main criticism is that communicative ethics pays insufficient attention to the context of unequal social relations in which speech is always situated and therefore underplays the possible barriers to equal or full political participation that flow from the embodied experience of domination. It effects a twofold depoliticization of the social context of interaction: political power relations are reduced to those of communication, which are, in turn, neutralized by being understood as reciprocal. The underlying cause of this depoliticization is that Habermas regards the political subject as a primarily linguistic being rather than as an embodied, socially situated one and, as a result, conceives of political deliberation as a matter of abstract linguistic competence, or, to quote Bourdieu, he presupposes 'that everyone participates in language as they enjoy the sun, the air, or water' (1991: 146). Discourse ethics presumes that individuals have, to a greater or lesser degree, a roughly equal linguistic capacity to participate in debate and, indeed, that all of them have accepted a priori the necessity of participation in the political realm. For Bourdieu, this separation of linguistic competence from embodied social existence is a theoretical artifice: a form of symbolic denegation that fictitiously brackets off relations of power and forgets that 'linguistic relations are always relations of symbolic power' and that 'the theoretically universal competence liberally granted to all by linguists is in reality monopolized by some' (1991: 146). Some of the deepest barriers to equal political participation cannot be discerned from the perspective of an abstractly endowed capacity to deliberate because they only ever emerge in an embodied context. What this linguistic universalism fails to acknowledge is that the capacity to speak is not a formal universal competence but a 'statutory ability' directly related to one's social situation, and in disregarding this it tacitly generalizes a dominant way of being as a universal norm. There are types of symbolic power inescapably associated with embodied being – one's sex, one's race, one's class – which means that not only will some speakers always be taken more seriously than others, but also that some speakers, even when they conform to the rules of dominant discourse, might not be heard at all (e.g. Sanders 1997). Prejudice, for instance the failure to take seriously some types of speakers, is triggered not by force of argument but by the colour of someone's skin, the timbre of their voice, the 'authority' of their demeanour, and so forth, and, more significantly, it operates below the radar of formal prescriptions that claim to guarantee in advance an equal right to participation. In short, Habermas's 'linguistification' of social relations allows him to substitute rational speech for embodied pain and to presume what Gayatri Spivak calls a naturally articulate subject of oppression (1987: 288).

Bourdieu is not alone in making such a criticism of Habermasian deliberation. The argument that it pays insufficient attention to the subtle relations of power that skew any speech situation in favour of some speakers rather than others is by now familiar (e.g. McNay 2008a; Rancière 1999; Sanders 1997). Furthermore, Habermas and his followers have gone some way in revising the strong rationalism of deliberation which is held to be the principal reason why certain groups have difficulty in articulating their experiences as moral claims and being taken seriously as political subjects. The critique of social weightlessness has more bite, however, than simply drawing attention to the suppressed context of power that subtly influences any speech act. For it also casts doubt on the rationale of theoretical approaches whose main aim is to isolate an essential political logic (deliberation or otherwise) and, on this basis, construct a definitive model of democracy. The focus on universally valid procedures may mean that the theorist prioritizes the integrity of the abstract model per se regardless of the conflicting evidence of practice. From this perspective, the 'silence' of oppressed groups is indicative not just of an inability to express oneself formally but also of the limits of the deliberative paradigm itself vis-à-vis certain radical demands. Even when marginal groups articulate their grievances in the prescribed manner, they are still often disregarded. The perspective of social suffering draws attention to the tacit norms that are set in play by supposedly inclusive models of the political that in fact may have deeply exclusionary effects. For instance, coercion, violence and the mobilization of extreme emotions are ruled out a priori by deliberative thinkers as illegitimate political strategies because of their potentially destabilizing effects on democratic debate. Yet, in the context of hierarchical social relationships, these strategies can be important, even necessary, political tools for rendering visible those oppressions and injustices that remain below the threshold of public perception or that, even when they have been given voice, have not been taken seriously by the dominant. Historically, as various thinkers have shown, marginalized and excluded groups have more often than not had to resort to what are deemed to be 'coercive' techniques – civil disobedience, strikes, boycotts, and so forth – to gain entry into democratic debate and be taken seriously (Medearis 2005; see also Stears 2010: 1–14). The resort to coercive, even violent, actions is testament to how, even when oppressed groups adhere to the rules of the political game, they are still just not heard: 'The social problems that they wish to address are effectively invisible to others' (Medearis 2005: 53). In short, there are aspects to the political process of challenging domination, things that need to be done to overcome it, that cannot be captured by simply putting them into words, by limiting them to 'the regulated confrontations of a rational dialogue that knows and recognizes no other force than that of arguments' (Bourdieu 2000: 73).

In presenting deliberation as beyond power, as grounded in abstract and supposedly neutral competences rather than as inseparable from contingent political struggles, Habermas and his followers are unwilling to consider deeply enough the limits of the universal validity of their paradigm. What is presented as an abstract capacity is in fact an expression of a linguistic universalism, the tacit generalization of a dominant way of being as a universal norm (Bourdieu 2000).The resort to coercive strategies on the part of subordinated groups to gain entry into democratic debate reveals ways in which deliberation may foreclose radical political challenge through the imposition of a priori sanctions on unacceptable modes of action. In this light, the resort to coercion represents not just a bid to be included in an established democratic order, but rather a challenge to the very parameters of the reasonable order itself. From the perspective of emancipatory power struggles, then, there is arguably a 'serious incompleteness' in the deliberative model of politics because it cannot really incorporate radical democratic challenge and transformative action within the limits of its linguistic universalism. As John Medearis puts it: 'What is at stake is *the structure of major institutions and social relations* (not just deliberative forums), their distribution of *power* (not just deliberative chances and capacities), and broad inclusion on equal terms in *political contention* (not just in deliberation)' (2005: 69). Habermas and other deliberative thinkers fail to sustain a moment of reflexive awareness with regard to their own idealizing presuppositions, with the consequence that discourse ethics can only be maintained as a universal norm by repressing thought about its own social and economic conditions of possibility.

The idea of social suffering stands as a challenge to the imperialism of the universal that arises from the separation of fact from norm, from the unhitching of formal models of democracy from the underlying context of power struggles between unequal groups in which they are always ineluctably situated (Medearis 2005: 71). No theory – the problem is not limited to ideas of deliberation – can hope to set up an a priori, universal model of democracy whose inclusiveness vis-à-vis radical political challenge is perpetually guaranteed. Universal norms – procedural or otherwise – cannot be asserted once and for all lest they become a closed theoretical paradigm that is more concerned with maintaining its own internal integrity than responding to concrete struggles. Conceptual closure is, as we shall see in subsequent chapters, a risk inherent even in radical theories that claim to install a sensitivity to power and struggle at the heart of their models of democracy but, in fact, finish by privileging certain ways of conducting politics and marginalizing others that may be fundamental to emancipatory change.

An obvious response to the charge of social weightlessness is that it undermines the task of political theory altogether by reducing its legitimate concern with how things ought to be to the social scientific analysis of how things are. Thought about the ought necessarily implies a move away from actuality to the construction of regulative ideals and abstract principles that can serve as a guide to democratic action. Such a response taps into a well-established criticism of Bourdieu's sociology of domination that in its determinism it not only fails to provide any resources for normative thinking but, worse, also denies the possibility of any kind of progressive social change (e.g. Rancière 2003). The criticism of social weightlessness does indeed cast doubt on certain modes of abstraction, but it does not necessarily undermine normative political theorizing altogether. It suggests a way of thinking about emancipatory social change that is more situated and gradual than one that operates through the construction of competing models of democracy. Such an approach could be termed that of disclosing critique, the idea that thought about social change proceeds from the attempt to describe the world in such a way that some new or neglected aspect is brought into focus which might, in turn, serve to shift or reorient theoretical reflection and debate. If thought is to be both epistemologically and politically effective, in Bourdieu's view, it must be exercised 'in the same direction as the immanent tendencies of the social world' rather than at great remove from them (2000: 5). It is through the attempt to comprehend the repressed material conditions from which it emerges that thought can begin to move beyond its limitations: 'There can be thought about the social conditions of thought which offers thought the possibility of a genuine freedom with respect to these conditions' (Bourdieu 2000: 118).[5] The idea of social suffering exemplifies the attempt to think reflexively in accord with the tendencies of the world rather than at one remove from them. The very act of identifying a layer of social abjection that ordinarily remains unnoticed reveals the inadvertently exclusionary nature of formal models of political participation and, at the same time, permits an 'unformulated repressed discourse' to emerge (Bourdieu 2000: 201). It is in this light that the idea of social suffering has significant implications for current political thinking because it not only alerts us to the existence of 'ordinary violences' that do not figure in established theoretical agendas, but it can also tell us something significant about agency or, more importantly, the social conditions necessary for effective agency. In Zygmunt Bauman's words: 'There seems to be little point in designing alternative modes of togetherness, in stretching the imagination to visualize a society better serving the cause of freedom and security . . . if a collective agency capable of making the words flesh is nowhere in sight. Our dependencies are now truly global, our actions however, as before, local' (2001: 149).

While a notion of disclosing critique is implicit in his work, Bourdieu is not especially interested in pursuing its relevance for political theory. To do so, it is necessary to turn to the work of the Critical Theorist Axel Honneth, who has elaborated the entailments of the idea of social suffering for political thinking. A focus on negative social experiences is a crucial element of disclosing critique and, moreover, represents a vital corrective to the procedural tendencies that dominate contemporary political theory.

DISCLOSURE AND SOCIAL JUSTICE

Honneth has claimed that the widespread preoccupation with procedural models of justice and democracy means that much contemporary political theory has become reified. It has lost sight of underlying issues of oppression, economic dependence and deprivation and the means with which to disclose and challenge them. In making this claim, Honneth is influenced by Bourdieu's idea of social suffering, but he develops it in connection with his more widely known social theory of recognition. Briefly, Honneth locates the origins of all social and political conflict in the experience of three fundamental types of misrecognition or disrespect visited on marginal and oppressed groups. Driving even the most fully organized and strategic forms of collective action is a submerged layer of 'social' suffering that arises from society's failure to recognize groups of individuals as worthy of esteem and respect. For individuals to acquire a secure sense of self and to develop their capabilities fully, they require meaningful acknowledgement from others in the three basic spheres of social action: affective recognition or love (family), cultural recognition or esteem and formal legal recognition (rights). When these forms of recognition are successfully instantiated in a society, the individual understands herself as 'both an equal and unique member of society' (Honneth 2007a: 74). If recognition is denied to individuals in any or all of these spheres, then their sense of self-worth can be profoundly damaged and these injuries of misrecognition are often lived, at a deep psychological level, as feelings of shame, anger, hopelessness, and so forth. All political conflict, even the most redistributive, can therefore, in Honneth's view, be typified as a struggle for recognition. At a societal level, when patterns of misrecognition become systematically entrenched, they engender widespread social suffering, and this speaks to something morally amiss with the logic of social relations. Suffering, then, on Honneth's view, has an intrinsically normative core because misrecognition violates the fundamental conditions necessary for healthy self-realization. To quote Honneth: 'If the adjective "social" is to mean anything more than "typically found in society", social suffering and discontent possess a normative core . . . such feelings of discontent and suffering . . . coincide with the experience that society is doing something unjust, something unjustifiable' (Fraser and Honneth 2003: 129).

Honneth's strong claim about the intrinsic normative core of suffering has proved to be contentious and has provoked criticisms that he indulges in a form of suffer-mongering that fetishizes the experience of injury as an incontestable indicator of injustice (Brown 1995; Brown and Halley 2002; Fraser and Honneth 2003). On the face of it, it is hard to see how claims about 'social suffering' forming the 'moral' core of all political struggle do anything other than compound a psychologically reductive account of politics. However, Honneth's idea of a phenomenology of injustice is in fact potentially less reductive than his critics allow in so far as he takes up Bourdieu's de-essentialized notion of social suffering and integrates it into the approach of disclosing social critique. Disclosing social critique represents his attempt to reinvigorate the post-Marxian tradition of Critical Theory, which has never, in his view, fully realized the radical potential of its insight into the intertwinement of fact and norm. What makes critique a compelling way of pursuing normative thought is its 'intramundane transcendence': that is, that its emancipatory norms are not free-standing or logically developed ideals but are derived from actual social practices. As Honneth puts it: 'Whatever its congruence with other forms of social critique, Critical Theory in its innermost core is dependent upon a quasi-sociological specification of an emancipatory interest in social reality itself' (2007a: 65). It is in part through attentiveness to the lived experience of misrecognition that an ' objective foothold in pre-theoretical praxis' is retained.[6] The primary task of a 'phenomenology of injustice' is to shine a light on unseen, neglected and emergent types of oppression, the 'social pathologies' that form the experiential substrate of hierarchical social orders. Like Bourdieu, Honneth maintains that there are aspects to oppression and inequality that cannot be deduced from the objective perspective of social structures but can only be discerned through an interpretative analysis of embodied experience. It is not possible to fully appreciate in what fashion and to what extent asymmetrical social arrangements are oppressive without an examination of how they are realized in the daily lives and practices of subjects. Contra his critics, then, Honneth's idea of suffering does not inevitably entail a moralistic and uncritical subjectivism; rather, following Bourdieu (1990a), it can be understood as a relational phenomenology that attempts to situate experience within the complex set of symbolic and material relations that explicitly and implicitly structure it. By unmasking previously unrecognized forms of domination, disclosing critique does not recover an authentic voice of oppression but rather expands existing accounts of social injustice and its possible remedies.

The difference that this focus on social suffering makes to political thought is brought out in Honneth's debate with Nancy Fraser over recognition and redistribution and, in particular, whether misrecognition is best understood as a form of psychological injury or as an institutional form of status subordination. Fraser redefines misrecognition in institutional terms as a violation of participatory parity in order to circumvent the problematic subjectivism that is a consequence of construing misrecognition in vague terms of psychological harm and injurious cultural representation. She maintains that by adding institutional specificity to the idea of misrecognition it becomes easier to adjudicate between genuine and opportunistic claims to recognition. In Honneth's view, however, Fraser's avoidance of an interpretative perspective on suffering is over-stated and conceptually limiting for not all forms of misrecognition can be adequately identified by considering only institutionally anchored types of parity violation. Fraser's non-identarian formulation of status subordination significantly constrains an account of misrecognition because it is unable to identify certain types of unthematized 'social suffering' which fall below the threshold of political articulation and therefore remain effectively invisible. What is lost in her objectivist reformulation of misrecognition is a perspective upon the submerged experiences of everyday life from which struggles for recognition arise, and this leads to its rather narrow focus on established movements that have already achieved public recognition (see McNay 2009).

In short, a phenomenology of suffering significantly expands a mainstream account of social justice by uncovering neglected types of social misery that arise from normalized structural inequalities. It is this concern with the neglected 'other' of justice that lies at the heart of Honneth's critique of Habermas's discourse, which has become so removed from such existential issues of domination that an 'extreme discrepancy' has opened up between it and the experience of the democratic subjects whom it is supposed to represent. Honneth appreciates the normative potential unlocked by Habermas's reformulation of reason in inter-subjective, dialogic terms, but he believes that it seriously underplays the distorting effects that entrenched social inequalities may have upon the capacity of individuals to act as deliberating agents. Many types of inequality are not revealed as, *pace* Habermas, violations of moral norms that may be formally expressed as justice claims but rather are experienced in a more immediate manner as types of psychological injury and suffering. In everyday consciousness, such injuries cannot easily be articulated as systematic normative demands but are felt in a more intuitive, inchoate and fragmentary way that may escape rational expression: 'The acting subject is in principle far too emotionally caught up in its situations, and has categorized its social environment too diversely into components capable of either moralization or strategic treatment, for us to assume that a consistent moral consciousness constitutes the norm' (Honneth 2007a: 85). The inchoate nature of certain injuries which leads to their lack of articulation is often compounded by socio-structural constraints, such as relative lack of social and educational capital, that do not expose particular groups to the need to 'depersonalize their own norms of action'. Lacking access to certain symbolically distinguished 'vocabularies of self-articulation', working-class people are often aware that they express themselves in a socially devalued manner, that they lack authority when they speak in public or semi-formal situations (Charlesworth 2000: 133–4). This lack of confidence in speaking – linguistic dispropriation – that ensues from tacitly knowing one's own social worth intensifies the silence of the dispossessed. As Bourdieu observes:

> The reality of linguistic legitimacy consists precisely in the fact that dominated individuals are always under the *potential jurisidiction* of formal law, even when they spend all their lives . . . beyond its reach, so that when placed in a formal situation they are doomed to silence or to the broken discourse which linguistic investigation also often records. (1991: 71–2)

Suffering is an expression of the way in which domination is maintained through embodied power relations and, in Honneth's view, this is better grasped by the conceptualization of social bonds as relations of recognition, rather than communication.

Habermas obliquely acknowledges some types of pathological and disempowering experience in the thesis of the 'colonization of the lifeworld' when the instrumental considerations (money and power) intrude upon and distort the communicative processes whereby societies debate the norms and values which should guide them. The difficulty with the idea of colonization is, however, that it views this distortion as extrinsic to social practices, as an external, invasive force emanating from 'systems' and warping the communicative processes of the lifeworld. The possibility not entertained by Habermas is that the lifeworld may itself give rise to forms of suffering through its own intrinsic pathological tendencies rather than through the exogenous distortions of money and power. Prejudicial and ideological beliefs, such as homophobia and racism, that construe certain individuals as less worthy of respect and esteem than others can't really be said to originate in an external realm but are deeply, if unevenly, embedded and reproduced in patterns of socialization and linguistic communication. As a result of this one-sided view of power, Habermas's definition of justice as reaching understanding free from domination is only tangentially related, at best, to such experiences of disrespect. It does not adequately penetrate the prior conditions in the lifeworld that affect entry into communicative relations, meaning that, for reasons of, say, prejudice, some speakers are never as equal as others.[7] The claim that norms of equality underpin communicative ethics becomes an empty formula if, in Honneth's words, these norms do not permit 'subjects to present themselves in intersubjective structures of public life without shame' (2012a: 8). Habermas in fact sidesteps such underlying existential issues with the repeated assertion that, by the time they have reached the point of debate, issues of misrecognition should have been solved, that recognition of the individual as a unique and autonomous being is a 'universal and unavoidable' presupposition of communicative debate (1992: 191). In making such an assertion, he implicitly ignores widespread forms of suffering that persist in diffuse feelings of humiliation and shame or silent forms of disapproval but that rarely erupt into forms of collective protest. 'Silence' is a frequent feature of oppression and may be understood as the effect of the incorporation of structural violence into the body which is then lived in the euphemized form of a habitus of acceptance or resignation. There is, for example, a literature on social oppression and age that draws attention to the silence that surrounds the experiences of loss, frailty and dependence that accompany growing older. The social denigration and fear of ageing mean that there is no adequate language in which it can be constructively expressed and it is therefore often lived as a socially negative or reviled subjectivity, 'a subjectivity that is the repository of the social terror of ageing and death, and therefore a place where one's own lived reality has to be constantly and insecurely denied' (Frost and Hoggett 2008: 448). Similarly, in her work on melancholia, Judith Butler (1997) talks about the way in which certain experiences of loss are symbolically obliterated because there is no public recognition or discourse through which they might be named or mourned. Many unjust and injurious experiences are hard to put into words because they are not so much temporally discrete events as persistent, lived background conditions of stigmatization and purposelessness – 'pathologies', as Honneth understands them, that do not exist in their details in consciousness. Continued unemployment, for example, is not so much a specific, identifiable injury to self-identity as a pervasive state of alienation that empties lives of social significance and purpose and is experienced at an embodied level as 'a vague, amorphous kind of confused abjection; as boredom; a dull ache; apathy and inertia' (Charlesworth 2000: 71). The accumulated effects of deprivation are pernicious precisely because they are taken into the body and internalized as feelings of worthlessness that distort the most basic sense of purposive being in the world.

Lacking an interpretative perspective, procedural deliberation is unable to discern these silences and interpret their significance; as a result, it loses sight of major social pathologies and the means with which to criticize them. One such cluster of pathologies pertain to class, which, in Honneth's view, has been wrongly displaced as a central concern of political theory despite the fact it remains fundamental to an understanding of social inequality. What Honneth finds especially helpful in Bourdieu's idea of social suffering, then, is the way it places a renewed emphasis on class inequality but in the reconfigured terms of the existential significance of labour for self-identity. Clearly, labour has always been central to Marxist thought, but since Arendt's separation of the realm of action and freedom from those of labour and work, it has been emptied of much experiential and political significance and, by and large, reduced to the status of merely instrumental activity. A phenomenological perspective rectifies this by disclosing the significance of work to self-esteem and to the process of healthy identity formation. It is a crucial underpinning of an individual's sense of being a valued member of society and also to her core ability to deal with the fears of living in an increasingly uncertain world. Although material compensation for labour is important, so too is its social recognition as fulfilling and worthwhile. For Honneth, it is, in particular, the changing nature of labour and its increased 'precarization' under neoliberalism that renders the workplace one of the primary loci for this new diffuse but widespread type of suffering. The increasing precariousness of work transcends established class lines, creating new forms of inequality as it pulls workers from across all strata into its short-term, unprotected and unpredictable conditions, exposing them to greater uncertainty about their future (LaVaque-Manty 2008: 107–8). The work itself offers neither any kind of career progression, nor any meaningful occupational identity, leaving individuals 'hovering between deeper self-exploitation and disengagement'

(Standing 2011: 20). It deepens existing inequalities of class, gender and race, and intensifies feelings of vulnerability and despair: 'The precaritised mind is fed by fear and is motivated by fear' (Standing 2011: 20). In the most fundamental sense, the inceasing precariousness of work weakens the capacity to hope (Deranty 2008: 456; see also Bourdieu 2000: 207–34). Thus, under the 'flexible' conditions of globalized capital, labour continues to be alienated in so far as it does not contribute to an individual's sense of being a valued member of society. Class deprivation persists in a symbolic form, in the 'asymmetrical distribution of cultural and psychological life chances', but, on the whole, it remains largely unarticulated, lying beneath more publicly visible forms of normative conflict and taking the form of 'unco-ordinated attempts to gain, or regain, social honor' (Honneth 2007a: 93–4). In order to keep such pathologies in mind, a positive theory of moral principles must be grounded in the experiences of social subjects, that is, in negative perceptions of misrecognition and injury, lest it become a purely formal universalism. Disconnected from such experiences, procedural accounts of justice lose sight of the way in which societies may 'demonstrate a moral deficit without violating generally valid principles of justice' and, therefore, often do not coincide with the normative expectations of individuals (Honneth 2008: 84). This is not to say that a realist moral theory attuned to social suffering is purely descriptive and that the validity of normative principles can be derived in a straightforward sense from empirical experience. Disclosing critique recognizes that its relation to 'truth' is indirect in so far as it seeks not to present a definitive account of the world but rather to expand the terms of social scientific analysis and debate (see conclusion). It remains the case that procedural theories of justice frequently presume the existence of ready-made political subjects who are able to understand their oppression, express it coherently and accept the importance of participating in the political game to effect progressive change. For Honneth, as for Bourdieu, this assumption is troubling because, in ignoring aspects of the lived reality of oppression such as vulnerability, entrapment and alienation, it disregards deep-seated barriers to effective political agency. Indeed, in focusing on 'ordinary' suffering, Honneth has arguably rescued the Critical Theory tradition from the arid Habermasian concern with deliberation and restored one of its original central concerns, namely the unmasking of domination.

MISERABILISM AND NEGATIVISM

The danger of an unremitting focus on suffering is, of course, that it can border on a miserabilism that over-predicts the powerlessness of oppressed individuals. Honneth, as we have seen, is widely criticized for suffer-mongering, and Bourdieu, too, is frequently castigated for a determinism that empties the lives of subordinated groups of meaning and vitality and denies them the agency to overcome their oppression (McRobbie 2002; Rancière 2003). It is undoubtedly the case that many disempowered groups can speak only too well about their oppression and are often motivated to do something about it, either through indirect methods of resistance or through direct political challenge. It is important, therefore, not to exaggerate levels of powerlessness and passivity. But the charge of miserabilism is also over-stated because it fails to appreciate the important role a social theoretical perspective on negative experience plays in keeping in mind the plight of the most oppressed groups in society. Arguably this is vital in the light of changing patterns of social control which render certain kinds of oppression and pathology less visible than they otherwise might be.

The criticism of miserabilism is levelled by Veit Bader (2007) at Honneth, who, he claims, 'victimizes the victims' by over-estimating the moral and psychological incapacitation that is supposedly the inevitable consequence of deep and enduring forms of collective misrecognition. Bader argues that there is little compelling sociological evidence for the existence of 'cultures of poverty' that are supposed to invoke in individuals the feelings of helplessness, resignation, dependence and marginality designated in the idea of social suffering. He goes on to maintain that, far from being passively endured, practices of collective injustice – exclusion, marginalization, domination, and so forth – are as likely to give rise to submerged forms of resistance. As evidence, Bader cites James Scott's celebrated study *Domination and the Arts of Resistance*, the central thesis of which is that 'the large historical forms of domination . . . are . . . unable to prevent the creation of an independent social space in which subordinates can talk in comparative safety' (Scott 1990: 85). In other words, to arrive at a realistic rather than exaggerated understanding of the nature and extent of oppression, it is important to focus on uncovering the 'hidden transcripts' of dominated groups rather than relying on the 'public transcripts' of dominant groups. The latter inevitably only provide limited insight into the ways in which powerless groups resist their subordination. Finally, even where incapacitation does exist, Bader maintains that it is not nearly as enduring and pernicious in its effects as 'misguided' structuralists like Honneth or Bourdieu suggest; indeed the evidence is 'that so-called internalised submission melts like snow in the sun if windows of opportunity to communicate and act are (left) open' (Bader 2007: 264).

The difficulty with Bader's critique is that, in the desire to rebut a sociological miserabilism, he perhaps too quickly endorses a naïve view of populist resistance. Contra his claim that there is little evidence for enduring incapacitation, one might point to a host of sociological studies that attest both to the persistence of cultures of poverty and cycles of deprivation and to the depth of their distorting effects upon embodied being. With regard to the use of Scott's idea of hidden transcripts as examples of covert defiance, it is important to bear in mind the dangers of romanticizing subaltern practices as inherently resistant. Resistance itself is a slippery concept, as a number of commentators have noted, that often imputes a vague contestatory force to ordinary practices without demonstrating what precisely is being resisted or indeed how exactly they disrupt the hegemonic culture of control. What is regarded as resistance from one perspective can be viewed, from another, as the making bearable of the otherwise intolerable (Frost and Hoggett 2008). This amounts to the difference, mentioned earlier, between first- and second-order notions of agency. Powerless groups may not lack the capacity to render their conditions of oppression tolerable, but whether this amounts to an assertion of political agency in terms of control or transformation of their conditions of existence is another matter entirely.

Of greatest significance, however, is Bader's failure to tackle directly widespread tendencies to social fragmentation that undermine the solidaristic forms of social existence that are a necessary underpinning of the group resistance he celebrates. What ideas of social suffering draw attention to above all is the corrosive effects of a marketized individualism that erodes collective bonds and other types of social solidarity.[8] One of the key features of the new urban poor is, for instance, a deep material and symbolic fragmentation that deprives them of any sense of group solidarity (Wacquant 2008). Similarly, by virtue of their internal division and disarray, the precariat are alienated from the main mechanisms of democratic representation and, as a result, lack political voice (Standing 2011: 77). In relying on Scott's idea of hidden forms of group activity, Bader assumes a holistic and simplified domination–resistance model of subordination that does not capture the complex reality of contemporary forms of oppression. It is to combat this problem of the internal disorder and ensuing political invisibility of certain groups that Nancy Fraser, for example, introduces the dimension of representation (along with those of recognition and redistribution) into her model of justice as participatory parity. Transnational flexible capitalism has had the effect of creating new exploited groups – such as, say, migrant care workers – who, because of their geographic dispersal and insecure work conditions, are effectively not visible as a democratic constituency and consequently undergo 'political death'. While it might be a straightforward matter to identify the objective mechanisms of their exploitation, it is not so easy to establish a political solution to their oppression precisely because, as a group, they are so dispersed. The claims of such groups are often channelled into the domestic political space of relatively powerless states, which has the expedient effect of preventing the issue becoming the responsibility of more powerful states and of shielding transnational powers from critique and control. In short, a politics of representation is important to challenge and rethink conventional constituencies and boundaries of the political in order to make visible this growing class of 'non-persons' whose social precariousness places them beyond the reach of justice. In the light of this kind of fragmentation, it cannot be assumed that oppressed groups necessarily possess the internal cohesion and resources for mobilization and resistance that Bader renders so unproblematic.

There is no intrinsic reason, then, why the focus on social suffering should be tantamount to an unacceptable paternalism, as Bader and others have it. Bourdieu emphatically rejects the accusation of failing to go beyond a cramped, defeatist social vision. Although there is no easy route from suffering to politics, he sees his ethnography as having potentially empowering and mobilizing effects upon the subjects whose lives it describes. As he puts it:

> [A]s skeptical as one may be about the social efficacy of the sociological message, one has to acknowledge the effect it can have in allowing those who suffer to find out that their suffering can be imputed to social causes and thus to feel exonerated; and in making generally known the social origin, collectively hidden, of unhappiness in all its forms, including the most intimate, the most secret. (Bourdieu et al. 1999: 629)

In this regard, there may be less distance between the positions of Bader and Bourdieu than initially seems. Bader himself has suggested that it might, in the end, be more productive for political theorists to start not with the ambitious aim of formulating positive ideals but with the negative one of identifying and avoiding serious harms. It is far easier, in his view, to agree on what constitutes serious forms of misrecognition and inequality than it is to reach agreement on a positive theory of what recognition and equality entail (Bader 2007: 248–51). Such a negative, minimalist approach doesn't preclude normative solutions but binds them to the analysis of oppression rather than assuming the form of abstract procedures. By defining effective political thought as fact-dependent and negative in nature, Bader is closer to the perspective of social suffering than he might chose to acknowledge.

RECOGNITION AND REIFICATION

If there are problems with Honneth's work, they lie not so much in the idea of social suffering per se but in the extent to which it is attached to an idea of recognition that is, in turn, generalized as the universal framework of ethical life. The critical potential of his early work on disclosing critique and social suffering is stymied by the ambitious claim, in his later work, that recognition is the foundational principle for a comprehensive social theory of modernity. Even as Honneth criticizes Habermas's communicative ethics for its unwarranted formalism, his work displays similar tendencies that undercut attention to the phenomenal specificities of social life. In order to sustain the assertion that recognition constitutes the normative kernel of social relations, Honneth deploys a reductive social theory grounded in a questionable ontology and a simplified account of power. This is where the work of Bourdieu and Honneth could be said to part company. On the former's ontology of complicity, power and embodied existence are coeval and therefore primacy must be given in any phenomenological account of experience to the dynamics specific to a given social location. On the latter's ontology of recognition, however, this social specificity is undercut by a teleology where power is only ever a *post-hoc* distortion of a primal empathetic link. Social relations are judged according to how far they stray from this primal empathy: that is, whether they are reified and genuine forms of recognition. Ultimately, then, the idea of recognition is a limiting, dualist theoretical construct that undermines the critique of power initiated by the idea of social suffering. In J.M. Bernstein's words: 'Although Honneth . . . gives a certain precedence to social suffering, his approach finally turns on providing a formal . . . reconstruction of the good life in recognitive terms; the price of this is to eclipse injustice and social suffering once again, and hence again to betray emphatic justice' (2005: 305).

Suffering, in Honneth's view, arises from misrecognition, and he makes the strong normative claim that modern societies can be understood as recognition orders. Recognition not only forms the basic structure of intersubjective social relations, but it also propels the overall direction of modern social development. Modern societies are imperfect realizations of a recognition order which, if it were to be fully realized, would represent the maximal conditions for positive self-realization and personal integrity. Indeed, in a Hegelian fashion, the development of modernity as a whole can be understood as the historical instantiation of ever more inclusive and capacious forms of recognition. Relations of recognition are accorded this teleological and normative pre-eminence over any other type of social interaction on the basis that they are constitutive of human development, and Honneth's primary source for this strong claim is the work of object relations theorists such as Winnicott and Benjamin (Honneth 1995: 96–107; 1999). Many problems arise from grounding a social theory in such a strong ontogenetic claim, and these have been extensively discussed by a variety of thinkers. A particular difficulty is that the normative and analytical senses of the idea of recognition blur into each other, with the effect that the positive valuation given to recognition as an ideal constrains its adequacy as a description of social relations (McNay 2008a: 132–8). Differently put, the normative monism of recognition does not really capture the multidimensional, complex nature of social relations of power without simplifying them, misrepresenting them or even sentimentalizing them (e.g. Bader 2007). It results, *inter alia*, in a psychologically reductive social theory where social relations are persistently viewed as extrapolations from the primary dyad of recognition. As a result, Honneth has rightly been taken to task for his misrepresentation of oppressive social hierarchies of gender, class and race as simply imperfectly realized relations of recognition (e.g. Van Den Brink and Owen 2007). For instance, an implication of his analysis is that if women's domestic labour were more positively recognized, then gender inequality in the family would diminish. As well as being a misleading way of framing the problem, recognition mystifies family relations as purely those of interpersonal dynamics of care, underplaying the extent to which they are also historically contingent, shaped by forces of money, social control and asymmetrical relations of power, often including domestic violence (e.g. Donzelot 1979; Fraser and Honneth 2003: 219–20; Shapiro 2001: 58–66; Thistle 2000).

A consequence of the reliance on an ontology that views all social relations as imperfect instantiations of a primal dyad of recognition is that Honneth is unable to acknowledge sufficiently how recognition can itself be distorted and normalizing. The normative pre-eminence of recognition is sustained by overlooking, for example, how the internalization of harmful norms might pervert prevailing standards of recognition such that, in conforming to them, individuals are subjected rather than empowered. For Foucault, for instance, the quest for recognition shares the same structure as the confessional – the paradigm of individualizing pastoral power – where individuals seek self-legitimation through being acknowledged within the disciplinary discourses of authority. From this perspective, what Honneth regards as the spontaneous and innate nature of the desire for recognition is an example of how, in late modernity, disciplinary structures have been so thoroughly internalized by individuals that they have become self-policing subjects. In his more recent work, Honneth addresses this problem of normalization through recognition, claiming that it is Foucault's work on the productivity of power that allows him to develop a more nuanced understanding of the potentially 'regulative patterns' of certain dynamics of reciprocal recognition (Honneth 2012b). As he puts it: 'Far from making a lasting contribution to the conditions of autonomy of the members of our society, social recognition appears merely to serve the creation of attitudes that conform to the dominant system' (Honneth 2007b: 323–4). In fact, his response to this dilemma of normalizing interpellation is decidedly unFoucauldian in that he breaks down the monolithic concept of recognition into a simplistic dualism of 'morally justified' and ideological forms. He acknowledges that it is not easy to distinguish between the two sorts of recognition because they are deeply intertwined. Like genuine types of recognition, ideological variants are not crudely negative but may have a positive appearance in that they are freely assumed and have a productive, evaluative content in terms of subject identification. Given these apparent similarities that make it difficult to definitively separate genuine from unjustified content from within 'the unbroken flow of a many-layered struggle for recognition', Honneth goes on to stipulate that it is only the former that will be reinforced by corresponding progressive changes in the material circumstances of society, for instance expansion of legal and political rights or economic redistribution (2007b: 342). Ideological forms of recognition are not underpinned by correlative changes in the concrete social world and, in so far as they lack material content and are illusory, an irrational core lies beneath their rational appearance:

Suffering and Social Weightlessness 59

'The deficiency by which we might recognize such ideologies could consist in the structural inability to ensure the material prerequisites for realizing new evaluative qualities' (Honneth 2007b: 346). Thus, along with consumer advertising, Honneth identifies the neoliberal discourse that positions individuals as entrepreneurs vis-à-vis the world of work as ideological forms of recognition in so far as an 'abyss opens up' between their 'evaluative promise' and 'material fulfilment' (2007b: 346).

An immediate difficulty with this distinction between genuine and ideological forms of recognition is its apparent resurrection of a reductive and untenable distinction between illusion and reality, the symbolic and the material, which Foucault and Bourdieu, along with many others, decisively deconstructed in their work on the corporeal internalization of power. A neoliberal discourse of entrepreneurship has many pernicious effects, but Honneth's idea that these are somehow ideological or illusory in that they are less instantiated in material institutions and practices is not really a satisfactory or convincing approach. While neoliberal governance of the self might be ideologically driven, its social effects are much more complex and deep. It forms part of a material reshaping of the social realm which controls individuals, not through explicit forms of domination, but through rationalized techniques and devices which orient action to certain socially useful ends – the conduct of conduct. It multiplies individual freedoms in the context of a notion of responsible self-management whilst at the same time depoliticizing the state's relation to the individual, attenuating its duties and responsibilities towards vulnerable groups and eroding collective social practices (McNay 2009: 10–1). In such a vein, Judith Butler (2000a) unpicks the ambivalent effects of a certain liberalizing move on the part of the state towards family life and sexuality. The very moment at which the state progressively extends kinship and family rights to gays and lesbians is also the moment at which a more punitive, neoliberal response is shown to those who choose to live outside a two-parent family unit. A similar 'double entanglement' is described by Angela McRobbie where globalizing capital brings 'young women forward, as individualised subjects and . . . as agents of change' (2008: 6), in so far as it creates a new feminized workforce, at the same time as it reworks gender hierarchies where women remain the most vulnerable and exploited subjects. An implication of such analyses is that neoliberal governance forces us to rethink issues of subjectivity and identity politics beyond the dichotomous formula, suggested in Honneth's dualism of genuine and ideological modes of recognition, that regimes of power necessarily acknowledge or distort human subjectivity. Rather, these styles of government produce new modes of subjectivity, ways of being and acting that 'make up subjects as free persons' in a manner that is neither authentic nor inauthentic, neither genuine nor ideological (Rose 1999: 95).

In a later work, Honneth (2008) refines the ideas of genuine and ideological recognition as the difference between antecedent and reified recognition. The two distinctions clearly overlap, but the subsequent one is elaborated more explicitly in terms of the ontological conditions necessary for healthy human development. But, like the previous distinction, this one also amounts to a simplistic holding apart of good from bad forms of recognition and is an equally reductive way of explaining the operation of power upon embodied subjects and the reasons why individuals may resist and comply with their oppression. Again, Honneth returns to the problem of normalization: how it is that structures of recognition can themselves be distorted and normalizing given their instantiation within hierarchical relations of power. In response to this dilemma of normative interpellation, Honneth reworks recognition through a developmental reinterpretation of the concept of ideology drawn from Lukács's labour-oriented idea of reification. In Honneth's view, this permits him to make a sharper distinction between types of recognition that are enabling and those that are potentially distorting and repressive. Primordial or 'antecedent' recognition is defined as a pre-cognitive emotional acknowledgement or care of the other – paradigmatically expressed in the pre-oedipal bond between mother and infant – and 'epistemic' recognition is defined as a cognitive detached grasp of the other which is catalysed by the acquisition of language. Antecedent recognition precedes and therefore forms the condition of possibility of epistemic recognition in so far as the ability to assume a detached perspective on the other is founded in the primal experience of empathetic engagement or pre-cognitive acknowledgement: 'Without this antecedent act of recognition, infants could not take over the perspectives of their figures of attachment, and adults would be incapable of properly understanding the linguistic propositions of those with whom they interact' (Honneth 2008: 52). To substantiate the 'generic and conceptual' ontological priority of antecedent recognition, Honneth draws on what he calls the 'evidence' of similar theories of a primal sympathetic mutuality found in object relations theory and in the philosophies of Heidegger, Dewey and Cavell, amongst others. Reification – 'forgetfulness of recognition' – occurs when epistemic forms of recognition become overly detached and rigid, forgetting their origin in this antecedent 'interaction of existential care'. Clearly, not all forms of socially objectified cognition are reified: the 'neutralization of recognition and engagement' is necessary for many types of formal knowledge and 'intelligent problem solving'. Reification occurs when a cognitive stance becomes rigid and over-emphasized or is based in a retroactive denial of recognition for the purposes of maintaining a stereotype or prejudice. In short, it can be a feature of an excessively objectified relation with the self, or others, or with the objective world, although one does not necessarily follow from the other. Consequently, an emancipatory social theory must strive to develop analytical criteria which help to understand and criticize possible reifying tendencies within society.

Although it is presented as a refinement of his previous argument, it is not clear whether Honneth's (2012b) distinction between antecedent, epistemic and reified modes of recognition really goes much further than his earlier work in adequately depicting potentially 'regulative patterns' of certain dynamics of reciprocal recognition (2007b: 323–4). Rather, it seems simply further to embed his social theory in a tendentious and romanticized ontology which resembles nothing so much as a 'secularized version of the fall' (Lear 2008: 131) and which creates problems at all levels of analysis. The idea of antecedent care is based in an emotionally one-sided ontology which universalizes the positive feelings of the primal bond but filters out the negative ones such as fear or hatred, which, according to many thinkers, are equally as elemental (Butler 2008: 103–4). It also reifies socially contingent parenting arrangements in the idealized archetype of the singular bond. For instance, as Winnicott himself came to realize, the maternal function could be distributed across several caregivers and therefore the primary bond need not always be dyadic (Butler 2008: 107). The dyad is also structurally skewed in that it emphasizes a primal mutuality when in fact other accounts of infant development might highlight the asymmetrical dynamics of being born into a world which is fundamentally alien and inaccessible, encapsulated in the enigmatic, even troubling, presence of the mother (e.g. Laplanche 1999). By tacitly eliding the idea of cognition with the idea of power, Honneth is able to defer these negative, asymmetrical aspects of infant experience to the second moment of epistemic recognition and can assert therefore a symmetrical mutuality as a primordial state. But this elision is misleading since, whilst it is reasonable to assume that cognition may indeed come after recognition, the same cannot be said for the asymmetrical social relations that pre-exist the infant and that shape the world into which she is born and of which she has to make sense. As Carolyn Steedman's (1986) work demonstrates, for instance, primary familial dynamics are marked, *ab initio*, by the dynamics of class, and, in her own biographical case, deprivation, in a way that problematizes archetypes of patriarchal authority and maternal care and, more generally, the uni-directional movement from psyche to society. In other words, asymmetrical power relations are arguably as much an intrinsic feature of primary, empathetic forms of recognition as they are of epistemic forms. To quote Butler: 'Why do we imagine that the primary structures of the social begin with the child? . . . what social relations make possible the emergence of the child, and what relations are in place, waiting for the child, when it emerges into the world?' (2008: 108). Honneth, however, obscures this co-originality of power and embodied being by setting up a questionable chronology that artificially detaches an untrammelled primal dyad from the context of hierarchical social relations in which it is ineluctably embedded, thus establishing the former's tendentious normative primacy.

Having been careful, in his earlier work on suffering, to avoid a subjectivist attribution of authenticity to embodied experience, Honneth seems to resort to such a problematic notion in the idea of antecedent recognition. The difference between the ontology of recognition and Bourdieu's ontology of complicity or mutual possession between body and world is instructive here. In the former, there is a problematic teleology where power comes *ex posteriori* to distort primal affectual relations, whereas in the latter, power and embodied being are coeval and thus there can be no access to a supposedly untrammelled mutuality underpinning social relations. The truth, so to speak, of embodied existence is bound up with analysis of its social location. The co-implication of body and power does not rule out the possibility of moving towards types of interaction that are less oppressive than others, but it would be a considerably more complex task than the retroactive retrieval of some kind of mythic, antecedent relation of care and acknowledgement. To begin to understand various experiences of deprivation and marginality requires a more nuanced and multi-layered account of the impoverishing effects of dispossession upon embodied being than Honneth's dualism of reified and antecedent recognition permits. This distinction tells us little of significance about the diverse forms of sociality it supposedly encompasses, how these are instantiated within asymmetrical social relations and how it may be possible to transform them. Any such nuanced analysis is obscured beneath an over-drawn, massified dualism. In an obvious sense, escape from the 'bleak instrumentality of a brutal world' would involve the establishment of more meaningful personal relationships and of a purposive sense of being in the world, but, beyond an asocial notion of mutuality, the idea of antecedent recognition doesn't help us understand any of the details of this process. It might involve, for instance, the transformation of a habitus born of disappropriation and the inculcation of a more empowered orientation towards the world that begins both in the ability to give voice to one's demands and in the confidence that what one says is taken seriously. For some deprived individuals, acquisition of such a privileged linguistic habitus is a remote possibility, not because they are not capable of it, but because their adaptation to the chronic realities of their lives in the form of dispositions of reluctance, frustration and shame can render such acculturation a fundamentally alien and intimidating process:

> It is as though these people are perceptually damaged, and what looks like a natural absence of capacity in fact emerges from a taught inability and the damage that comes from being made to be intimidated by the expressive medium itself, such that they remain ... alienated from a range of perceptual and expressive tools that enable one access to the possibility of founding worthwhile relations. (Charlesworth 2000: 283)

In failing to address such phenomenal intricacies, Honneth's social theory of recognition reveals its central difficulty, namely its over-extension as a universal paradigm. His claim is that recognition yields a 'formal conception of ethical life' that bypasses the split between procedural but phenomenally empty notions of autonomy, on the one side, and determinate but relativist ethics, on the other. The assertion that recognition forms the necessary ontological grounds for healthy self-realization enables Honneth to elevate it to the status of a hyper-good towards which all concrete struggles and ethical conflict are oriented: '[Recognition] has to do with the structural elements of ethical life, which, from the general point of view of the communicative enabling of self-realization, can be normatively extracted from the plurality of all particular forms of life' (Honneth 1995: 172). Yet, just as the drive to transcendence in Habermas's formulation of discourse ethics weakens its understanding of the existential depth of certain types of oppression, so an analogous drive in Honneth's 'recognition theoretic approach' leads to a simplified account of embodied social relations. Recognition–misrecognition cannot be elevated to the sole underlying principle around which all negative social experiences and struggles turn without considerably reducing the latter's historical variability. The discernment of a single stable norm within the morass of historical struggles over diverse social goods denies their heterogeneity and also the extent to which they may, in themselves, be conflict generating. Rather than these struggles reflecting a single hyper-good of recognition, they may in fact represent a multiplicity of competing goods and hyper-goods that are deeply antagonistic to, even irreconcilable with, each other:

> Honneth does not sufficiently appreciate the extent to which the plural meanings of this ideal undermine the normative stability he ascribes to it. . . . A 'formal' conception of the good cannot overcome this stubborn fact. . . . Any conception of the good may be challenged to such an extent that its status as an idea of the good can be considerably devalued or simply discredited. (Kompridis 2004: 335)

Not only does it underplay questions of 'deep difference', but it is also questionable whether, as Honneth claims, such a universal, context-transcending perspective is necessary for a social theory to have critical purchase. A false choice seems to be set up between universalism and historicism, thereby negating the types of critical insight delivered by a number of more hermeneutically informed perspectives, including comparative, historical and genealogical approaches and, ironically, Honneth's own earlier phenomenology of suffering. As Nikolas Kompridis puts it: 'Ideas of the good do not need to be universalised to provide sufficient normative power for social criticism; quite the contrary, the attempt to universalise ideas of the good renders them less rather than more effective for purposes of social criticism' (2004: 336). What may be required instead is an historicization of what is more usually conceived of in formal, abstract terms, something that Bourdieu calls a 'Realpolitik of the universal' (2000: 80) but might also be thought of as a renewed effort to think through the dialectic of fact and norm suggested in disclosing critique.

Honneth's claim is precisely that his idea of recognition does straddle this line between universalism and specificity; it is not a straightforward ontology in that it is never fully independent from specific cultural and social contexts. Although the need for recognition is pre-social, it is only ever manifested in variable and socially specific forms (Fraser and Honneth 2003: 131–2). Yet, at the same time, recognition is not entirely a contingent construct: the psychological need for recognition is not relative to a given culture but is the fundamental prerequisite of healthy human self-development. Through this equivocation, Honneth appears to want to have it both ways: recognition is both a universal, transcendental structure and a contingent one. It is hard to see, however, how this circular logic is anything but self-cancelling. The claim to historical specificity – that forms of recognition are entirely shaped by social forces – is surely undermined by the positing of a self-same dynamic of the desire for recognition that is the unvarying psychological cause behind social conflict and transformation. Furthermore, given Honneth's claim that recognition provides a universal model of ethical life, it empties it of much content as a meaningful normative ideal. As critics such as Foucault and Bourdieu would argue, acts of recognition can be as normalizing as they are liberating, depending on who is doing the recognizing, what is being recognized and the particular form the act itself assumes. Honneth's unwavering investment in the idea of recognition as a universal norm leaves him unable to address these political dynamics in anything but the most simplistic terms and he finishes by espousing precisely the type of idealized abstraction that his earlier work on disclosing social critique set out to avoid.

CONCLUSION

Despite these limitations, Honneth's early work on disclosing critique stands as an important corrective to socially weightless tendencies in contemporary political theory. When read in conjunction with Bourdieu's ideas on social suffering, it serves as a reminder of the deeply depoliticizing effects of certain types of domination which, when internalized as embodied dispositions, can undermine the capacity and willingness of individuals to act as autonomous political agents. Their work underscores the point that formal assertions of democratic equality risk being empty formulae unless accompanied by thought on the social conditions necessary to realize effective agency. In questioning this presumption of agency, Bourdieu and Honneth bring to the fore a cluster of ethical and existential issues that have been relatively neglected in recent years because of a somewhat exaggerated fear, on the part of democratic theorists, of the dangers of a politics of pity. The work of these two thinkers shows that, when it is elaborated through an account of power, a phenomenology of social suffering has the potential to be more than an unmitigated miserabilism and becomes an effective tool for challenging settled views of the world and theoretical orthodoxies.

It is a phenomenological perspective on negative social experiences, understood as a vital element of disclosing critique, that informs my discussion of social weightlessness in subsequent chapters. Bourdieu and Honneth's criticism of the neglect of embodied experience is directed primarily at Habermas's work on communicative ethics and the notions of deliberative democracy that it has engendered. In this respect, their work adds to a well-established corpus of debates where deliberative thinkers have also responded in some detail to the critique of their paradigm. Rather than go over ground that has already been extensively covered, I use the perspective of social suffering to critically interrogate social weightlessness in a different body of work, one that is frequently opposed to deliberative theory, namely agonist accounts of democracy. There are various intellectual routes into the ideas of agonism, each giving rise to different notions of radical democratic politics. Associative ideas of agonism derived from Hannah Arendt are as dissimilar to the more conflictual formulations of agonist democracy found, say, in Chantal Mouffe as they are to the existential kind of agonist politics proposed by William Connolly or the ruptural agonism of Jacques Rancière. Despite their differences, however, they share an underlying scepticism about the deliberative elevation of consensus as the goal of democratic debate. Agonists highlight instead that disagreement is a necessary, even desirable, feature of any democratic order in so far as it reflects the inescapable centrality of struggles over power to political life. Within this general emphasis on power, radical agonists argue that it is vital to attend to struggles from below, the struggles of disempowered and excluded groups that any established order necessarily downplays or ignores in the attempt to maintain its own legitimacy. It is by being perpetually attentive to these marginalized voices that tendencies within established political community to reification and exclusion may be resisted and its inclusiveness sustained. Yet my claim is that, despite the explicit concern with challenging exclusion and inequality, agonists remain wedded to theoretical accounts of democracy that prevent them from realizing this aim in crucial respects. In particular, their understanding of political dynamics is so formulaic and socially weightless that, albeit unintended, they are unable to attend to the experiences of oppression of the very groups they wish to address. It is not clear, ultimately, what relevance their models of agonist democratic practice have to the conditions that govern the lives of disempowered individuals.

2
The Unbearable Lightness of Theory: Mouffe's Dissociative Agonism

INTRODUCTION

Ideas of agonist democracy are emerging as significant alternatives to those of deliberation that have, for some time now, dominated discussion amongst political theorists. Agonists reject the deliberative proposition that politics should be oriented towards the achievement of consensus, arguing instead that conflict is both an ineliminable and desirable feature of any democratic order. Some agonists formulate this argument in the largely realist terms of the unavoidable centrality of disagreement and conflict to politics. From this perspective, it is naïve, even normatively dangerous, to think that it is ever possible to translate deep difference and struggles over power into enduring political agreement. Even if it were possible to achieve such a consensus, then, in the view of agonists, this would undoubtedly depend on the assertion of power and not, as deliberative theorists have it, on the uncoerced use of public reason. Other agonists understand the definitive nature of struggle to democratic practice as an ontological rather than an empirical issue, claiming that it is a symptom of the radical indeterminacy or lack that underpins any socio-political order. From the perspective of this foundational indeterminacy, there can be no natural or given order of things; things could always be otherwise. Any social-democratic regime only ever represents a contingent and temporary crystallization of power that in order to maintain hegemony conceals its fundamental arbitrariness behind assertions of its supposed consensual and fair nature. Even democratic regimes that appear to be fully inclusive cannot lay claim to an incontestable legitimacy for, in the agonist view, they are always predicated on latent or unforeseen exclusions that render them vulnerable to contestation and challenge. Given the insuperability of conflict, the task of the agonist theorist is not to propose ways of overcoming it but rather to discover means of channelling it into safe and productive forms of disagreement that are compatible with democratic commitments to freedom and equality. Institutionalized struggle, not consensus, speaks to a democracy that is vibrant, alive to demands from below and perpetually alert to its own limitations and how to overcome them.

It is this second ontological strand of thought that is the focus of this chapter and, in particular, the work of Chantal Mouffe on dissociative agonism. A potential problem for Mouffe and other agonist theorists is that the claim that empirical struggle is symptomatic of the radical contingency of social life may lead to an undiscriminating pluralism where all hegemonic regimes are regarded as equally as arbitrary as each other and conflict is valued as an end in itself regardless of its outcomes. Mouffe explicitly rejects such relativism and asserts the radical thrust of her notion of agonist pluralism, which, in the final instance, is intended to promote the inclusion of oppressed groups and expand an understanding of possibilities for emancipatory transformation. The agonist emphasis on conflict is of value not in itself, but in so far as it shines a light on the struggles of marginal and oppressed groups to overcome inequality and achieve political recognition. It also suggests new ways of understanding political identities and alliances that may reinvigorate the commitment to inclusive democratic values. Underlying this is the claim that ontological reflection on the political is in itself radicalizing in so far as it sharpens the critique of power and discloses new possibilities for democratic practice.

Whilst, in principle, reflection on foundational political dynamics may be compatible with a radical critique of power, I argue that in fact Mouffe falls into an abstract and self-referential logic whose relevance to concrete issues of exclusion, oppression and democratic practice is questionable. She recognizes that the mere assertion of the arbitrariness of all democratic orders is not sufficient to sustain radical democratic critique. It is little more than an empty formula if it is not accompanied by an attentiveness to the specific mechanisms through which certain groups are denied democratic parity and also to citizen struggles for inclusion. Accordingly, Mouffe draws on phenomenologically oriented thinkers such as Ludwig Wittgenstein and Stanley Cavell to highlight the diversity and creativity of the practices of daily life which are the ultimate source of democratic legitimacy. It is reference to this phenomenological substrate that is also a central plank of Mouffe's critique of deliberative proceduralism. Unfortunately, it is precisely this invocation of embodied praxis that reveals a fundamental discontinuity in her thought. For despite the repeated claim that agonist democracy is sustained by ordinary citizen practices, Mouffe reverts to a rigid anti-essentialist logic that cannot treat the former as anything other than an uninteresting positivity or essentialism. The one-dimensional anti-essentialism that governs her reasoning turns the distinction between the ontological and the ontic, the political and the social, into a conceptual hierarchy where the former term is granted absolute priority over the latter. The primacy of the 'necessary' logic of the political over the inert realm of the social enables Mouffe to close off issues of power that are crucial to her account of agency. She finishes with an account of democratic agonism that is so far removed from the actual practices and dynamics of everyday life that its radical credentials are thrown into question.

ANTAGONISM, AGONISM AND DELIBERATION

As we saw in the introduction, a distinctive feature of some leftist democratic theory is the elaboration of ideas of the political in explicitly ontological terms (e.g. Marchart 2007; Strathausen 2008; Tønder and Thomassen 2006; White 2000). These notions of the 'political' are not ontological in a strict philosophical sense, but they are in the sense that they start from claims about fundamental existential features of social being and then, from these claims, derive models of democracy which arguably best enshrine, contain or draw out these features. Unlike what Stephen K. White terms the cast-iron certainties of strong ontology, these more open-ended ontologies highlight in one way or another the fundamental contingency of social existence and the consequences that this constitutive indeterminacy may have for an understanding of democratic ethics and politics. The appeal of this ontological focus for radical democrats is that it is held to be a powerful way of contesting some of the central presuppositions of conventional political theory about supposedly given, inevitable features of the social order (rational individualism, for example) and, thereby, of generating new ways of thinking about political transformation. The ontological turn allows radical democrats to, in White's words, 'think ourselves, and being in general, in ways that depart from the dominant . . . ontological investments of modernity' (2000: 4). Thus, although radical democrats diverge in their precise understanding of the nature of the 'political', many of them currently deploy some kind of distinction between the 'ontological' and the 'ontic', the 'political' and 'social', the 'transcendental' and the 'empirical', to further the ends of progressive critique.

Mouffe's work on agonism is a paradigm of this form of ontological reasoning, which is held to give rise to a revivified understanding of radical democratic politics. Her claim that conflict is an ineradicable feature of politics is based less on a sociological observation about the inescapability of power, as it is for realists such as Raymond Guess and Bernard Williams, than on the ontological assertion that socio-political being itself is constituted through antagonism. On this view, the political cannot be restricted to determinate forms, whether it be a certain type of institution, specific sphere of activity or mode of behaviour. Rather, it is a dimension of antagonism inherent in every human society and that forms the condition of possibility of social existence; the political 'determines our very ontological condition' (Mouffe 1993: 3). We live, however, in an era of profound depoliticization exemplified in what Mouffe regards as the prevailing post-political zeitgeist. This is the view that those in Western democracies can anticipate a cosmopolitan future based on 'peace, prosperity and the implementation of human rights world-wide' because of the decline of sharp divisions between left and right, the spread of economically productive, post-conventional social orders and the globalization of democratic values (Mouffe 2005: 1). Such ideas typify not just common-sense apprehensions of the world but also democratic theory that turns around notions of global justice, the public use of reason and universal human rights. It is a world-view that presumes the prevalence of co-operation, consensus and stability and that underplays, even arguably ignores, deep difference, hostility and violent conflict. In so far as it is blind to the irreducible presence of antagonism in politics, democratic theory is unable, in Mouffe's view, to deal with many of the most fundamental and pressing problems facing contemporary societies. In an increasingly fractured and unstable world order, the liberal preoccupation with impartial procedures of reconciliation not only seems naïve but also runs the risk of aggravating the violent forces and deep divisions at work in society. What is needed instead are theories of democratic politics that tackle conflict and antagonism head on rather than seeking to overcome them or set them outside the parameters of reasoned debate. This theoretical acknowledgement that antagonism is the constitutive feature of political life leads, in Mouffe's view, to a renewed understanding of the radical possibilities for democracy.

What does it mean to understand the political in terms of a foundational antagonism? According to Mouffe, it is precisely the failure to understand the political in its ontological dimension that remains at the root of our 'current incapacity' to think about politics in a genuinely radical way (Mouffe 2005: 8). Mouffe's ontological account of antagonism was originally most fully developed in her influential early work with Ernesto Laclau, *Hegemony and Socialist Strategy* (1985), and is sufficiently well known to only briefly need restating. The idea that antagonism is constitutive of socio-political being is based on the anti-essentialist, relational account of meaning taken partly from structural linguistics and partly from Lacanian psychoanalysis. Conventional accounts of conflict and disagreement, captured in, say, liberal ideas of pluralism, rely on an 'essentialist' logic of the social that regards objectivity as residing in 'things themselves', the idea of 'being as presence'. On an anti-essentialist account, social being has no intrinsic meaning, 'pure presence or objectivity'; rather, things (elements) only acquire an identity and significance from the way in which they are organized in relation to other elements. When this relational logic is generalized, the social realm comes to be conceived of as a kind of negative essence, a potential infinitude of elements – the 'impossibility of society' – that only acquires meaning as a set of fixed relations through an act of political institution (the moment of the political). In other words, there is a foundational indeterminacy or 'undecidability' that underpins social being. By organizing elements according to a particular set of signifying relations, the political realm brings the social into being and conceals its mutable and lack of foundations beneath the appearance of a stable and self-evident order of things, a domain of 'sedimented' practices (Mouffe 2005: 17). Drawing on Carl Schmitt's famous friend/enemy distinction, Mouffe argues that a political order achieves this stabilization or hegemony through the successful organization of relations around a 'we/they' distinction. In this regime of inclusion/exclusion, some individuals are incorporated as legitimate citizens under the symbolic imaginary of 'the people'/the 'nation', and so forth, and others are barred and constituted as non-citizens. Given, that such types of collective identification could always be arranged otherwise, that the friend/enemy distinction may take a number of imaginary personifications, the legitimacy of any hegemonic political order is also always open to contestation on the basis of the exclusions upon which it is necessarily predicated.

A hegemonic political order is always therefore both contingent and coercive; it is an arbitrary but forced stabilization of what is, at base, the open-ended flux of social being. Underpinned as it is by a radical undecidability, there are no final grounds that an order can appeal to in order to provide itself with an incontestable legitimacy (Mouffe 2005: 17). Inevitably, any order will try to conceal its essential contestability by presenting itself as the outcome of consensus or natural law or some other legitimating principle. Ultimately, however, such attempts can only ever temporarily bring to a halt the process of contestation and antagonism from which it has emerged. On this relational logic, even the most apparently inclusive and consensual order is necessarily founded (albeit unwittingly) on unforeseen, potentially unjust exclusions that, in due course, will be subject to challenge and contestation: 'Every order is the temporary and precarious articulation of contingent practices. The frontier between the social and the political is essentially unstable and requires constant displacements and renegotiations between social agents' (Mouffe 2005: 18).

It is this political ontology as the 'ever present possibility' of antagonism that distinguishes Mouffe's idea of agonistic democracy from consensus-oriented accounts of deliberation (Mouffe 2005: 16). The stress on impartial reasoning and agreement that runs through ideas of deliberative democracy represents for her a profoundly anti-political vision. By downplaying agonism and contestation, it fails to recognize what is really at stake in politics, namely the struggle to achieve and maintain power in the face of perpetual challenge. Furthermore, in misrecognizing the constitutive nature of antagonism, ideas of deliberation also deny their own 'political' nature by presenting consensus as rationally attained and therefore as beyond hegemony, a pure space of freedom. Agreement, on Mouffe's view, is never the product of rational and voluntary deliberation but the result of the imposition of authority, a coerced and temporary cessation of struggle. The deliberative occlusion of power engenders its much commented upon tendency to substitute morality for politics. Whether in its first-order Rawlsian or second-order Habermasian form, deliberative theory assumes that significant political problems can be dealt with through the direct application of moral principles or, failing that, through the application of procedures that are capable of delivering such principles. Mouffe here adds her voice to the already extensive criticism of this applied ethics approach to politics as, at best, naïve in its belief in the integrative force of rational universalism. At worst, it is potentially dangerous in so far as the misrecognition of Western norms as supposedly transcendental and impartial runs the risk of intensifying social and political conflict through the marginalization and exclusion of dissenting others. Dissent can take on violent forms if it is not accommodated sufficiently into legitimate political channels.

It follows, then, that the essence of a vibrant democracy resides not in reconciliation and the supersession of conflict but rather in the flourishing of disagreement and struggle. A central task for the agonist theorist is to work out how potentially unruly and violent antagonisms can be channelled into a framework compatible with democratic values. What forms should the tamed we/they antagonism take so as to encourage the expression of difference whilst not violating a genuinely pluralist ethos? Mouffe understands this passage from antagonism to agonism as involving the transformation of enemies into adversaries: 'The aim of democratic politics is to construct the "them" in such a way that it is no longer perceived as an enemy to be destroyed, but as an "adversary", that is, somebody whose ideas we combat but whose right to defend those ideas we do not put into question' (Mouffe 2000: 102). Antagonistic opponents do not share a symbolic space in which to discuss their differences, whereas agonistic adversaries do but have differing conceptions of how it should be organized (Mouffe 2000: 13). An adversary is someone whose ideas we oppose but whose right to hold those ideas we do not question. Unlike enemies, adversaries 'have a shared adhesion to the ethico-political principles of liberal democracy: liberty and equality. But [they] disagree concerning the meaning and implementation of those principles' (Mouffe 2000: 102).

Needless to say, Mouffe's assertion that organized dissensus should be the structuring principle of radical democracy has provoked a strong critical response from deliberative thinkers. They have a number of complaints, chief amongst which is that she misrepresents the status of consensus in their thought by reifying it as an absolute category. Most deliberative theorists recognize that consensus is a regulative ideal to guide deliberation rather than an actual outcome. In actual political practice, its function is more likely to be pragmatic, open to revision and renegotiation and able therefore to accommodate conflict (Erman 2009: 1056). Although consensus is never purely rational and is always, to some degree, an expression of power relations, it does not follow that all forms of consensus are equally as bad or lacking in justification as each other. Conversely, it is not clear how the perpetual conflict that

Mouffe propounds would promote the values of tolerance, open-mindedness, respect and co-operation that are necessary to sustain agonistic debate and, consequently, why it is a desirable characteristic for radical democracy (e.g. Crowder 2006). Deliberative thinkers also take issue with the ontological priority that Mouffe accords to antagonism and, against this, they claim that it is, in fact, consensus that must be constitutive of the socio-political order. On Mouffe's view, the central aim of radical democracy is to convert social antagonisms into political agonism, but this can only be feasible on the presumption of an a priori agreement amongst political subjects to abide by the rules of the agonistic game, or, in Mouffe's terms, the shared underlying commitment to the ethico-political principles of liberal democracy. Persons must have agreed beforehand to represent their disputes within a common symbolic framework, to accept the terms of the framework and to respect the other's right to do so similarly. Since the assumption of this prior agreement is unacknowledged by Mouffe, her theory appears, on the face of it, to be incoherent because it lacks any mechanism to explain how the consensual move from antagonism to agonism is achieved. She has to presume a priori some shared interpersonal structure of norms already at subjects' disposal if agonistic political agency is to be intelligible. Without such a shared structure, the decision to move from antagonism to agonism remains opaque to others; it can only be understood as a kind of a solipsist decisionism: that is, a form of ungrounded subjectivism that would appear to contradict Mouffe's avowedly anti-essentialist theoretical commitments (Erman 2009; see also Norris 2006: 121–3).

The deliberative response to the agonist critique is not without grounds, but, in general, the debate over the ontological priority of consensus versus dissensus tends to become misleadingly polarized. Indeed, in the view of some, the debate turns around a 'false problem' in so far as it is not really an issue that can necessarily be determined in advance and in an abstract manner, nor does it necessarily amount to a zero-sum choice between agreement or conflict. Rather, the choice between conflict or consensus always emerges in a specific political context and makes sense to the actors involved, who make a practical decision in favour of one or other strategy according to the logic of circumstances. Indeed this reduction of relational political complexities to misleadingly dichotomous debates is, in Ian Shapiro's view, symptomatic of the flight from reality widespread amongst political theorists who take refuge behind 'gross' or simplifying abstractions that divert attention from 'first-order questions about the world which they purport to be interested in, diverting it to second-order questions about concepts' (2007: 14).

It is, however, with regard to such questions about the world, particularly issues of power and agency, that Mouffe's agonism can be understood to pose a more substantial challenge to deliberative theory, although it is one that gets somewhat lost in the dissensus–consensus opposition. The challenge pertains to the issue of agency and whether, in rendering debate the ultimate form of democratic action, deliberative theory is skewed towards maintaining the status quo or existing political community and is biased against challenges that call this community into question. In short, it finishes in a politics of resignation, of accommodation to the prevailing order, rather than one of potentially radical transformation (e.g. Scheuerman 1999). It is Mouffe's claim that an agonist politics that accepts the inevitability of conflict and the fundamental openness of democratic structures to challenge of any type – not just those that take the form of rational justice claims – is far more receptive to a radical politics from below. This acknowledgement of the contestability of all political structures renders agonism, in principle, sensitive to the myriad, heterogeneous and often provocative forms of speech and action that marginal and excluded groups may deploy in their attempt to acquire political voice. As we will see in the next section, Mouffe draws on the work of Cavell and Wittgenstein to demonstrate the theoretical sensitivity of agonist democracy to the dynamics of ordinary practice. In the final instance, however, she is unable to develop the insights implied in this turn towards practice because it conflicts with, and is ultimately undermined by, the one-dimensional anti-essentialism that rigidly governs her paradigm.

POWER, EXCLUSION AND PRACTICE

The kind of institutionalized dissensus that lies at the heart of Mouffe's agonist democracy is, according to some commentators, not really that different from the competitive dynamics of established ideas of liberal pluralism (e.g. Crowder 2006; Deveaux 1999). Mouffe emphatically rejects such a criticism, repeatedly asserting that agonist democracy is radical not liberal because it is inextricably linked to the struggles of marginal and subjected groups against inequality and exclusion. Agonist pluralism is intended to celebrate conflict and difference not for their own sake but rather only in so far as they are symptoms of challenges to hierarchical social relations from marginal and disempowered groups. Agonist pluralism, then, is intrinsically connected to the critique of power in so far as it should 'differentiate between differences that exist but should not exist, and differences that do not exist but should exist' (Mouffe 1992: 13). The flourishing of conflict is, in Mouffe's view, a guarantee that the democratic order is alive to demands from below, that it is alert to the ever-present possibility of challenge from those it has marginalized and excluded.

It follows from this attentiveness to marginal voices that agonist politics should not assume a permanent form or require groups to follow a particular procedure or pre-established pathway in making their demands. This would be to assert the closed logic of the democratic space over the fluid logic of contestatory practice. Conflict and challenge are not just external disturbances that can ultimately be rendered compatible with the established order; rather, they may call into question the very legitimacy of the order itself. As Mouffe puts it: 'There is no threshold of democracy that once reached will guarantee its continued existence' (1993: 6). She draws on Cavell's objection to Rawls's formulation of the conversation about justice to illustrate the dangers of theoretical closure with respect to radical democratic challenge. Cavell's focus is on Rawls's specific argument that it behoves those who object to the principles of justice agreed upon in the original position to show why certain institutions are unjust or how others have injured them. If they are unable to do so, then, according to Rawls, we can consider that our conduct is above reproach and bring the conversation on justice to a close. In response, Cavell claims that Rawls fails to appreciate the 'context of violence' in which all contracts are made and which means that we can never bring the conversation of justice to a close because there is always the possibility that a voice has never been heard properly in the first place, that someone has been excluded from the conversation at the outset: 'What if there is a cry of justice that expresses a sense not of having *lost* out in an unequal yet fair struggle, but of having from the start been *left* out' (Cavell 1990: xxxviii). Put differently, by unhitching deliberation from the underlying power relations in which it is always situated, Rawls blinds himself to the extent to which deliberation not only conceals domination but can itself be constitutive of it: 'Deprivation of a voice in the conversation of justice is not the work . . . of the scoundrel . . .; deprivation here is the work of the moral consensus itself' (Cavell 1990: xxxvii).

On the deliberative perspective, exclusion is something that happens beyond the established political community and can be rectified through inclusion within that same community. In contrast, for the agonist, exclusion is something that arises within the political community itself; indeed, for Mouffe, an internal frontier is a necessary condition for the establishment of a cohesive democratic space. In so far as these internal restrictions are naturalized or unacknowledged, they may have oppressive, undemocratic effects. In this respect, Mouffe's thought aligns itself with the social suffering critique discussed in chapter 1 that claimed that deliberative democrats are insufficiently attentive to the exclusionary implications of their framing of political disagreement as the regulated confrontation of words. Like Bourdieu, Mouffe understands this theoretical closure as the result of an abstraction away from the specific power relations in which the subject is always ineluctably embedded: 'They are abstracted from social and power relations, language, culture and the whole set of practices that make agency possible. What is precluded . . . is the very question of what are the conditions of existence of the democratic subject' (Mouffe 2000: 95–6). These displaced social conditions of possibility are not, in Mouffe's view, second-order concerns but are, in fact, central to the viability of first-order normative thinking itself. In her words: 'The free and unconstrained public deliberation of all on matters of common concern is a conceptual impossibility, since the particular forms of life which are presented as its "impediments" are its very conditions of possibility' (Mouffe 2000: 98).

In other words, the critique of power that flows from the insistence on the ineradicable presence of struggle enables agonism to avoid the kind of theoretical closure that limits other models of democracy. Accordingly, Mouffe emphasizes the openness and responsiveness of her account of agonist democracy to the diversity of practices and ways of being – 'conditions of existence of the democratic subject' – that subtend it: 'It is much more receptive than the deliberative model to the multiplicity of voices that contemporary pluralist societies encompass and to the complexity of their power structure' (2000: 105). Agonist citizenship, for instance, draws its inspiration from the multiplicity of ordinary, citizen activities to offer a more heterogeneous and dynamic account than the legalistic notions that prevail in liberal and deliberative theory. Commitment to democratic arrangements is understood not in terms of potentially arid notions of consent to the force of the better argument, but rather as deep-seated investments in values and ideas that are contiguous with individuals' daily lives and practices. Here, like other agonist theorists, Mouffe productively draws on Wittgenstein's practice-based account of rationality to challenge a tacit presupposition of democratic proceduralism, namely the idea that action is based on the interpretation and application of rules (e.g. Heyes 2003). When individuals follow a particular procedure in common, it is not on the basis of rational consent to its validity but rather on the basis of a more immediate resonance with the practical exigencies of their daily lives. Rules are not general principles which are then rationally applied to particular circumstances; rather, they are generated in part by particular modes of being and are abridgements of practices. Consensus is, then, inseparable from the pre-political ethical commitments and specific forms of life which define the individual's social context. Consequently, for Mouffe, it is not possible to set justice over the good as a set of transcendental norms independent from particular ethical world-views. Justice is never impartial; it always presupposes and, in fact, is dependent upon commitment to a particular set of concrete values. When these values clash, there can be no ultimate appeal to some conciliatory, neutral framework. To quote Mouffe: 'Taking pluralism seriously requires that we give up the dream of a rational consensus which entails the fantasy that we could escape from our human form of life' (2000: 98).

In short, democratic citizenship should be understood in an enlarged sense as a set of multifaceted and dynamic practices. It does not revolve around ideas of rational consent, nor should it be conceived in passive terms as a place-holder for legally ascribed rights. The job of radical democracy is to enshrine 'the diversity of ways in which the "democratic game" can be played' (Mouffe 2000: 73) within the context of an overall pluralist ethos of accommodating 'the multiplicity of present democratic demands' (Mouffe 1993: 83). It does this, in part, by creating political identities that engender new bonds of solidarity – radical chains of equivalence – between citizens, foster deep commitment to democratic values and promote full participatory parity within the polity. In so far as it is understood as the creation of strong identifications and alliances, agonist citizenship also breaks with the post-conventional emphasis on reason to highlight instead the central role played by emotions. After all, what makes a strong democracy is not just a reasoned acceptance, on the part of citizens, of the procedural fairness of a given order but also a 'passionate' commitment to pursuing the values of freedom and equality.

Put differently, in developing the link between agonist democracy and the context of power and struggle, Mouffe makes a turn towards practice. The lesson she draws from Cavell and Wittgenstein is of the importance of close attention to the dynamics of sociality, to the patterns and complexities of ordinary practice that sustain the abstract forms of democratic life. It is not so much for Mouffe, as it is, say, for James Tully, that theory should follow practice, more that theory should be sufficiently 'thin' as to render itself attentive to the often submerged dimensions of mundane social existence and, thereby, to ensure its receptivity to renewal from below. It is, however, in this turn towards practice that Mouffe sets up a troubling disjunction in her work between the gesture towards a phenomenology of embodied being, on the one side, and the unswerving adherence to a rigid anti-essentialism, on the other. In the end, the latter prevails, rendering Mouffe's agonism a socially weightless paradigm closed off from the very practices that are supposed to give it its radical political impact.

DEMOCRATIC IDENTITIES

This deep incompatibility between the gesture towards concrete practice and the reliance on an invariant anti-essentialism is manifest in Mouffe's discussion of the agonist creation of political identities. Part of the problem stems from her deployment of a theory of power which, in fact, is not a theory of power at all. Rather, it is a generalized theory of signification that is unable to capture embodied dynamics of oppression and inequality in anything other than the most formulaic dualisms of stasis and flux, inclusion and exclusion, essentialism and anti-essentialism. The creation of new forms of citizen identity is not, of course, a straightforward task, partly because of the ways in which individuals are always-already situated in entrenched social relations that precede, shape and limit possible political commitments. Mouffe briefly acknowledges the determining force of such pre-political forms of sociality, but tends to skirt round such issues, deploying instead the well-known structural logic of the 'constitutive exterior' to explain the process of identity formation. On this anti-essentialist view, social being has no intrinsic meaning; things only acquire significance from the way they are organized in antagonistic relation to other elements. Stable identity, at the level of the individual, is achieved through a process that exactly parallels the establishment of a hegemonic order, namely the positing of an other whose difference is not, as it may appear, external and alien to myself but forms, in fact, the condition of possibility of my existence. All identities are based on a disavowal of the very otherness that lies at their heart and that, were it to be acknowledged, would throw their seeming stability and integrity into question: 'Since the constitutive outside is present within the inside as its always real possibility, every identity becomes purely contingent' (Mouffe 2000: 21).

Once the 'precarious and temporary' nature of identity is properly appreciated, ideas of democratic citizenship need not be constrained by having to appeal to the supposed fixed and pre-given interests of subjects. Instead, political interests can be performatively reconfigured along solidaristic and progressive lines. Subaltern movements may be liberated, for instance, from the constrictions of a politics based on the recognition of authentic identities and the troubling drift towards particularism and separatism that this is often held to entail. On Mouffe's relational view, counter-hegemonic movements should struggle against the 'authoritarian' tendency to invoke singular and stable categories of identity and experience as some kind of guarantee of progressive intent. Thus, she warns feminists against grounding notions of democratic practice in essentialist identity claims, such as the ideas of maternal care invoked in some theories of ethics; rather, 'the pursuit of feminist goals and aims' should take place in the context of 'a wider articulation of demands' (Mouffe 1992: 87). Linking this anti-essentialism to a more general argument against the gender differentiation of citizenship, Mouffe claims that 'in the domain of politics, ... sexual difference should not be a valid distinction. ... What a project of radical and plural democracy needs is not a sexually differentiated model of citizenship in which the specific tasks of men and women would be valued equally, but rather a truly different conception of what it is to be a citizen' (1993: 82). Instead, subaltern movements should embrace the destabilizing implications of a foundational undecidability by creating cross-cutting identities and new political alliances. On the face of it, then, Mouffe's anti-essentialist formulation of democratic identification seems to have potential for radical democratic movements, and although she does not elaborate in any substance what she means by a 'truly different' conception of citizenship, others in related areas have taken up the challenge (e.g. Norval 2007; Ziarek 2001). Inspired by Mouffe, Moya Lloyd argues, for example, that feminist politics should be more than 'putting into action the demands of a pre-existing community of women' (2005: 1). It should instead become outward looking and oriented to coalitional forms of action; it should understand itself as a moment in a larger, solidaristic democratic movement. Ideas of agonist contestation liberate feminism from limiting and potentially dogmatic identity claims, creating a space for a politics based around the dynamic idea of the 'subject-in-process', which transcends false antitheses of essentialism versus anti-essentialism and establishes 'political friendships' across gender lines (Lloyd 2005: 161–9). In a similar fashion, Kate Nash (1998), for example, sees in arguments against gender-differentiated forms of citizenship a challenge to think feminist politics beyond the assertion of identity and instead as the formation of 'multiple and contextually sensitive' alliances with other groups also struggling for the radical extension of the democratic principles of liberty and equality. On this view, politics becomes a good deal messier and combative, more partial and erratic than some feminists allow, but also potentially more productive.

Any potential that Mouffe's ideas may have for radical politics, however, is significantly undercut by the narrowly linguistic terms in which the process of identification is conceived and which forecloses sustained consideration of related issues of disempowerment and mobilization. To be effective and truly galvanizing, the creation of new democratic identities must not simply be an imposition from above but must also engage with pre-established social practice, and this involves, *inter alia*, the objections and reluctances that individuals may present to the process of politicization. Individuals are not *tabula rasae* or docile subjects waiting passively to be pulled into new radical democratic alliances, but are embedded in ways of living that may present considerable obstacles to radical democratic mobilization. Whilst the logic of signification might be able to explain certain dynamics of social existence, it leaves many others unexplained, especially those that pertain to the ways in which persistent inequalities and enduring forms of oppression are realized in embodied being. Given that agonist democracy is supposed to appeal above all to marginal and disempowered groups, such issues of internalized inequality are particularly salient. When viewed from the abstract perspective of a relational theory of meaning, it is no doubt the case that identities might lack fixity. Emerging as they do from an essential non-fixity or undecidability, identities are always potentially open to reconfiguration, and Mouffe frequently repeats the claim that all identities are 'contingent and precarious articulations', that 'every identity' has a 'nomadic structure' and that 'the history of the subject is the history of his/her identifications and there is no concealed identity to be rescued beyond the latter' (1992: 236–7; see also Mouffe 1994). When viewed, however, from the perspective of embodied power relations, identities are often found to have a phenomenal depth and durability that, whilst not making them inevitable, does not necessarily render them easily amenable to agonist reconfiguration.

Take, for instance, Bourdieu's idea of habitus, which proceeds from the same initial assumption as Mouffe that identities are contingent in that they are culturally arbitrary norms, but also stresses that these contingent norms are realized as deeply entrenched, bodily dispositions. Unlike Mouffe's etiolated discursive account, which empties identities of any existential depth, on this view they have an entrenched historicity in so far as the objective tendencies of the world are incorporated into the body and lived and relived as inevitable, natural dispositions; in Bourdieu's words, 'The body believes in what it plays at: it weeps if it mimes grief' (1990b: 73). When identity is understood not just as a position in discourse but also as an embodied orientation to the world, the process of creating radical new forms of citizen identification becomes considerably more complex. Is it really the case, for instance, that identities are so fragile and transient that the process of their formation and reformation 'must be seen as one of permanent hybridization and nomadization' (Mouffe 1994: 110)? In contrast to this idea of unbounded linguistic flux, the logic of embodiment speaks to the systematic and relatively predictable way in which many types of subordinate identity – those related to gender, race and class – are reproduced and endure from one hegemonic order to another and can be roughly anticipated. Shifts between hegemonic regimes, then, are not, as Mouffe states, radically contingent, an abrupt shift from one arbitrary configuration of identities to another. Rather, any process of democratic transformation must have to deal, *inter alia*, with certain forms of persistent powerlessness that may create potential intransigencies and resistances on the part of dominated subjects to politicization. Mouffe rightly identifies depoliticization as a central problem for democracy, although she does not discuss it in any detail. The causes of depoliticization are complex (cynicism, affluence, individualism), but, as we saw in the previous chapters, one set of reasons why individuals often fail to engage as political agents relate to the internalization of inequality, and deprivation as a dominated habitus. The internalization of domination may create complicities on the part of subjects with their own oppression, which are often lived as profound psychological and emotional dispositions, feelings of powerless, resignation or lack of hope, for instance, which present considerable barriers to political mobilization. Mouffe is unable to address any of these underlying issues because the privileged terms of her paradigm – undecidability, contingency and flux – are insufficient to describe what often appears, at the level of lived social reality, as the stasis and intransigence of many social identities. Indeed, at points, her anti-essentialist nominalism seems to reduce social experience to little more than a place-holder for linguistic indeterminacy.

The logic of signification cannot be generalized, then, in the way Mouffe hopes it can as the basis for a comprehensive account of power. Her purely discursive account of citizen identification offers no insight into the potential barriers posed by such problems of depoliticization and powerlessness or how it might work to overcome them in order to engender new forms of democratic agency. In the abstract, Mouffe acknowledges the entrenched nature of many identities, talking in passing of how it is important to comprehend processes of over-determination and 'the complex dynamic of complicity and resistance which underlies the practices in which . . . identity is implicated' (Mouffe 1994: 110). But her anti-essentialist theoretical armoury lacks the appropriate interpretative tools to take this insight any further, relying instead on a 'simplistic analogy between the contingency of signification and the contingency of socio-cultural formations' (Cheah 2006: 84). The grounding of a theory of power in a relational theory of meaning locks Mouffe's theory of identification into a sterile logic of essentialism and anti-essentialism, fixity and flux, inclusion and exclusion that rules out precisely the kind of differentiated, multidimensional analysis that the idea of agonism really requires to have some analytical bite. Many forms of subordination are the result not of exclusion from a political order, as Mouffe's relational logic suggests, but of domination within an order in which one has been formally included, or, as it is often put, being a second-class citizen: 'Second-class citizens are invisible *within* the political realm, not outside it. . . . Invisibility is itself a *political* phenomenon' (Macedo and Williams 2005: 8). These forms of domination are often less visible and more insidious than the relatively obvious mechanism of exclusion because they work through the body and are thereby naturalized, creating what Bourdieu calls the complicity of the oppressed with their own oppression. It is impossible, of course, to draw a clear line between exclusion and domination, which often intersect in a complex fashion, and Mouffe may well intend the inclusion–exclusion dynamic to stand in for a more complex web of the dynamics of subordination. But the etiolated nature of linguistic constructivism prevents her from analysing the circuitous and often difficult passage from the experience of oppression to political agency, despite the numerous ways in which her theory inevitably circles around such issues.

In the final analysis, this lack of social depth means that the supposedly key strength of Mouffe's democratic agonism, namely that it is driven by an attentiveness to the voices of the marginalized and the excluded, is, in actuality, its central failing. There is a deep discontinuity between the phenomenal realm of embodied practice towards which the idea of agonist practice repeatedly gestures and her adherence to a theoretical framework governed by an invariant relational logic. This discontinuity means that she leaves hanging the very issues of subordination and inequality that she claims her theory addresses. To adequately tackle the issue of democratic identification, an agonistic approach should be able to engage with the 'ordinary violences' and deep-rooted injuries of misrecognition that may leave individuals with feelings of neglect and resentment and that prevent them from embracing the new citizen identities created for them in radical 'chains of equivalence'. In order to ensure that no social sphere remains immune from what Mouffe terms a 'scrutinizing concern' with injustice, agonist democracy has to be permanently attentive to the experiences of individuals in the pre-political sphere where domination and political exclusion have their roots. Agonistic citizenship involves a restructuring of the fixed boundary between the public and private around which liberal concepts of citizenship are organized and which, of course, has been so problematic in so far as it obscures certain kinds of oppression, most notably that of women in the domestic sphere. In Mouffe's idea of radical democratic citizenship, the public and private are not fixed domains each with an associated ethos and distinct duties; rather, they are conceived as aspects of any given action which exist in a tension that can never be reconciled and which are expressive of the larger tension that exists between the principles of liberty and equality (1992: 235–8). The discursive logic that Mouffe deploys, however, forbids her from examining any concrete instance of such tensions and the possible implications they have for the realization of agonistic democracy. Some kind of interpretative examination of the ordinary, pre-political register of experience is also necessary to identify the submerged 'ensemble of practices' that operate below the threshold of established political agendas but form the basis of a counter-hegemonic political challenge (Mouffe 2000: 95). Indeed, according to James Tully, a phenomenological sensitivity to this experiential substrate is an indispensable element of agonist political philosophy which aims both to reveal oppressive forms of governance and ultimately to enable subjects to see 'possibilities of governing themselves differently' (2008a: 16). Yet even as Mouffe frequently evokes this excluded experiential substrate in her discussion of expanded forms of citizenship, her adherence to a rigid anti-essentialism prevents her from addressing the underlying issues of empowerment and agency that this inevitably entails.

REGISTERS OF EMOTION

The seemingly unbridgeable gap between the appeal to the realm of embodied practice and the reliance on an intractable anti-essentialism is replayed in various ways throughout Mouffe's work. Time and again, an investigation of the social conditions necessary to realize effective agonistic agency is passed over in favour of a reassertion of what is held to be the 'necessary' logic of the political. This tendency to resort to a theoretical formula rather than consider the specific issues of power and inequality that pertain to agonistic practice is particularly evident in Mouffe's treatment of the emotional dimensions of political life. As we saw, a shortcoming of theories of deliberative democracy is, in her view, that they promote a troubling privilege of reason over emotion. Both Rawlsian and Habermasian variants do not sufficiently acknowledge that what moves individuals to participate politically is not rational interests or consensually achieved notions of truth but emotional convictions and passionate beliefs. In failing to grasp the central role of emotions as one of the 'main moving forces' of political behaviour, deliberative democrats find themselves 'disarmed when faced with its diverse manifestations' (Mouffe 2005: 24). They lack an adequate theoretical response, for example, to the rise of 'extreme' political movements such as populist far right groups or the emergence of ethnic and other nationalisms. Deliberative thinkers often morally condemn such movements as backward from the perspective of a post-conventional cosmopolitanism which, according to Mouffe, is frequently based on questionable ethnocentric assumptions. Perhaps more crucially, the deliberative assumption that passions are essentially destabilizing of reasoned argument means that they also disregard a central problem facing established democracies, namely that of declining interest and participation in politics. 'In the present conjuncture, characterized by an increasing disaffection towards democracy – despite its apparent triumph – it is vital to understand how a strong adhesion to democratic values and institutions can be established' (Mouffe 2000: 69). Allegiance to democracy does not require dispassionate theories of truth or reasoned consent but, rather, involves strong identifications with democratic values and institutions which are, more often than not, emotional rather than rational in nature. Mouffe is not alone in making this critique of the deliberative discounting of the importance of the affectual dimensions of political practice. It is not just that deeply held emotional convictions produce virtuous democratic citizens, it is also that the opposition between reason and passion maintained by many deliberative thinkers is misleading. As thinkers such as Martha Nussbaum (2003) have argued, passion is tightly interwoven with reason in that it incorporates cognitive judgements about what is valuable and good.[1] If individuals did not feel passionately about values and issues of social justice, then democractic regimes would be in danger of fostering passivity and civil and familial privatism amongst their citizens. As Cheryl Hall puts it: 'Total political dispassion ... would result in a polity characterized by apathy, immobility, and, ultimately, disintegration' (2005: 4).

In keeping with her linguistically derived anti-essentialism, Mouffe claims that it is a psychoanalytic model, specifically a Lacanian one, that offers the most compelling account of the intense, catalysing force of what she calls 'passions' upon political practice. She argues, for example, that the attraction and destructive force of nationalist movements can best be understood through the psychoanalytic frame of a collective fantasy that mobilizes an irruption of enjoyment/*jouissance* into the social field (Mouffe 2005: 25–9). *Jouissance* or enjoyment also has a role to play in democracies, where the passions and desires of citizens should be channelled into enjoyable political practices, thereby disarming the 'libidinal forces leading towards hostility which are always present in society' (Mouffe 2005: 26). It is easy to see why the Lacanian model has such an attraction for Mouffe, because its theory of symbolization around the primal lack of the Real is the psychological correlate to her theory of the radically contingent nature of identity formation. The thesis of the impossibility of society – that is, that it is never possible to overcome the latent antagonism that pervades social existence – finds its parallel in the Lacanian notion of misrecognition: that all stable identities are precarious illusions vulnerable to the perpetual disruptions of the primal void of the unconscious. This Lacanian logic undoubtedly offers insights into 'extreme' political phenomena, such as certain ethnic nationalisms, whose violent emotions fit into a model of the eruption of unconscious forces. The difficulty with it is, however, that it has its own inexorable logic about how emotions operate in relation to any established order: that is to say, they are unruly libidinal energies whose destablizing effects periodically unsettle the symbolic order that they subtend. Mouffe both uncritically accepts this depiction of emotions as a disorderly libidinal force and also elides it with her idea of latent social antagonisms. This elision is expedient because political resistance to a hegemonic order becomes an inevitability rather than being something which has to be created laboriously through various mobilization strategies. Just as suppressed unconscious desires will always make themselves felt through disruptions of the symbolic order, so it seems that social antagonisms, *qua* libidinal forces, will inevitably rise to the surface one way or another to disrupt any hegemonic political order. This psychoanalytic figuration of affect as a return of the political repressed is particularly convenient for Mouffe because it forecloses other ways of understanding how emotions operate with regard to social hierarchy. For instance, if we consider emotions not just as intra-psychic dynamics but, in the more sociocentric fashion suggested by habitus, as embodied, practical dispositions and tendencies, then we finish with a different account of how they may bolster and sustain social hierarchy rather than disrupt it. Generalizing Bourdieu's work, the psychoanalyst Lynne Layton (2004) has shown how, for example, emotions keep class alliances in place. Class identities are established by processes that involve the repudiation of the attributes of other classes: for example, fractions of the bourgeoisie build their identity on 'distinction' from the lower classes. One of the interesting implications of Layton's work is that class antagonisms are not expressed as hostility between groups but are taken into the self as split identifications and experienced as fear, anxiety and self-hatred. Similarly, as we saw in chapter 1, the idea of social suffering draws attention to how domination is lived as a kind of latent emotional paralysis that sustains social hierarchy and renders certain types of everyday oppression 'invisible' in that they drop below a threshold of public visibility. On this account, a common characteristic of the lived reality of domination is that it may be experienced in a fragmented, episodic manner, as 'senseless', as that which eludes coherent expression. The apparent senselessness of lived oppression does not, of course, mean that such experiences permanently defy coherent expression, but the unspeakable aspect of certain types of suffering may be deepened by the individualized nature of the experience. Many individuals are often reluctant to articulate, or even acknowledge, their suffering, because it is often experienced as personal failure, shame of failure to cope, and so forth. Thus, suffering is intensified because its unthematized nature means that, at the level of the individual, it is taken into the structure of consciousness itself as a form of personal denial and may result in depression and anxiety.

The emotional paralysis or silence that often accompanies domination is noted by Cavell in his critique of Rawls, although, significantly, Mouffe does not take this particular aspect up in her use of his work. The problem with Rawls's claim that justice requires that inequalities should be justified to the least advantaged is that the least advantaged often do not demand such justification but rather mutely resign themselves to inequality. In Cavell's words: 'Those who are least advantaged are apt to put up with the way the way things are, keep quiet about it, not initiate the conversation of justice. Their silence may be a sign of demoralization, or it may signal a belief that whatever can be done for them is being done by the normal political process' (1990: 108). Unlike unruly, eruptive passions, Mouffe has nothing to say about this muted register of embodied emotion, about persistent feelings of resignation, despair, demoralization, and so forth, whereby individuals accommodate themselves to suffering and entrenched social inequalities. Lacking a theory of embodiment, she is able neither to grasp the nature of such types of internalized domination nor to pursue the implications of their emotional reality for her theory of agonism. What drives her work is an assumption that social antagonisms, like repressed emotions, are unruly and violent and will inevitably rise to the fore in some kind of conflict or zero-sum tensions between groups. She has little to say about social antagonisms that are mute, that are latent structural strains, incorporated into the body and lived as seemingly natural and inevitable physical and psychological dispositions. How are such embodied antagonisms to be converted into a productive form of political agonism when they are largely silent, pre-rational or unarticulated?

Ultimately, then, for Mouffe, as for Lacanians, the specificities of embodied existence have theoretical significance only in so far as they confirm in an explicit or disavowed way the central impossibility of any stable social identity. To quote Nancy Chodorow: 'Evidence cannot oppose this logic, since it is a logic, and Lacanians even have a language for dismissing evidence. Anything given, natural, or "real" is repudiated by definition on the symbolic level' (1989: 124–5). The tacit assumption underlying this repudiation of the given that runs through Mouffe's work is that the phenomenal realm lacks significance or complexity; indeed, that these qualities are only imputed to it by the workings of the unconscious, or, in her political analogous terms, a foundational undecidability. By construing practice and experience in such a flattened-out manner, she loses any way of explaining the historicity of social being and how it is constituted by different types of power that do not operate according to a relational logic of signification. Consequently, her version of agonism finishes in a rarefied form of social weightlessness that is unable to capture basic dynamics of oppression and inequality in anything other than the most formulaic dualisms.

She thus defaults on the purported central concern of her theory of radical democracy, that it is supposed to speak on the part of what Rancière (1999) has called those who have no part.

THE SOCIAL, POLITICAL AND ETHICAL

Ultimately, the failure to bridge the gap between the logic of embodied practice and that of antagonism is symptomatic of a hierarchical skewing in Mouffe's understanding of the relation between the social and political realms. To put it bluntly, a hierarchy prevails where the latter is accorded a primacy that is ultimately unjustified and the former is treated as a residual category, devoid of any intrinsic properties or complexity. As Hannah Pitkin (1988) famously observed of Hannah Arendt's thought, the social is treated as a kind of alien 'blob', as an inert, faintly threatening (exemplified in the notion of the 'rise of the social') but, ultimately, uninteresting positivity. Devoid of any autonomous logic or specificity, social being comprises the inert realm of sedimented practices that acquires significance only when elements of it are taken up by the political, denaturalized, so to speak, and rendered a point of antagonism and struggle ('the moment of the political'): 'The social is the realm of sedimented practices, that is, practices that conceal the originary acts of their contingent political institution and which are taken for granted as if they were self-grounded' (Mouffe 2005: 17). Indeed, the domain of the social is so weightless and passive that it presents no resistance to the one-way process of political articulation. As Andrew Robinson and Simon Tormey put it: 'The social is so meaningless and inadequate in itself that it will look to anyone and anything to provide the political content it needs' (2008: 137). Not only does the realm of social practice lack immanent complexity, but also any attempt to attribute it with an intrinsic positivity or autonomous logic inevitably falls into the error of positivism or essentialism. In his well-known intemperate attack on post-Marxism, Norman Geras observed long ago that the way in which Laclau and Mouffe use the term 'essentialism' lacks much analytical precision. In his view, it seems to be deployed in a random and fairly indiscriminate fashion, to dismiss analyses that attribute a logic or positivity to the social realm that does not correspond to their extreme discursive constructivism: 'Their constant cry of "essentialism"... resembles nothing so much as an obfuscatory curse' (Geras 1987: 57). One doesn't have to be as angry as Geras to recognize that the logic of social being exceeds the explanatory force of the one-dimensional antagonistic logic of signification and its impoverished dualisms of essentialism and anti-essentialism, fixation and flux, stasis and change.

The absolute priority accorded to the abstract logic of the political, combined with an over-reliance on a catch-all notion of essentialism, prevents Mouffe from recognizing the immanent density and complexity of social practice. For example, as we saw earlier, she dismisses the ethics of care as a suitable grounds for a radical democratic feminism because of the way in which it seems inevitably to entail essentialist identity claims. The problem might be, however, not so much that the issue of care is inherently essentialist but rather that Mouffe's attenuated notion of the social prevents her from treating it in any other terms. It is no doubt the case that grounding an ethics of care in a psychoanalytic account of subject formation, as thinkers such as Carole Gilligan have done, can have potentially reductive political entailments. But it is also possible, as other feminists have shown, to develop a socio-centric perspective on care which unyokes it from dogmatic identity claims and analyses it as a social practice that is connected to wider issues of social transformation, justice and equality. When it is viewed as the social practice of care work, which is largely undertaken by women and is systemically devalued and unsupported, it emerges not as a narrow identity issue (even though it may be couched in such terms in the first instance) but as a major cause of gender inequality.[2] Furthermore, when care work is de-linked from the expression of supposedly innate maternal qualities and related to the condition of dependency which affects all humans at some point in their lives, then arguably it also emerges as a universal political good that should be distributed more equitably around society. In short, a more mediated account than Mouffe deploys of the relation between social practices and structures would avoid the over-rehearsed and simplistic criticism of essentialism, revealing instead that care is one of the central political problems facing both traditional and post-traditional societies. As Diemut Bubeck (1995) has shown, an ethics of care perspective leads directly into issues of justice: how to avoid the exploitation of women as carers, how to address inequalities in meeting people's need for care, how to promote an equal distribution of the burden of caring.

This is not to dismiss Mouffe's anxiety about the fragmenting effects of a certain dogmatic type of identity politics on wider democratic alliances. The problem is that her attenuated conception of the social as the 'blob' and the subordinate position it is accorded with regard to the political do not get us very far in thinking through the complex relation between care and gender equity, or indeed equality more generally. Mouffe states that 'as long as feminists focus only on questions of social and economic concern – questions about children, family, schools, work, wages, pornography, abortion, abuse – they will not articulate a truly political vision' (1992: 76). In the face of such a list of proscriptions, it is difficult to avoid wondering what would in fact make up the substantive content of her 'truly political vision'. Indeed, although Mouffe insists that her idea of political agonism is very different to Arendt's, she seems to finish here very close to the latter's purified, but ultimately empty notion of politics.

Above all, Mouffe's etiolated conception of the social creates difficulties for her idea of political agency. For, if the social is as sedimented and doxic a realm as Mouffe repeatedly claims, where does counter-hegemonic agency come from in the first place? Either it is created *ex nihilo* through the operations of the political, or the logic of social existence must be considerably more complex than Mouffe allows to permit the seeds of resistant agency to emerge in the first place. Indeed, with regard to the emergence of agency, Mouffe's conception of the social seems to be profoundly aporetic. The social lacks any phenomenal depth or significance, on the one hand, and yet, on the other, as the site of manifold citizen practices that ceaselessly energize agonist democracy, it seems to have a mysterious density and vitalism. The effect of this aporia is to foreclose precisely the kind of sustained engagement with the realm of the ontic and its underlying power dynamics that Mouffe claims distinguishes agonism from the exclusionary proceduralism of other democratic theory. The denial that meaning can be constructed immanently in social life means, according to Richard Day (2005), that Mouffe is unable to appreciate the significance of many important new forms of radical activism. She denounces new social movements as obsessed with reductive identity issues but fails to appreciate that many of the newest of these movements do not operate in such a fashion. Consequently, her anti-essentialist analysis is both outdated and theoretically inappropriate. Anti-globalization protests, or the Occupy movement, for instance, do not turn around the confrontation and the seizure of power, following the logic of hegemony, but instead seek to construct alliances and forms of mobilization around a non-hierarchical logic of 'affinity' (Day 2005). Similarly, Robinson and Tormey provide numerous examples of radical action – both within and beyond established political channels – that are testament to the intrinsic complexity of social action but which are ruled out a priori as non-political by the restrictive logic of antagonism. When movements do not correspond to her blueprint of the political, Mouffe can only denounce them as post-political and, in failing to appreciate their diverse contestatory rationales, she tacitly aligns herself with a liberal politics based on 'a logic of representation of interests within a state-regulated system of hegemonic struggles' (Day quoted in Robinson and Tormey 2008: 149).

It is not just an empty proceduralism that is a potential danger for Mouffe's socially weightless account of agonism, but also relativism. As we have seen, agonist conflict is valued not as an end in itself but only in so far as it furthers progressive democratic ends. In Mouffe's view, democracy involves a 'manifold of practices and pragmatic moves aiming at persuading people to broaden the range of their commitment to others, to build a more inclusive community' (2005: 66). Given that not all practices routinely exemplify these qualities of inclusiveness and responsibility, it is necessary to pay attention to their specific dynamics in order to discriminate between more and less progressive types of action, those that challenge the existing order in the name of equality and those that do not. But such discriminations depend, to some degree, on a more substantive account of social practices than Mouffe is prepared to envisage.

One way in which Mouffe tries to forestall the slide to relativism is by sketching out a radical democratic ethos that is supposed to serve as a kind of ballast for the otherwise empty logic of perpetual conflict and agonism. Extrapolating again from Cavell, she argues that the idea of responsibility for our decisions is crucial for a democratic ethos: 'We should never refuse bearing responsibility for our decisions by invoking the commands of general rules or principles' (Mouffe 2000: 76). A lot hangs on this idea of responsibility for decisions because it is one of the features that distinguishes Mouffe's version of dissociative agonism not only from deliberative proceduralism but also from other 'associative' versions of agonism. By this she means thinkers ranging from Arendt to Bonnie Honig and William Conolly, who are overly concerned with maintaining the open-ended, contestable aspects of political agonism. By keeping identities and practices perpetually open to challenge and disruption, they avoid the essential moment of decision that brings debate to an end and ushers in action.[3] This negative moment of exclusion is both unavoidable and necessary for radical democrats given that they wish to intervene in the world in order progressively to transform it: 'The hegemonic space periodically disturbed by agonism's valorization of multiplicity and contestability must eventually be filled by *something*. Associative agonism ... seems unwilling or unable to tell us what that something might be – a framework completely incapable of setting limits to democratic discourse and standards for legitimacy' (Glover 2012: 90). The important thing, then, for radical democracy, in Mouffe's view, is not perpetually to defer decisions, but to take responsibility for making them. Yet although she emphasizes an ethics of the decision as a distinctive feature of dissociative agonism, she does not ever clarify what this might mean practically beyond the abstract claim that it brings a democratic space into being. There is no discussion of how decisions are to be made in the first place, given the discordant process of dissensus and hegemonic struggle in which they are enmeshed. Nor is their discussion of which normative criteria they might invoke, which institutional procedures might be better suited than others to sustaining an ethos of responsibility, which levels of the polity decision making should take place, and so forth. It is not clear, moreover, how this ethics of the decision fits in with arguments Mouffe makes elsewhere that agonistic democracy must be accompanied by an 'ethics of disharmony' which creates a bond not around an ethical unity but around the recognition that we are 'divided subjects' (2000: 139). She is rather vague about what such an ethics might entail other than that it would enable individuals to accept the conceptual impossibility of reconciliation, that 'antagonism and violence are ineradicable' (2000: 139). One possible interpretation of this idea would be of the type given by Levinas or Butler that draws attention to the experiential impossibility of full, symmetrical recognition between self and other. Given her theoretical commitments, however, such a phenomenological account is clearly not available to Mouffe and, consequently, it is difficult to see how this assertion of the ineradicable nature of violence and antagonism amounts to anything more than a negative formulation of the perpetual contestation that she deplores in associative agonism.

From the perspective of embodied power relations, one might ask what kind of capacities Mouffe is tacitly attributing to her citizens to be able to endure perpetual agonism. At the very least, the toleration and celebration of conflict as a necessary democratic ethos assumes a certain level of political virtuosity and articulacy that, arguably, in an era of declining political participation, is not especially evident amongst citizens. More importantly, one cannot escape the suspicion that Mouffe's idea of the conceptual impossibility of reconciliation perpetuates a tendency in much post-foundational political thinking of fetishizing the non-identical, *qua* conflict or indeterminacy, as an apodictic source of radical politics. But, in

Pheng Cheah's words, 'emancipatory consciousness cannot subsist on linguistic dynamism or cultural-symbolic flux alone' (2006: 90). Why should the ability to tolerate conflict be a self-evident political good? At some level, would the ability to operate in this manner not speak to being in a position of relative power and privilege vis-à-vis political norms and practices rather than in a position of relative powerlessness where permanent contestation may be profoundly alienating? How does the acceptance that 'chaos and instability' are irreducible help us with Mouffe's other claim, from Cavell, that an ethics should be about responsibility. Surely responsibility for our decisions might entail facing up to the social context of inequality and trying to foster, *inter alia*, enduring relations of care, dependency, trust and understanding (e.g. Geras 1999). It is not possible to capture the complexities of such an ethico-political labour by filtering it through the lens of the over-stated dilemma of choosing between reconciliation or accepting its perpetual impossibility. In favouring the latter over the former and elevating non-identity as an apodictic source of radical ethical practice, Mouffe turns away from thinking meaningfully about issues of inequality, domination and exclusion in the context of embodied social relations. Hampered by this social weightlessness, her claim that the agonist challenge to an established order is always conducted in the name of marginal and oppressed subjects remains, ultimately, empty. It falls back into a relativism that values conflict as a political end in itself rather than in so far as it is connected to the struggles of oppressed and excluded groups.

ONTOLOGICAL AND ONTIC

Mouffe might respond to the above criticisms by restating that her primary concern is with the ontological realm of the political not with the ontic realm of concrete practices. In this light, the criticism of social weightlessness would seem to miss the point of her analysis for 'the ontic has to do with the manifold practices of conventional politics, while the ontological concerns the very way in which society is instituted' (Mouffe 2005: 8–9). On this basis, it is reasonable to argue in relation to the issues of power and agency raised here that it is impossible to foretell, from the perspective of a general theory of social foundations, all the possible barriers that prevent individuals acting as agents in their own interests or to prescribe the forms that democratic agency should take. Agency has its own singular logic and emerges unpredictably from the realm of the ontic. As Moya Lloyd puts it: 'The activity of politics is contingent and contextual and it cannot therefore be predicted or prescribed but rather is dependent upon decisions taken at opportune political moments' (2005: 173). But, in the light of the theoretical discontinuities that mark Mouffe's work, one might ask whether the distinction between the ontological and the ontic is in fact a helpful way of thinking through the parameters of radical democracy. For radical democrats, as we saw at the outset, the delineation of the ontological category of the political is not intended as a straightforwardly transcendental move. Although the realm of the political is irreducible to the ontic realm of the social, it is also inseparable from it in so far as it is inextricably tied to the critique of domination. The moment of the political – that is, the revelation of the contingency of being – only ever occurs when existing determinate social inequalities are challenged: 'The encounter with contingency ... must depend on specific circumstances for contingency to be realized. It must depend on what we can call the historical constellation whether or not that "moment" of contingency will arise' (Marchart 2007: 30). But, in fact, in the hands of Mouffe, this supposed circularity or intertwinement of the ontological with the ontic becomes a hierarchy where the former is systematically prioritized over the latter. In other words, Mouffe's idea of the political turns into an empty abstraction rather than, as it intended to be, a 'quasi-transcendental' category oriented to radical social critique. This reification of the political is evident in the primacy Mouffe repeatedly accords to abstract dynamics of undecidability, non-identity and indeterminacy over the analysis of determinate social forms. She seems to attribute to the political dynamics of indeterminacy and dissensus a self-evident radical quality that is unsupported by any sustained justification. It does not necessarily follow from an ontology of radical contingency that real-world emancipatory practices should somehow reflect this in the weaker form of perpetual agonism, struggle and conflict. Indeed, although he shares with Mouffe a foundational notion of undecidability, Laclau disagrees that radical democracies necessarily have to promote openness or agonism as an ethical disposition: 'From the fact that there is the impossibility of ultimate closure and presence, it does not follow that there is an ethical imperative to "cultivate" that openness or even less to be necessarily committed to a democratic society' (Laclau 1996: 77). In so far as Mouffe's agonism erroneously tries to replicate the dynamics of an abstract political inderminacy in concrete democratic practices of perpetual dissensus and agonism, she effects a kind of ontological reduction upwards.

CONCLUSION

This turning away from an analysis of determinate social relations because it is deemed to be somehow reductive compared to discussion of ontological political dynamics is, as I go on to show in subsequent chapters, not a feature peculiar to Mouffe's work. It reflects a tendency in post-foundational thought on radical democracy to get stuck in an abstract mode of reasoning that conceptualizes progressive politics not as interventions in the world but according to a transcendental logic of undecidability. The tacit privileging of ontological dynamics over ontic practices downplays the logic of existing struggles in favour of abstract but ultimately empty notions of radical change which rest on, to quote Stephen K. White, '"messianic" appeals to an indefinite, but somehow redemptive, future' (2000: 151). Existing attempts to change the world appear to lack intrinsic interest and have significance only in that they are incomplete empirical instantiations of a foundational undecidability. In the light of what Bruno Bosteels has described as this 'eschatological even catastrophic desire for radicalization', a focus on the actual dynamics of domination and emancipation often becomes tantamount to a reductive metaphysics of presence. The risk of this turning away from the actual is that 'the gesture of radicalization may very well have disabled in advance the pursuit of truly emancipatory actions in so far as the latter will necessarily appear far less radical' (Bosteels 2009: 247). Ultimately, Mouffe's socially weightless account of democratic agonism is a particularly stark expression of a phenomenon that Nancy Fraser has, in the context of another debate, called politicism. This is the tendency to accord primacy to the political realm over other social practices and identifications without offering any compelling justification of why this should be the case (Fraser 2008: 343). Perhaps, then, radical democrats should relinquish the misguided desire to rescue purified models of the political from the miasma of social issues. Instead, maybe they should endeavour to do more or less the opposite, namely concentrate on situating ideas of the political more securely within the social context in order to reflect in a more concrete way on issues of agency and change. The lineaments of radical political agency cannot be arrived at simply through reflection on supposedly foundational ontological dynamics. Although necessary, this type of reflection on radical agency is deeply insufficient if it is not accompanied by an attentiveness to the political struggles of the age and, perhaps even more importantly, by a negative sociological scrutiny of existing power asymmetries, how they are anchored in daily experience and how they may prevent powerless groups of individuals from acting in their own interests.

3

Freedom beyond the Subject: Feminism, Agency and Agonism

INTRODUCTION

This chapter examines the issue of social weightlessness in certain types of feminist political theory. Over the last few years, influential feminists have argued that feminism should shift its central focus from issues of gender identity to a more general set of 'post-identity' concerns. The claim is that the preoccupation with gender identity has enmeshed feminism in a parochial politics of recognition whose limited aims constrain its political imagination and prevent it from engaging in broader democratic debates. These post-identity arguments have considerable force, but I argue that they are weakened in the extent that they explicitly or implicitly raise questions about political agency that they cannot answer. They are unable to do so because the critique of identity upon which they rest is overstated and results in a theoretical anti-subjectivism that erroneously construes agency in abstract discursive terms rather than also as a capacity of embodied subjects. The anti-subjectivist rejection of interpretative approaches to lived dimensions of embodied being fails to appreciate the latter's analytical centrality for explaining issues related to the creation and mobilization of effective political agency. It is not possible to understand what makes an action political or not, or indeed what disinclines individuals to behave in a political manner in the first place, without engaging with their own understandings and interpretations of self and world. Contra post-identity assumptions, such an interpretative approach to agency need not necessarily involve a retreat to problematic subjectivism, if it is construed in terms of a relational and materialist phenomenology in the fashion suggested, as we saw in the previous chapter, by the Bourdieusian idea of habitus.

In this chapter I focus on the work of Wendy Brown and Linda Zerilli, both of whom have made influential interventions in the post-identity debate. I examine how the anti-subjectivist tendencies of their work are expressed in formulations of the idea of radical political agency through the trope of indeterminacy. This trope allows them to capture the idea that radical political practice consists in a turning away from the doxic experiential certainties of the self to take the form of a ceaseless contestation of boundaries and exploration of unforeseen modes of being. Although this conveys an undoubtedly valuable democratic ethos, the implied idea of radical agency as indeterminacy lacks phenomenological grounding and, as a result, fails to advance thought about the social conditions necessary for the emergence of effective political action. It is important that post-identity theorists deal with underlying questions about the mobilization of political consciousness and agency, given that identity politics are often rooted in deeply felt injuries of misrecognition. It is necessary to engage with this experiential substrate in order to understand how it may be possible to convince individuals to move beyond a politics of recognition. By disregarding the social conditions of possibility for effective agency, the important arguments of post-identity feminists remain rather ungrounded exhortations that do not connect to the embodied experience of the very subjects they wish to mobilize.

FROM IDENTITY TO POST-IDENTITY

For some time now, identity politics has been a troubling issue for democratic theorists. There is a widely held concern that the particular and self-referential nature of identity claims stands in tension with – indeed, may even be destructive of – a world-oriented and solidaristic democratic politics. Demands for recognition are frequently couched in emotive and narrowly self-interested terms that may lack objective warrant and also conflict with the kind of impartial and outward-looking deliberation required to deal with matters of the common good. As a result of these fears, political theory tends to operate within a post-identity frame which aims to integrate but also subordinate identity concerns within a more general and inclusive model of democratic community. In this way, tendencies to balkanization and separatism are neutralized. Proceduralists such as Habermas and Rawls, for instance, define identity politics as intrinsically substantive issues of the good that, by virtue of their non-generalizable nature, can be legitimately excluded from public deliberation on the just. Agonists such as Mouffe seek to empty identity concerns of a politically dangerous dogmatism by reconfiguring them as relational constructs that are compatible with a wider politics of democratic alliance (see chapter 2). Others, such as Rancière, take a more stringent line, arguing that the particularism of most identity claims means that they have no place in a genuine democratic politics which is defined by challenges issued in the name of the radical equality of 'all and everyone' (see chapter 4). The shared presumption underlying these different theories is that it is of paramount importance to shore up democratic universalism in the face of the destabilizing and fragmenting effects of an essentially myopic identity politics.

If anything, this 'aversion' to identity and turn to a post-identity perspective has been even more pronounced in some quarters of feminist theory given that its historical development has been so closely bound up with the often fraught debates on essentialism and difference. A number of influential thinkers have expressed the idea that feminism needs to move beyond its narrow preoccupation with issues of gender identity and subjectivity and adopt instead a more outward-looking perspective oriented towards coalitional forms of political action. The adoption of a post-identity agenda is hardly straightforward for feminists given that ideas of identity have played such a pivotal role in their project of uncovering and revalorizing women's experience. Nonetheless, despite the undoubted importance of this work, it is felt that a narrowly conceived focus on gender identity has been somewhat superseded by a new set of pressing political issues connected with the social transformations set in train by globalization. Phenomena such as increasing social inequality, the privatization of wealth and the socialization of risk, ecological depredation and the rise of political fundamentalisms mean that feminism risks being side-lined as a parochial politics of recognition if it does not attempt to broaden its horizons and somehow incorporate such issues into its thinking. It is not that questions of gender and identity are necessarily irrelevant to these emerging new problems – indeed, they are often implicated very deeply within them – but rather that they need to be radically rethought in the light of changing structures of power. Nancy Fraser has argued, for example, that much of the emancipatory promise of second-wave cultural feminism has been undermined by its apparent co-optation into the new recuperative spirit of neoliberal capitalism. Many of its seemingly progressive ways of thinking about identity have been de-radicalized in so far as they have become elements of a neoliberal governance of the self that promotes women's autonomy whilst simultaneously enmeshing it within a reconfigured disciplinary matrix.

Take, for instance, Kate Bedford's study of the World Bank's social provisioning policies that aim to restructure intimate relations between men and women to enable families to endure the effects of poverty (Fraser and Bedford 2008). On the face of it, these policies appear to break down entrenched gender roles and identities by encouraging men to take on care work to enable women to move into paid labour. However, this apparent egalitarianism can also be viewed as part of a more general re-privatization of social welfare that operates through the indirect adjustment of intimate relations. In other words, this seemingly progressive policy might be seen as a way of embedding neoliberal governance in a more sustainable way through the insidious reshaping of social practices. Or consider, for example, Carla Freeman's work on the production of female workers' pink-collar subjectivities in the informatics industry in Barbados (Freeman 2000). The symbolic differentiation of their identities from blue-collar workers speaks to the pervasive and insidious operations of globalizing capital, which shapes the subjectivities of women around an illusory 'status' of professionalism that in fact makes them a source of docile, productive and cheap labour. Studies such as these force us to reconsider ideas of freedom and constraint in ways that are complex and destabilizing of conventional political categories. In short, in Fraser's view, the cultural discourse of identity politics has 'gone rogue' in so far as ideas of emancipated womanhood have been deployed by neoliberalism to insert women as disciplined and exploited subjects into their new regimes of work: 'The dream of women's emancipation is harnessed to the engine of capitalist accumulation' (Fraser 2013: 221). For Fraser, then, a politically effective feminism turns around the extent to which, in the most general sense, it can reconnect its ideals to a broader critique of neoliberal capitalism and, in a more specific sense, replace its narrow discursive critique of identity with a more developed materialist analysis of social relations as a whole: 'Grounding those indispensable aspects of feminist critique in a robust, updated sense of the social totality, we should reconnect feminist critique to the critique of capitalism' (2013: 225).

Running parallel to such sociologically informed arguments for post-identity feminism is a philosophical strand of argument that focuses on the impoverishing effect that the preoccupation with identity imposes upon the feminist political imagination. Such arguments often focus on the conceptual limitations of the subjectivism that underlies identity politics and frequently take the form of a critique of 'suffer-mongering'. From this perspective, the politics of identity uncritically elevates the experience of suffering to the status of incontestable indicator of injustice, where, in Lauren Berlant's words, 'trauma stands as truth' (2000: 41). Its moralistic subjectivism binds groups to a cramped and retributive politics of the wound and stymies the political imagination in so far as it forecloses bolder and more creative visions of action as a radical reshaping of the world. In this respect, the suffer-mongering critique reawakens a long-standing worry of feminist theorists, namely that by over-stating the extent of patriarchal domination, it risks imprisoning women in the powerless position of universal victims. And it is perhaps precisely because of the way it powerfully reformulates this long-established concern with exaggerated notions of powerlessness that the critique of suffer-mongering has had so much influence in feminist thinking (e.g. Badinter 2006).

On the face of it, these sociological and philosophical arguments for post-identity feminism appear to converge and reinforce each other. But, in fact, their implications for feminist theory and how it might approach issues of identity are quite different. The former tend towards a revisionism that urges feminists to develop a renewed understanding of identity in the context of changing power structures and the new forms of gendered autonomy and domination that are emerging. The latter tend towards a more definitive rebuttal of the category of identity altogether in favour of formulating new ways of thinking about feminism beyond the 'subject question'. There is no doubt that, in many respects, this philosophical strand of argument is compelling, but it is also problematic in so far as its exaggerated critique of identity politics leads it into alternative formulations of the political that are socially weightless. It is not difficult to agree with the claim made by post-identity thinkers that feminism should aim to detach itself from the preoccupation with identity in order to develop a more creative, world-oriented political praxis. There is undoubtedly a troubling tendency in feminist theory to reduce politics to issues of identity, and this, in my view, often proceeds from a reductive understanding of agency as directly governed by sexuality (McNay 2008a: 162–97). Yet, although it may be relatively straightforward to concede, in principle, that the feminist political imagination might benefit from broadening its theoretical horizons, it is more difficult to see how this transformation might be realized in practice, because of the abstract way in which these post-identity arguments are often framed.

At the heart of this impasse stands the issue of agency. Any move from identity to post-identity politics necessarily relies on a certain type of political agency which, given that its existence is not assured, must be created in individuals through, *inter alia*, the formation of critical self-understanding, the mobilization of political consciousness and the fostering of a willingness to engage in counter-hegemonic action. Identity politics often emerge from the deeply felt injuries of misrecognition, and it is imperative therefore to engage with this experiential substrate in order to understand, and possibly change, individuals' perceptions of themselves and their oppression. To move towards the broader concerns of a post-identity paradigm, it is not enough to simply urge individuals to lay aside a politics of personal injustice without inquiring first into how the rhetoric of suffering gives shape to embodied experience and how it might be necessary to transcend its deeply felt constraints. The abstract terms in which post-identity arguments are framed tend to foreclose these issues and thus to presume the pre-existence of ready-made political subjects rather than considering more closely the underlying social conditions that may either hinder or facilitate the emergence of effective types of political agency. As I argue in the next sections, the concern to avoid an uncritical subjectivism has led some feminist post-identity theorists to take an anti-experiential turn in their work that results, ultimately, in the deployment of ideas of agency as a discursive abstraction rather than as a capacity of embodied subjects. The overly precipitate association of identity concerns with subjectivism pre-empts the recognition, on the part of post-identity thinkers, of the importance of an interpretative perspective on embodied identity for understanding agency and prompts a turning away from an analysis of the given in favour of socially weightless ideas of otherness.

POLITICS OF SUFFERING

Arguments for post-identity feminism take their inspiration from a variety of sources, but two key influences are the work of Foucault and Arendt. Although each thinker starts from a critique of politics based on identity claims, their work gives rise to very different ideas of democratic praxis in terms of both scope and content. Foucault construes democratic praxis as a contestatory ethos that operates primarily at the micro level of self–other relations, whereas Arendt outlines a more formal notion of political participation oriented to the establishment of radical new collectivities. While it is important to appreciate the divergences between their respective accounts of political action, each in its own distinct way proceeds from a distrust of the experiential dimensions of embodied existence, *qua* suffering. When this is taken into feminist post-identity theory, it takes the form of a turn away from the given that, ultimately, has theoretically limiting effects in terms of an understanding of agency and power.

The Foucauldian critique of suffer-mongering takes its cue from his well-known argument that disciplinary power subjugates individuals by tying them to their own identities and to a 'law of truth' that has profoundly normalizing effects and obscures more radical notions of political practice and freedom (Foucault 1994: 331). A politics of suffering focuses individuals inwards upon the hidden causes of their pain and, in this solipsistic turn towards the 'truth', blinds them to possibilities for more radical, world-oriented rather than self-oriented modes of action. Following Foucault, Wendy Brown (1995) has formulated one of the most devastating, and justifiably influential, critiques of identity politics as a politics of the wound which binds individuals into moralistic and politically regressive assertions of victimhood and reparation. In her view, feminist identity politics too often attributes an incontestable moral legitimacy to the idea of personal suffering, where it is taken as irrefutable evidence of oppression and injustice. Not only is suffering far from being an automatic guarantor of social injustice, but the persistent focus upon injury also sets up a negative psychic dynamic that shackles individuals and groups to their own subjugation and consequently stymies the political imagination. In this masochistic dynamic, subaltern identities are fetishistically constructed around the compulsion to repeat and relive the primal injury of oppression or exclusion. The symbolic and actual violence that gives rise to politicized gender and racial identity is constantly reiterated through repeated acts of racism and sexism and also through the subject's own compulsion to re-experience that punishment. This repeated restaging of the original trauma generates a quasi-erotic gratification and also certain psychic and political reassurances, one of which is that, in an era of declining community, there exists an imaginary bond with others who share in the suffering. The cost of this psychic investment in reliving the primal injury, however, is a political paralysis of the subject. Individuals remain in thrall to a compulsive oscillation between desiring to be punished through the replaying of their injuries and aggressively desiring the punishment of others for this humiliation. In the meantime, wider ideas of political action and progressive intervention in the world are lost, or, to quote Brown: 'Freedom, as a wish or a practice, is nowhere to be found' (2001: 61). In order to enlarge its understanding of freedom, it is imperative for feminism to break out of the masochistic logic of suffer-mongering and resituate itself within a broader, political conversation (Brown and Halley 2002: 33).

Of course, Brown and other critics of suffer-mongering do not deny the pain that arises from oppression; rather, they object to a subjectivist, psychologically reductive mode of analysis which attributes the experiential aspects of suffering with an apodictic truth status. In other words, a methodological objection to subjectivism underpins the political critique of suffer-mongering. To avoid this subjectivism, some critics have argued that there are more objective indices against which claims of unwarranted suffering and unjust treatment can be measured. Nancy Fraser, for example, famously redefines misrecognition in non-subjective, 'non-identarian' terms as various types of institutional, and hence measureable, status subordination to escape the vagueness of the free-floating idea of psychological injury (Fraser and Honneth 2003: also Williams 1998: 178–202). Brown also speaks of the need to distinguish between genuine and false forms of suffering, although, unlike Fraser, she does not indicate specific criteria upon which such an adjudication could rest. The overall thrust of her critique is, however, towards transcending any kind of subjectivist focus on suffering because of its potentially regressive political effects. Ultimately, even those whose suffering has a legitimate basis are exhorted to move beyond the balkanizing language of identity claims and to embrace a more solidaristic and universal politics oriented towards 'diversity and the common, toward world rather than self, and involving conversion of one's knowledge of the world from a situated (subject) position into a public idiom' (Brown 1995: 51).

Arendt's work initiates a different critique of the politics of identity and suffering that accords with her general attempt to rescue an emancipatory conception of political activity from the instrumental social concerns that have swamped it in modernity. Unlike Foucauldians, Arendt does not distrust the discourse of suffering per se, for there is no doubt that it attests to enduring structural inequality and injustice. For her, however, the proper response to suffering is one of compassion, and this is, in essence, an intensely private experience which cannot be extended beyond the interpersonal dynamic where one individual acknowledges the plight of a singular other: 'Compassion, by its very nature, cannot be touched off by the sufferings of a whole class, or a people ... it cannot reach out further than what is suffered by one person and still remain what it is supposed to be, co-suffering' (Arendt 1973: 85). The immediacy of the emotional response to the suffering other means that it defies generalization, even to the point of it being difficult often to put into words. Compassion is ultimately 'closer to a gesture than to a speech' (Arendt 1973: 86). Compassion also expresses a logic that is fundamentally antithetical to that which governs Arendt's ideal political realm and, therefore, it has no role to play there: 'Because compassion abolishes the distance, the worldly space between men where political matters, the whole realm of human affairs, are located, it remains politically speaking irrelevant' (1973: 86). On the historical occasions, when suffering has been depersonalized (the suffering of the masses) and a collective public response has been orchestrated, it assumes the perverse form of the sentiment of pity. Sentiment, as opposed to passion, is inauthentic emotion and can be cynically manipulated as a way of galvanizing political action through the glorification of the 'suffering multitude'. When it loses its intense singularity and takes on this pathological public form, the response to suffering may become a dangerous instrument of mass-manipulation, a boundless emotion that can be exploited to justify all kinds of brutality, exemplified, for Arendt, in the revolutionary excesses of Robespierre's Terror (1973: 90). In short, for Arendt, suffering and the response to suffering, in both its authentic particularity and perverse public form, have no place in politics. Suffering touches on social matters, those of poverty, maldistribution, and so forth, and these can only be solved by administrators and experts, not by actors in the political realm, whose quest for freedom should not be hampered by such worldly concerns (Arendt 1973: 91).

Arendt's view on suffering is of course influenced by her famous argument about the rise of the social and is of a piece with her more well-known claim that identity concerns belong to the pre-political 'sphere of the household' and therefore also have no role to play in political action. This insight has proved extremely fruitful for post-identity feminism, enabling it to put aside earlier feminist concerns with what Bonnie Honig terms the 'Woman Question in Arendt' and to focus instead on the 'Arendt Question in Feminism' (1995: 3; also Dietz 2002). The Arendt Question entails the reconfiguration of the central concerns of feminism in political rather than social terms, as ideas of action and creation and not of identity and recognition.

For Honig, for instance, Arendt's performative notion of the political suggests a feminist politics of agonism that 'presupposes not an already known and unifying identity of "woman" but agonistic, differentiated, multiple nonidentified beings that are always becoming, always calling out for argumentation and amendment' (1995: 156). In a similar vein, Linda Zerilli argues in *Feminism and the Abyss of Freedom* that the relentless focus upon 'the subject question' has hampered feminism's ability to think about the nature of freedom and action beyond the assertion of identity (2005: 9). Real women cannot identify with the one-dimensional figure of the oppressed victim that permeates feminist identity politics. Perpetual victimhood is not a liveable social position (Zerilli 2005: 100). In so far as it is wedded to a 'victim discourse', feminist identity politics remains stuck in the assertion of the 'I can' rather than considering the possibilities of the 'I will'. This preoccupation with the 'vicious circle of agency' ultimately pre-empts any consideration of how feminist politics could ever be 'a truly transformative practice that might create something new, forms of life that would be more freedom enabling' (Zerilli 2005: 12).

This concern to reinvigorate the feminist political imagination leads Zerilli to criticize Judith Butler's work on performativity, for example, which, even as it undoes essentialist ideas of identity, remains ultimately within the strictures of the feminist preoccupation with subjectivity and agency. The central problem with the idea of the performative is, in Zerilli's view, that the essentially reiterative structure that Butler attributes to gender identity forecloses a more radical concept of change. Although heteronormativity can be denaturalized and disrupted through subtle processes of resignification, this subversion still operates ultimately within the terms of those hegemonic norms, thus excluding a concept of change as the radically new or unanticipated: 'The only alternative to a hegemonic application of a rule is to see it as something that is open to transformation insofar as it can be endlessly interpreted' (Zerilli 2005: 53). Against this rule-bound, interpretative model of change, Zerilli invokes Arendt's future-oriented, inaugural notion of action which rethinks freedom outside the parameters of established subjectivity and agency. Arendt questions the idea that politics is a rule-governed activity whose outcomes can be known in advance of the activity. From Arendt's assertion that political actors 'know not what they do', Zerilli argues that political action must be a future-oriented, world-building practice that seeks to instate as yet unanticipated modes of being (2005: 37). As a world-building practice, feminism should base itself not on the assertion of pre-given differences – the 'what' of identity – but on the quest to establish the newly thinkable in gender – the 'who' of politics: 'that which cannot be proved like a truth or possessed like a substance, but only practiced or enacted by present and future generations of feminists' (Zerilli 2005: 182). Zerilli concludes that feminists should no longer be content to ask '"the woman question" in political theory'; rather, they should 'ask the political theory question in feminism' (2006: 120).

The critique of suffering, then, gives rise to two significantly different feminist visions of post-identity politics. Foucauldians would reject the language of suffering because of the way it reinforces naturalized notions of identity and consequently prevents subjects from recognizing and resisting the subtle strategies of normalization that underpin the government of individualization. Although the Foucauldian critique moves beyond notions of fixed identity and its symptom of incontestable suffering, it still operates within the general terrain of the 'subject question', albeit one that is deconstructed and open to a process of perpetual critique. From an Arendtian perspective, this type of critique does not go far enough, however, because, in as much as it retains a focus on a cluster of issues associated with identity and subjectivity, it improperly accords social issues a political status. On the Arendtian view, feminist politics must break out of the logic that links freedom to the subject question and instead reconceive itself as a form of collective praxis that seeks to 'start something new' (Zerilli 2005: 23). The aspiration to reinvigorate feminist understandings of radical action is undoubtedly admirable, and both formulations of post-identity politics are compelling in many respects. However, when they are unmoored from a focus on embodied experience, these ideas of politics tend towards social weightlessness. The emphatic critique of identity and suffering in which they are grounded results in a one-sided focus on the politics of the potential unmediated by any analysis of the dynamics of the actual. This lop-sided focus obscures, *inter alia*, issues of power and agency that are crucial to any move from identity to post-identity feminism.

ACTUALITY AND POTENTIALITY

Brown's critique of recognition as suffer-mongering undoubtedly has much force, but there is something troubling, nonetheless, about its rather over-emphatic rejection of the discourse of suffering as an impediment to wider democratic aims. For a start, there is an uncomfortably dismissive and aristocratic connotation to the Nietzschean construal of recognition claims as *ressentiment*. To quote Susan Bickford: 'To see identity claims as obsessed with suffering is to overlook the fact that it is the perspective of the dominant culture that marks them out that way' (1997: 117). The very vehemence of the critique precludes an acknowledgement that the tendency to masochistic suffer-mongering is not an inevitable feature of identity politics but a contingent effect sporadically generated by the specific, often hostile, context of any given struggle for recognition (e.g. Medearis 2005). What follows from the dehistoricized terms of the critique of *ressentiment* and suffer-mongering is that there is a foreclosing of an analysis of how the experience of suffering may reveal important aspects to oppression. Manufactured as it may be, the language of suffering attests, at least in part, to the way in which oppression and inequality are internalized by individuals as symbolic violence and lived within the body as certain dispositional tendencies that may leave them feeling unable to take control of the conditions of their lives. In other words, suffering may tell us something significant about the nature of social inequality and domination, and the Nietzschean-style critique marginalizes this type of analysis in its over-hasty eschewal of the category.

The theoretical cost of this rather precipitate association of the experiential with a politically and methodologically dangerous subjectivism is that those influenced by the Foucauldian critique fail to appreciate sufficiently that a focus on subjective experience may be analytically crucial for explaining aspects of domination. This critique is oriented primarily to a generic analysis of the intra-subjective effects of disciplinary subjugation – namely that it produces docile subjects. As valuable as this general theory of normalization has been, it has not been tied particularly closely to other dynamics of inequality, such as class, race and gender, and what the experience of suffering might tell us about them. For Foucault, the language of suffering speaks to an inculcated confessional urge to speak the 'truth' about our innermost experiences. What this blanket, existential critique underplays is the fact that some types of suffering are not evenly distributed around society but are closely correlated to class inequality, deprivation and social exclusion.

The phenomenon of power cannot therefore be dealt with from a purely external, discursive point of view; the subjective experience of exclusion, marginalization and domination is also crucial to understanding its operations. In Hans Herbert Kogler's words: 'Subjects may not have the adequate conceptual tools to thematize how power relations actually function, yet, to be evaluated by the interpreter as oppression, the subjects' assessement and experience of them as oppressive is indispensable' (1996: 262).

The hostility of Foucauldians towards the language of suffering and attendant methodological aversion to subjectivism is strongly informed by a notion of critical knowledge as a break with the given, a deconstruction of the experiential in order to explore aspects of freedom that transcend present actuality. Ideas of freedom as non-identity are central to post-foundational political thought, and Foucault provides a paradigmatic formulation in his notion of a critical ontology of the present. This involves a scrutiny of modes of being intended to 'separate out, from the contingency that has made us what we are, the possibility of no longer being, doing or thinking what we are, do, or think' (Foucault 1984: 46). Ethics of the self encapsulates a 'limit attitude' where a critical relation to self is established that explores the possibility of going beyond what seems natural, authentic or inevitable in identities and behaviours: 'The critique of what we are is at one and the same time an historical analysis of the limits that are imposed on us and an experiment with the possibility of going beyond them' (Foucault 1984: 50). Critique, then, as a practice of freedom, is, in some fundamental sense, anti-experiential and anti-subjectivist; it is a 'possible transgression' that undoes phenomenological certainties (Foucault 1984: 45). It is a refusal of the given: 'the art of voluntary insubordination' whose aim is 'the desubjugation of the subject in the context of . . . the politics of truth' (Foucault 2002: 194). This idea of a break with the given informs feminist formulations of post-identity politics as the exploration of the non-identical, the hybrid, the indeterminate, and so forth. As Butler puts it, for instance, critique takes place beyond 'any received understanding of intention and deliberation' and involves 'risking the subject at the limits of its ordering' (2002: 225). Analogously, thinkers such as Aletta Norval (2007) and Ewa Ziarek (2001) argue that feminist politics must participate in a wider 'ethics of dissensus' or 'aversive' democratic ethos characterized by a perpetual struggle against conformity and interrogation of doxic attitudes and modes of behaviour.

There is indisputably much value in Foucault's formulation of ethical practice based on a deconstruction of prevailing norms and an openness to other potential ways of being. What gets lost, however, in this critique of the experiential in the name of non-identity is an alternative, socio-centric mode of analysis which explores not so much the potential for otherness in the actual but the dimensions of the actual itself and what they might tell us about domination and social inequality. To be sure, Foucault's ontology of the actual does not rule out a priori such systematic social critique, and, indeed, he is in many respects the theorist of domination *par excellence*. The idea of docile subjects is tremendously important as part of a general account of normalizing governance, but Foucault's analysis of modernity tends to be broad-brush and not oriented to the specific ways in which established social hierarchies of class, race and gender are realized in daily life. As a result, Foucauldians have chosen to interpret his idea of an historical ontology of the self not so much through a focus on actual dynamics of inequality, but more through notions of non-identity in the present and explorations of other ways of being (McNay 2012). In the light of this orientation towards potentiality and non-identity, a focus on the actual often becomes tantamount to a reductive and potentially essentializing recovery of the given. In other words, there is a tacit discounting of the given as an uninteresting positivity, which is somewhat ironic for, to quote Bruno Bosteels, 'Foucault's provocation ... also consisted in enabling an historical ontology of ourselves that would not have to shy away from speaking about the present situation in the name of some knee-jerk aversion to the metaphysics of presence' (2009: 244–6).

One of the effects of this turning away from the given is that agency is assumed as unproblematic and questions pertaining to its underlying conditions of possibility are too easily displaced. Consider, for example, what kind of capacities must necessarily be attributed to citizens for them to be able to implement the perpetual self-critique that is a crucial part of Foucauldian ethical self-formation. As a way of expressing an ideal of democratic openness, the interrogation of the limits of identity is, of course, desirable. But, from the perspective of embodied individuals, what does this configuration of agency in terms of a process of 'voluntary insubordination' mean as a pragmatic strategy for action? At the very least, the elevation of the limits of intelligibility as a cipher for the openness of the democratic ethos assumes a certain level of political virtuosity and articulacy that, arguably, in the context of the unequal distribution of symbolic resources is not evenly spread amongst citizens. From this perspective, there is a discontinuity between, on the one hand, the abstract negativity of non-identity as transgression that informs ideas of progressive ethical practice and, on the other, the social negativity of non-identity as experiences of isolation, resignation and disempowerment which often accompany the lived reality of domination. Non-identity as transgression speaks to being in a position of relative power and privilege vis-à-vis social norms where subjects can afford to run the risk of testing the limits of identity. Non-identity as embodied domination speaks to dynamics of powerlessness where subjects struggle and often fail to make much sense of their experiences within the matrix of established social norms. In short, the concern that a focus on embodied experience leads to a reductive subjectivism means that the idea of non-identity gets detached from any grounding in the phenomenal realm and is held up as an emancipatory, if rather vague, end in itself. A hiatus consequently emerges between the abstract negativity of transgressive critique and the social negativity of the experience of oppression. How do disempowered individuals who do not necessarily have the privileged detachment to experience their lives as sufficiently contestable to accommodate ethical re-fashioning begin to move towards such a goal?

ACTION AND THE ABYSS

It is important to note that the Foucauldian turn away from the given is not inherent in his work on critical ontology; rather, it is the effect of a certain post-foundational interpretation of the idea. In Arendt, however, the turn away from the given is intentional and explicit in so far as she holds that social concerns limit the political imagination and prevent us from appreciating the true nature of freedom. Whilst Arendt might have good reasons for her socially weightlessness conception of emancipatory action, this hardly lessens the problems that arise from such a strict partitioning of the political realm from its underlying conditions of possibility. The troubling emptiness of her idea of the political has prompted extensive discussion amongst commentators. In her own lifetime, it caused Arendt to seriously misjudge some of the most important struggles of the day, exemplified, for instance, in her response to the Little Rock desegregation episode. Arendt's stance on this event was, as Danielle Allen (2005) documents, highly problematic in so far as she accused the parents of the African American students, who tried to attend the previously whites-only school, of seeking social advancement through the exploitation of their children. For Arendt, school desegregation was a 'private' identity issue belonging to the order of the social and therefore an inappropriate focus for political action, which, in her view, should only pertain to public and collective issues. As Allen discusses, Arendt's refusal to see the actions of the civil rights activists as progressive is troubling in many respects, but not least because it illustrates the naïvety of her own rarefied and heroic notion of political action which is somehow intrinsically redemptive and emancipatory regardless of social context.¹

Feminist post-identity theorists are of course aware of the problems inherent in Arendt's undetermined idea of the political but, nonetheless, ultimately make the judgement that this is more enabling than constraining when it comes to rethinking progressive practice. For Zerilli, for instance, not only does the 'subject-centred' way of thinking about social transformation prevent feminism from imagining political intervention in the world in a radically creative manner, but it is also conceptually misguided. To configure critique and change as the interpretation and reinterpretation of rules, in the manner that, say, Butler does, is to fail to grasp what we actually do when we follow or criticize social norms. Using Wittgenstein, Zerilli contends that the following of social rules is predicated not on acts of interpretation or knowing but on a more immediate type of action, a spontaneous form of doing. The breaking of rules does not involve so much an act of critical reinterpretation or resignification as a type of imaginative exercise that operates beyond the alternatives of truth and falsehood: 'Imagination allows us to think the possibility of something beyond the epistemic demand of deciding the true and the false' (Zerilli 2005: 59). Drawing a parallel between the immanent creativity of practical reason and Castoriadis's idea of the radical imagination, Zerilli argues that the faculty of the productive imagination ensures the capacity to think of forms or figures *ex nihilo*: that is, forms or figures that do not already exist in embodied experience and thought but which cannot be said to be 'false': 'This figure of the newly thinkable does not inhere in the object itself' (2005: 61). It is this creative ability to posit an object outside the 'use-economy' of an instrumentalized gender politics that is, in Zerilli's view, crucial to a freedom-centred feminism. Changes in ideas of gender emerge not from counter-hegemonic resignifications but from an inaugural act of the imagination which projects 'a word like women into a new context, where it is taken up by others in ways we can neither predict or control [and] which has the potential power to change every political, worldly constellation' (Zerilli 2005: 65). To speak about women as a political collectivity is not to make a truth claim but rather to make a political claim about the nature of a given community – 'with whom am I in community'. Such political claims have an inherently anticipatory structure; to posit a prospective commonality with others raises the possibility of those others speaking back and either accepting or refusing these claims. The predicative structure of political claims encapsulates the paradox of openness and closure that is constitutive of all democratic political movements. Political action, then, is radically indeterminate in that the openness of its future orientation tests the limits of 'every claim to community, [it is] about testing the limits and nature of agreement and about discovering what happens when the agreement breaks down' (Zerilli 2005: 172). It is this unconstrained indeterminacy that Zerilli names the 'abyss of freedom'.

It is not difficult to recognize in Zerilli's image of the abyss the expression of a desirable ethos in democratic practice of an open, critical and creative orientation to the world that seeks not to pre-empt unforeseen modes of political action. In this respect, the image follows a well-established route in radical political thought of using tropes of liminality and indeterminacy to encapsulate a non-sovereign, ethical predisposition to the other (e.g. Markell 2003; Oliver 2001). It is also no doubt the case that the future-oriented dimensions of action hold open the promise that engagement with the world is always potentially unpredictable and creative and that political thinking should seek to refresh itself around the vertiginous possibilities of these indeterminacies. In short, it is easy to accept the normative force of formulations of political agency as indeterminacy in so far as they challenge the settled and doxic ways in which we think about ourselves and intervention in the world. The question is, however, whether Zerilli is right to attribute the critical limitations in thinking about freedom that she does to subject-centred modes of thought and also whether her own, phenomenologically de-centred 'world-building' alternative has much political meaning apart from as a utopian cipher. It could be argued, for example, that the freedom-centred approach espoused by Zerilli presupposes, rather than dissolves, the subject-centred frame. It is hard to see, for instance, how intersubjective debate about the nature and extent of community and about the social impact, liberating or otherwise, of the 'newly thinkable' can be resolved without some detour through the subject paradigm that Zerilli so strongly criticizes. In Amy Allen's words: 'Simply claiming that freedom is a world question rather than a subject question does not obviate the need for thinking about the individual subject and its capacities for critical reflection and self-transformation, nor does it establish that such matters are not properly political' (2008: 16). In her account of the formation of the feminist movement in the late 1960s, for example, Juliet Mitchell shows how the emergence of this new political collectivity is underpinned by the process of 'speaking bitterness': that is, the translation of personal experiences of suffering into an impersonal analysis of subordination: '"Speaking bitterness" is the bringing to consciousness of the virtually unconscious aspects of oppression: one person's realization of an injustice brings to mind other injustices for the whole group' (Mitchell 1971: 62). It is hard to see how any emerging movement can acquire the mobilizing force to become a significant political movement without some kind of detour through a 'subject-centred' focus on experience. Drawing somehow on experiences of oppression seems to be a crucial part of the creation of effective political agency amongst disempowered groups. What is more, it is not always correct to assume, as Zerilli does, that the detour through experience is necessarily a dead-end, trapping groups in the self-referential language of victimhood and stymieing their ability to participate in wider democratic politics. There is good reason to question the causal chain where strongly felt identity politics are held to lead inexorably to, at best, politically limited movements and, at worst, more extreme forms of separatism. Indeed, as Linda Alcoff notes, there is evidence to suggest instead that for many groups identity politics in fact fosters an enlarged perspective that enhances their participation in wider egalitarian politics (2006: 38–40).

In the final analysis, Zerilli's insistence that the 'subject question' and the 'social question' form part of the same 'instrumental and adjudicative' frame that 'minimizes the possibility of freedom as action' leads to the lionization of a peculiarly abstract notion of agency as indeterminacy (2005: 10). Indeterminacy – whether it be epistemological, social or temporal – is certainly a necessary condition for individuals to be able to effect political change; however, detached from the context of embodied social practice, it takes the form of a reified abstraction. Without phenomenological content, the idea of world-building creativity says little about the substantive contours of radical political agency other than a vague gesture towards unanticipated otherness. In short, action is wrongly conceived of as pure indeterminacy, *qua* the paradox of openness and closure, rather than as a capacity of embodied subjects. This phenomenological abstraction is exemplified in the way Zerilli derives the capacity of the productive imagination from Castoriadis but, in doing so, unharnesses it from the account of subject formation which is central to his project. In Castoriadis, the idea of the unconscious as radical imagination is used instead of the Lacanian idea of the unconscious as lack to explain why it is that individuals have the ability to act in spontaneous and unpredictably creative ways. Precisely because it is the unconscious, however, the radical imagination is never fully accessible in social life; rather, it is a disruptive ontological plenitude which manifests itself only ever partially in often surprising human acts of creation (McNay 2000: 133–54). In Zerilli, however, the productive imagination is detached from subject formation, becoming a free-floating capacity which can somehow be directly accessed in the radical political imagination. This is not to question the iconoclastic force of the 'newly thinkable' on the rare occasions when it arises, but the emergence of the radically new is almost always mediated through, and therefore constrained by, the confines of embodied existence and understanding. If political praxis is to transcend these confines in order to intervene more creatively in the world, then their limiting effects must be explored more fully rather than be dismissed in favour of the postulation of an inchoate potentiality. As Bourdieu says: 'Even the most subversive symbolic actions, if they are not to condemn themselves to failure, must reckon with dispositions, and with the limitations these impose on innovative imagination and action' (2000: 234–5).

The abstraction of the capacity for radical action from the parameters of embodied existence may be suggestive but it falls short of being a meaningful account of the possibilities for effective political intervention in the world. The elevation of an unqualified idea of indeterminacy as a cipher for political subversion disregards certain parameters of embodied existence and, in doing so, empties itself of praxeological relevance vis-à-vis the idea of agency. It is indeed the case that the future-oriented dimensions of action render social existence more fragile and uncertain than is often acknowledged and may also reveal, in the abstract, an ever-present potential for change. It is one thing, however, to assert an essential temporal indeterminacy as an abstract condition of possibility of action and interaction, it is another to trace out what this might mean at the level of social relations, which, even at their most informal, are ineluctably embedded in entrenched hierarchies of power. Social action and interaction are certainly indeterminate to some degree and this is what gives social life its open-ended quality. However, action and interaction are also determinate in that they are mediated through embodied tendencies and social structures and are therefore relatively predictable and conformist and routinely contribute to the reproduction of systemic inequalities of race, class and gender. Even the most radical account of political action must reckon with this 'resistance of "reality"' if it is to have critical purchase (Bourdieu 2000: 108). For example, what is the meaning of thinking outside of the parameters of the subject-centred frame or 'testing the limits of every claim to community' given the predisposition of social actors to configure the flux of existence into determinate patterns, such as narrative? From a lived perspective, there is a deeply entrenched resistance to temporal and epistemological uncertainty because individuals seem to require a certain degree of coherence and stability in order to make sense of themselves and their environments (e.g. Ricoeur 1983). These tendencies may not be innate or inevitable, but they nonetheless impose significant limits on action and change which cannot be dislodged simply through exhortations to embrace uncertainty and mutability. As David Couzens Hoy puts it: 'One difficulty that arises with the ... emphasis on the historical malleability of subjectivity and embodiment is that pluralism seems to turn into sheer, unconstrained proliferation. The task then becomes to explain why a thousand possibilities are not simply actualized, and why instead societies manage to be fairly stable' (2005: 15). If the idea of agency is to have substantive force in terms of helping us to think about how we move from identity to post-identity politics, then it must be thought through more carefully in relation to the determinate nature of many dimensions of social existence which pertain, in part, to the insidious operations of power upon the embodied subject.

RIGHTS AND INDETERMINACY

Viewed from a phenomenological perspective, political agency is not an abstract competence or universal capacity but a set of embodied potentialities the realization of which is contingent, to some degree or another, upon the relations of power specific to a given situation. Furthermore, agency is more than a single capacity – for example, the capacity for critical self-scrutiny or creation *ex nihilo* – rather, it encompasses a spectrum of embodied capacities that in voluntarist, rational accounts are often conflated with each other. To quote Diana Coole: 'Modern ideas of agency have elided a series of phenomenal processes – such as consciousness, meaning generation, interiority, reflexivity, will, reasoning – that are then unified in the figure of the ontological individual or transcendental subject' (2005: 128). Post-identity theorists such as Zerilli do not make this error of condensing the agentic spectrum into the conventional figure of the sovereign subject, but, arguably, instead make a not dissimilar error of projecting it into the impersonal category of indeterminacy. This transfiguration of the property of persons as the property of structures closes off the underlying context of power and, by implication, important issues pertaining to the emergence of agency. How is it, for example, that individuals may have a critical understanding of their situation in the world (the 'lucidity of the excluded') but nonetheless may still be deeply disinclined to engage in political action? Willingness to act cannot be taken as a given but is an essential precondition of the implementation of radical political practice. The subjective representations that individuals have of themselves and the social world, their intentions and aims, perceptions and evaluations form the fundamental substrate of effective agency and must be taken into consideration if 'one wants to account for the daily struggles ... which ... transform or ... preserve ... [social] structures' (Bourdieu 1990b: 125).

By relegating such issues to the limiting frame of the 'social and subject question', Zerilli's fetish of indeterminacy comes perilously close to endorsing something that is not intended, namely the voluntarist fiction of unencumbered agency. As Moya Lloyd puts it: 'Without an explanation of how people are able to transcend their circumstances, in order to constitute a new world, it might appear that humans are in fact sovereign individuals able to do what they want' (2007b: 242). In short, an interpretative perspective is not necessarily the theoretical dead-end that Zerilli portrays it as but rather may be crucial to throwing light on the dispositional underpinnings of agency, of how individuals might be empowered and persuaded to overcome the practices and beliefs in which they are enmired in order to participate in progressive political practice. Trauma may not equate to truth, as Berlant (2000) has it, but by connecting the language of complaint to a phenomenological analysis of oppression it is possible to acquire insight into potential sources of and barriers to the emergence of effective political agency.

The difference that a phenomenological perspective has for an understanding of agency can be illustrated with reference to an exchange between Wendy Brown and Annabel Lever on rights discourse as a means for challenging gender oppression. In her article 'Suffering the Paradoxes of Rights', Brown (2002) considers some of the inconsistencies and contradictions of the language of rights for articulating and addressing women's inequality in Western democracies. Her critique is familiar in that it stems from the basic discrepancy, originally pointed out by Marx, between formal and substantive rights. For Brown, as for many feminists, the central paradox of rights is that the more they are formulated in an abstract or gender-neutral way, the more likely they are to enhance the privilege of men and eclipse the needs of women as subordinates. The necessarily abstract nature of universal rights renders women's subordination such a thin concept that the particulars of women's inequality vanish from the content and justification of the right. The difficulty is that the effort to redress this empty impartiality leads to a second paradox, namely that the articulation of more gender-specific rights risks encoding a definition of women premised upon their subordinate status. Not only will such a definition inevitably be partial – that is, it will be based on the needs and experiences of only some women – but also it risks binding women into a status as subordinates, with the possible effect, as we have seen, of engendering a masochistic attachment to victimhood and suffering. These tensions may be compounded by a further paradox, again proceeding from a central objection of Marx's, that the individualistic form that rights take inevitably limits their efficacy vis-à-vis overturning systemic inequalities, including gender subordination. Despite the fact that these overlapping paradoxes appear 'endlessly self-cancelling', Brown does not altogether abandon rights-based approaches as a vehicle of political struggle. Rather, she finishes with an injunction to consider how the indeterminate nature of paradox might 'gain political richness when it is understood as affirming the impossibility of justice in the present and as articulating the ... contours of justice in the future' (Brown 2002: 432). In a manner that echoes Zerilli, Brown holds up an abstract notion of indeterminacy, *qua* paradox, as a metonymic representation of radical political agency.

In response to Brown, Lever (2000) argues that it is only from a certain abstract perspective that paradox appears to be the central feature of rights. There are undeniable tensions and shortcomings in using rights discourse as a means to secure the overcoming of systemic oppressions. Nonetheless, in Lever's view, many of the so-called 'paradoxes' highlighted by Brown are not necessary to the structure of rights themselves but can, in fact, be overcome through political judgement and strategy. Lever claims, for example, that the ways in which rights currently work against women's interests is a concrete indication of how both the form and substance of existing rights might be transformed. For such transformative strategies to be effective, however, it does not help particularly to see rights as inherently paradoxical. Rather, existing practical limitations should force us to think more carefully about what is necessary to see and treat men and women as equals, within and beyond a discourse of rights. It pays to regard rights, in Lever's words, 'as the more or less predictable result of, and guide to, the forms of inequality in our society – both the ones of which we are already aware and those of which we still have to learn' (2000: 245). Ultimately, for Lever, the problem with Brown's analysis of rights is that it is abstracted from any political or institutional context, and this abstraction means that she reifies paradox as the essential feature of rights. One of the assumptions driving this paradox, for instance, is that the instantiation of rights within law is inevitably constraining and that it is the push from below via social movements that mitigates these constraints and forces the law to change. Whilst this dialectic of freedom and constraint captures some aspects of the struggle for social change, however, it also risks simplifying a far more complex political and legal reality into a single dynamic of domination from above and resistance from below (e.g. Passavant and Dean 2001)

In other words, there may indeed be features of rights that are paradoxical, but these are not necessarily the most central or the most relevant features that oppressed groups should focus on in their struggles to attain equality. One way of considering how rights-based approaches might be rendered more effective in overcoming gender inequality is to consider the reasons why women and other subordinate groups are disinclined to seek legal remedies in the first place. Rather than looking at rights as paradoxes, it might be more fruitful to examine, through a materialist phenomenology, how individuals relate, or, more pertinently, do not relate, to rights-based political discourse. In her study of attitudes towards the legal regulation of offensive public speech, Laura Beth Nielson (2000) found that there were significant differences between how various groups thought about the way in which such speech should be dealt with by the law, and these differences correlated to differences of class, race and gender. Although there was widespread agreement across all social groups against the legal regulation of speech, the only group that articulated this opposition through rights-based reasoning (along First Amendment lines) were the white male respondents to her survey. Perhaps surprisingly, the groups of individuals who were much more likely to be the targets of offensive speech on a daily basis – women, people of colour – were not only opposed to the legal regulation of such speech, but did not even construe it as a problem that pertained to the law and legal remedy at all. In the case of women, Nielson traces this reluctance to see public verbal harassment as a problem into which the law could helpfully intervene to the convergent effects of overarching norms about appropriate feminine behaviour. On the one hand, women are expected to be 'good girls' and avoid public harassment by dressing and behaving correctly. On the other hand, a gendered expectation emerging from the individualizing tendencies of late modernity is that women are expected to be autonomous in the sense that, confronted with harassment, they should be able to stick up for themselves without making a fuss or construing themselves as victims. These gender norms are of course not experienced as external expectations but are internalized in the form of practical dispositions and commonsensical views. It results in a form of what Bourdieu would call misrecognition or the partial complicity of the oppressed with their own oppression. The female respondents of Nielson's study disconnected the problem of harassment from the broader social apparatus of gender subordination and fell back on a doxic interpretation of verbal harassment as isolated incidents unconnected to the social institution of sexism.

Nielson draws various conclusions from her research about the contingent and iterative nature of legal consciousness, which varies according to social position and life-course. From the perspective of this book's central concern, the interesting implication of this work on legal consciousness is how self-identity and understanding affect agency – in this case, the individual's willingness to even consider certain types of action over others, or indeed to prefer inaction to any kind of action. From this perspective, it is not the paradoxical nature of rights that is the main problem confronting feminist activists, but a host of more basic problems pertaining to political mobilization. These include levels of oppositional consciousness and dispositional disinclination amongst many women to construe problems related to gender inequality as legally or politically redressable. This perspective draws attention to one of the main insights of habitus: that social constraints such as gender and class are lived as profound psychological dispositions or structures of feeling. It is important to attend to these embodied dispositions, not to elevate them as some kind of experiential 'truth', but rather to understand potential barriers and resistances to the formation of political consciousness and agency. The political consciousness that is an important precondition for any type of radical political change cannot be taken as an unproblematic given. There are many different types of oppositional consciousness, none of which occur spontaneously but which are the effects of certain kinds of social and political intervention. Jane Mansbridge, for example, identifies at least six types of oppositional consciousness, which are never manifest in a pure form, because they are interwoven with hegemonic types of consciousness. Furthermore, the passage from critical consciousness to action is not automatic (Mansbridge 2001: 238). There are considerable differences between recognizing injustice, identifying systemic domination and common interests, devising strategies for action and finally feeling able to act. Often, in Mansbridge's view, the most effective way of inducing individuals into wider, deliberative political debate is, at the outset, to engage individuals and groups through a direct appeal to their own experiences and narrower concerns of recognition and interest. In other words, an initial route into post-identity politics is not through the abandonment of the politics of identity but precisely the opposite, through an appeal to it. By creating what Mansbridge calls 'deliberative enclaves', marginal and oppressed groups are given the opportunity to formulate politicized understandings of their identities, interests and needs. The challenge for wider political deliberation becomes that of ensuring that these enclaves don't become self-enclosed ends-in-themselves, that dialogue across enclaves is guaranteed and that, ultimately, identity claims are oriented to 'broader surroundings in which they can test those ideas against the reigning reality' (Mansbridge 1996: 57).

In sum, political consciousness is a complex, socially specific phenomenon that has to be carefully created by critically engaging with and often transforming individuals' interpretations of self and world. The abstract ideas of agency as indeterminacy deployed by Brown and Zerilli are conceptually unable to deal with such underlying issues of consciousness and mobilization because their critique of subjectivism means they fail to appreciate the analytical importance of a concept of self-identity for an account of agency. By disregarding issues pertaining to the social conditions necessary for effective agency, the important argument that feminism should move towards a post-identity politics remains an ungrounded exhortation that does not connect to the embodied experience of the very subjects it wishes to mobilize.

INDETERMINACY AND RESISTANCE

Perhaps the ultimate difficulty with Brown's and Zerilli's formulations of political agency as indeterminacy is that they tacitly rest on a questionable valorization of non-identity as inherently radical. This holding up of indeterminacy as a political good in itself is familiar from poststructural thought, whose critique of identity thinking often leads to a fetishization of the non-identical and inchoate, *qua* desire, as the source of subversion. This tendency to attribute an apodictic radical status to indeterminacy is particularly evident in some accounts of agency as resistance. Although ideas of resistance have moved away from the uncritical populism for which they were extensively criticized, they have been reformulated in recent theory on identity in terms of ideas of unruly emotion, disruptive desires and other indeterminate features of social existence (see, e.g., Probyn 2004; Skeggs 2004). These moments of non-identity are thereby implicitly invested with a contestatory status that is far from self-evident. This is not to deny that certain ineffable and indeterminate aspects of existence might be harbingers of change, in the sense that they are indicative of profound shifts in structures of emotion. It is certainly the case that everyday life is frequently marked by emotional and corporeal experiences whose meaning is opaque but which are profoundly felt and disrupt the closure of routinized existence. But to herald these inchoate and ineffable emotions as resistance is problematic because it is far from clear what is being 'resisted' and what, if any, are the 'political' effects of these phenomena. It is also to reduce the logic of agency to a conceptually limited dualism of conformity and subversion, domination and resistance. In Saba Mahmood's words: 'To analyze people's actions in terms of realized or frustrated attempts at social transformation is to necessarily reduce the heterogeneity of life to the rather flat narrative of succumbing to or resisting relations of domination' (2001: 222).

Following on from their critique of identity and the subject-centred frame, Brown and Zerilli are also hostile, at least on the face of it, to the construal of political agency as resistance. Ideas of resistance, in Brown's view, form part of a wider postmodern sensibility that is wary of the authority of any type of normative critique, and takes refuge instead in the 'local viewpoint and tendency toward positioning without mapping' (1995: 49). This deliberately constrained perspectivalism renders ideas of resistance ineffectual as coherent political responses to types of social injustice: 'Resistance goes nowhere in particular, has no inherent attachments, and hails no particular vision . . . resistance is an effect of and reaction to power, not an arrogation of it' (1995: 49). Rather than being driven by the parochial logic of resistance, feminist political praxis should engage in the wider use of public reason, in processes of democratic deliberation. Yet, despite the explicit opposition to ideas of resistance, Brown's construal of political agency is closer to them than she might care to acknowledge in so far as she appears to invest notions of indeterminacy, fluidity and flux with an inherent radical force. For example, although she espouses a version of deliberative democracy, the form and content of this deliberation remains undefined except in the negative terms of a ceaseless testing of limits and crossing of boundaries. Feminists should learn the 'pleasures of public argument', but this public use of reason cannot take the form of a Habermasian purified communication, or, contra Zerilli, the form of a pristine Arendtian political space held apart from the embodied concerns and constraints of the social realm. Deliberation somehow involves a constant movement across boundaries: '[T]hese spaces ... are necessarily cluttered, attuned to earthly concerns and visions, incessantly disrupted, invaded, and reconfigured. ... They must be heterogeneous, roving, relatively noninstitutionalized, and democratic to the point of exhaustion' (Brown 1995: 50). Echoing Brown's work on rights, political agency is configured, once again, in the appealing but elusive terms of indeterminacy and paradox. As an image of a desirable democratic ethos of self-questioning, it is undoubtedly attractive, but from the perspective of embodied agents, what does this ceaseless crossing of boundaries and challenging of certainties mean in terms of furthering progressive action, and why, as is implied, is it necessarily radical? How do the claims that progressive political agency must be 'incessantly disrupted, invaded, and reconfigured ... heterogenous, roving ... noninstitutionalized' cash out as pragmatic strategies for embodied political subjects? This elision of counter-hegemonic challenge with indeterminacy that Brown is not alone in making is the result of an abstract discursivism which views social reality through the narrow lens of the stability of meaning and its disruption.

Once one switches, however, from this essentially linguistic world-view to a phenomenological perspective on embodied existence, then the celebration of indeterminacy as radical becomes much more problematic. So too does the correlative assumption that associates determinacy with the 'constraints' of identity thinking. Davina Cooper, for example, has criticized the tendency in radical theory to elide oppositional politics with the spontaneous and the relatively ephemeral and the linked assumption that the institutionalization of such practices necessarily constrains and may even eradicate their radical impact. Against this celebration of the inchoate, Cooper argues that a certain degree of routinization and entrenchment is crucial to ensure that the radical thrust of counter-hegemonic practices endures. The establishment of 'new routinized pathways', for example, is crucial for oppositional practices, 'from recycling to lesbian motherhood', to maintain pressure on the established order to change (Cooper 2004: 143). They constitute practical exemplars of other possible ways of being that potentially have more persuasive effects than abstract exhortations to embrace an openness to new, uncertain modes of existence. The sedimentation of everyday practices as pathways also renders them potentially less vulnerable to attack from opponents. Pathways may take a *de facto* form, in that they come from below, from the emergent repetitive practices of everyday life. However, the term is not based in an uncritical populism – of which post-identity thinkers would be rightly suspicious – because access to different pathways is determined by power inequalities. They may also take the form of *de jure* processes of sedimentation: that is, pathways that are organized from above that may have normative effects, for example legislation in the UK on civil unions which establishes some kind of institutional pathway for what has been for a long time the *de facto* practice of same-sex couples. Cooper's idea of routinizing radical practices throws into question the tendency, in much post-identity theory, to construe radical agency in the overplayed opposition between determinacy and indeterminacy. The metaphor of pathways designates how important it is for informal radical practices to become durably sedimented in order for counter-hegemonic options to gain a wider political currency. It represents an alternative way of thinking about the contours of political action from the perspective of embodied subjects rather than through socially weightless notions of indeterminacy. From the former perspective, the idea of radical action as ceaseless critique, transgression of boundaries and the living through of paradox is a one-sided phenomenological abstraction that fails to address the 'reality' of embodied agency. The risk entailed in this turning away from the actual is that practical attempts to intervene in the world and change it in a progressive manner may inevitably seem less radical than ideas of freedom as unconstrained indeterminacy and creation *ex nihilo*. In this way, post-identity theorists defer the moment of democratic action from the present instant to a perpetually forthcoming one that, despite its supposed imminence, never quite arrives.

NEW UNIVERSALISM

In the final analysis, the tendency of post-identity thinkers to view indeterminacy as inherently radical forecloses an examination of the specific social conditions that engender or hinder the emergence of political agency. By locating the source of emancipatory political action in free-floating ideas of indeterminacy, they finish by universalizing the conditions of possibility of a phenomenon which is, in fact, more local and contingent upon a given configuration of power relations. To quote Mahmood: 'The desire for freedom and liberation is a historically situated desire whose motivational force cannot be assumed a priori' (2001: 223). Both Brown and Zerilli repeatedly acknowledge that political agency is a socially specific entity, but this is undermined by the abstract and socially weightless manner in which they thematize the idea. Ironically, Zerilli criticizes Butler's idea of the performative on precisely these grounds, namely that it attempts to provide a universal guarantee for counter-hegemonic action when, in fact, none exists given that agency is always situated and historically singular. She takes issue with Butler's claim that it is the imitative structure of gender itself – its intrinsic repeatability – that renders it open to subversive resignification. The generic structure of drag, for example, highlights the performative and artificial nature of all gender identity: drag is an imitation without an original. The attribution of an intrinsic subversive force to this a priori structure is erroneous, in Zerilli's view, because, in fact, political effects are only generated by the specific contextual conditions of a given action, the nature of the audience, for example, or the site of the performance. There is nothing intrinsic to the structure of drag itself that will ensure its counter-hegemonic interpretation:

> There is nothing in a drag performance that guarantees I will see drag and gender as the same kind of object – see, that is, the drag performance as the display of what gender really is. . . . It is just as likely that I will see drag when I see drag and see gender when I see gender. . . . To see drag, after all, is to know that gender is being performed – otherwise we would simply see gender. (Zerilli 2005: 57; also Lloyd 2007a)

The claim that it is the imitative structure of gender itself that assures its own disruption is misguided in so far as it seeks to formulate the radically contingent conditions of doubt as a universal, generalizable proposition. Although Zerilli's critique is not without grounds, she appears unwittingly to reproduce a reification similar to that which she accuses Butler of making when she locates the source of radical political intervention in the world in a quasi-transcendental notion of future uncertainty rather than in the actions of embodied subjects. Consequently, there is an unresolved paradox in her work between, on the one hand, her critique of the hypostatizing tendency to displace the locus of emancipation from practice to the structure of gender itself and, on the other hand, her substitution of a disincorporated idea of indeterminacy as a cipher for embodied agency.

A similar paradox also marks Zerilli's work on political judgement, potentially undermining her interesting attempt to move feminist critique beyond overplayed dilemmas of relativism and universalism. The issue of judgement is of fundamental importance for feminist politics given its intrinsic normative commitment to overcoming the subordination of women. Yet, from an anti-foundational perspective, the grounds on which such judgements should rest are unclear given the equally as inescapable commitment of post-conventional feminism to respecting the differences of others. Such dilemmas are paradigmatically expressed in debates on multiculturalism, where a central issue for feminists is how to respond to the potentially oppressive practices of non-Western cultures towards women without invoking the kind of ethnocentric assumptions that, in their view, often underpin liberal ideas of impartiality and value neutrality. If, however, judgements are understood to always proceed from a situated perspective, this seems to potentially limit feminist critique to a relativism that works against a commitment to overcoming gender subordination. Influential feminist thinkers, such as Martha Nussbaum (2000) and Seyla Benhabib (2002), have tried to solve these dilemmas by redefining universalism in sufficiently anti-essentialist and weak procedural terms as to provide quasi-transcendental criteria on which to base political judgements. Their central claim is that cultures are not self-enclosed, internally unified totalities that are fundamentally alien to each other, but are hybrid, mutually permeable entities that have as many features in common as they have differences. The identification of shared, trans-cultural features provides the grounds for arriving at consensual political judgements that simultaneously do not violate respect for cultural pluralism. For Zerilli, however, it is the very anti-essentialism of this 'new' universalism that, far from overcoming the ethnocentric prejudice of 'decayed rationalism', proves to be the vehicle for reintroducing it in a more subtle guise. Anti-essentialism leads to a theoretical bias that lionizes cultural practices and beliefs that accord with cosmopolitan notions of hybridity, fluidity and openness whilst tacitly discounting those other, say, more traditional practices and populist movements (e.g. nationalism) that do not necessarily display such qualities: 'Ethnocentrism reappears in these new universalists' anti-essentialist view of culture in the form of local contexts that have been rendered politically superfluous from the standpoint of any articulation of shared normative criteria' (Zerilli 2009: 302; also Cheah 2006; Kompridis 2005).

This post-foundational universalism is, in the view of Nussbaum and Benhabib, the only viable theoretical route for culturally sensitive feminist critique that wishes to avoid sliding into a politically debilitating relativism. Zerilli, by contrast, rejects this choice between universalism or relativism as a false antithesis and uses Wittgenstein's practice-based idea of rationality to reveal its basis in a faulty understanding of what it is that we actually do when we make judgements. To make a judgement is not a question of rule-following, of applying established criteria to particular instance as if pre-given guidelines could always be guaranteed to accommodate the multiplicity of practical problems thrown up by complex and pluralistic societies. It is rather a practical, first-order issue of discernment in political discourse. The ability to discern something arises from the immediacy of a given situation where the subject takes a view on something without the reassurance of inherited criteria: 'an ability to form an opinion about the particular qua particular precisely in the absence of known rules' (Zerilli 2009: 307). Combining this idea of practical discernment with Arendt's idea of representative or enlarged thought, Zerilli argues that judgement involves the gesture of empathic understanding with an 'other' yet fused with a simultaneous awareness of the impossibility of such a gesture. The exteriority of the other renders it always ultimately inaccessible to the subject's own perspective. At the same time, however, it is this very exteriority that enables the moment of judgement itself, understood as a reflexive understanding of one's own positionality: 'a way of expressing the specificity of one's own rootedness elsewhere as the condition of understanding and judging what is foreign' (Zerilli 2009: 312). The inability to fully assimilate the other to one's own perspective engenders the distantiation necessary for an enlarged awareness of the strengths and limitations of one's own standpoint with regard to understanding. Judgement, then, necessarily involves the capacity to bring together these perspectives of identification and estrangement and to hold them in tension rather than reconcile them; it is the attempt to 'see from multiple standpoints in order to form a critical opinion and to make a judgement'(Zerilli 2009: 313).

Zerilli's redefinition of judgement in situated, processual terms rather than teleological ones may solve the false antinomy of universalism versus relativism, but it raises another problem that is more difficult for her to overcome. If her version of judgement as enlarged thought is to have any bite, it seems to require a movement towards precisely the issues of sociality – of power, identity and social position – from which elsewhere she wishes to escape. Here a comparison with Bourdieu is instructive for although, like Zerilli, he thinks that understanding and, by implication, judgement flow from the ability to hold in tension multiple standpoints, his approach requires the type of engagement with the social context that she explicitly rejects. For Bourdieu, reflexive understanding is knowledge of the sociological other generated neither by ostensibly neutral methods of sociological inquiry nor by phenomenological projection of self into other (Bourdieu et al. 1999: 613). So-called 'neutral inquiry' always involves, at an unspoken level, a 'social relationship' between subject and object, and it therefore behoves the sociologist to examine, as far as possible, the 'distortions . . . embedded in the very structure of the research relationship' (Bourdieu et al. 1999: 608). It is just as naïve, however, to jettison the pretence to objectivity in order to launch into an emphatic liaison driven by the 'spontaneistic illusion' that the perspectives of the sociologist and object of study perfectly coincide (Bourdieu et al. 1999: 621). Understanding of the other is created not through a vague act of empathy – 'immediate half-understanding'– but through a careful reconstruction of the space of points of view, or, as Bourdieu puts it, a *'generic and genetic comprehension* of who these individuals are, based on a . . . grasp of the social conditions of which they are a product' (Bourdieu et al. 1999: 613). At the same time, the sociologist must also be mindful of the possible distorting effects of her own unavoidably distantiated perspective on such a reconstruction. Understanding, then, emerges from a process of reflexive self-scrutiny situated somewhere between objectivism and subjectivism, between, in Zerilli's terms, identification and estrangement, where the sociologist attempts to hold together, in as rigorous a fashion as possible, multiple points of view:

> Sociologists cannot be unaware that the specific characteristic of their point of view is to be a point of view on a point of view. They can re-produce the point of view of their object and constitute it as such by resituating it within social space, but can only do so by taking up that very singular (and, in a sense, very privileged) viewpoint, being obliged to place themselves there in order to be able to take . . . all the points of view possible. (Bourdieu et al. 1999: 625)

For Bourdieu, reflexive understanding emerges from a reconstruction of the very social conditions of possibility of action and interaction that, in her Arendtian mode, Zerilli views as pertaining to the constraining 'frames of the social and the subject'. Yet, if Zerilli's idea of political judgement is to amount to more than a formal oscillation on the part of the theorist between acknowledging the relation with the other and the simultaneous impossibility of that relation, then it is precisely this type of socio-centric analysis that is required to give it substance. To be more than an ungrounded imaginative projection, political judgement must proceed in tandem with a close attentiveness to the underlying social conditions that are generative of different perspectives. In short, Zerilli appears to propose an idea of political judgement that, if it is to be effectively realized, stands in conflict with her understanding of political freedom. Although, in principle, the moments of judgement and freedom are not intrinsically incompatible, it is not clear, on the basis of what Zerilli says about the limiting nature of the social and the stringent fashion in which she holds it apart from the political, how they can be reconciled. In theory, deeper knowledge of the parameters of social existence may give rise to how it is possible to transcend those parameters. This is precisely why Bourdieu argues that effective political thinking has to be exercised in the direction of the tendencies of the world, not against them. In contrast, the disconnected and tacitly hierarchical nature of Zerilli's account of the social and the political undermines any substantive basis for her otherwise interesting formulation of judgement.

CONCLUSION

More generally, in its detachment from the parameters of phenomenal existence, Zerilli's idea of political action is in danger of being little more than a socially weightless fantasy of freedom from determination. In the light of this social weightlessness, it would seem precipitate for feminists to follow her exhortation to relinquish the woman question in political theory and to ask instead the political theory question in feminism. This does not mean to say that Zerilli is necessarily wrong to identify the limiting effects of a narrow preoccupation with identity on thought about democratic freedom or to argue that feminism should try to embrace more fully a post-identity politics. But perhaps the critique of identity is exaggerated; indeed, as Linda Alcoff observes, it has in recent years become something of a shibboleth for democratic thinkers in general, where it is 'blamed for a host of political ills and theoretical mistakes' (2006: 15). The challenge for feminist theorists may lie then not so much in abandoning ideas of identity and subjectivity as a conceptual dead-end, but instead in reconfiguring them in materialist and relational terms in order to work towards an enlarged understanding of the conditions needed for effective political agency. Rather than embark on the quest to conceive of political freedom beyond the social and subject questions, perhaps feminists should begin with the attempt to resituate the personal within the impersonal, to reconnect 'struggles against personalized subjection to the critique of the capitalist system' (Fraser 2009: 115). Indeed, if, following Fraser, Foucault, Bourdieu and others, we understand some of the most insidious effects of neoliberal capitalism to reside in a depoliticizing governance of self, then the subject question and associated ideas of identity and agency should perhaps have a renewed rather than diminished significance in feminist political thought about freedom. These challenges are not captured in the post-identity equation of freedom with the escape from identity concerns and, as a result, some feminists find themselves stranded in a socially weightless paradigm that poses questions of undoubted importance but which it has little hope of beginning to answer.

4
All or Nothing: Rancière's Ruptural Agonism

INTRODUCTION

Jacques Rancière describes the animating concern of his work on the political as an attestation of the agency of the oppressed. In realizing this concern, however, he avoids many of the established routes in democratic theory. He does not sketch out, for example, an inclusive procedural framework which aims to guarantee that oppressed and marginal groups will always be granted participatory parity. Nor does he undertake an analysis of the obstacles that confront disempowered groups in their struggle for recognition in order to suggest ways in which they may be overcome. Nor, finally, does he attempt to outline the type of ethical attitude that virtuous citizens should adopt towards each other in order to sustain the open and egalitarian spirit necessary for democratic life. Indeed, Rancière would reject all such options as excessively prescriptive for, like other intellectuals of the post-Althusserian generation, he rejects the Leninist view that the task of the intellectual is to show the oppressed the way towards their emancipation. It is not the job of the intellectual to speak for others, for they are perfectly capable of speaking and acting for themselves. Rather, the task is, in part, to retell history in such a way that the demands for equality made by oppressed groups are heard clearly once more and stand as a reminder of the deeply challenging nature of genuine democratic conflict.

Given that the role of the intellectual is not to recommend in advance the rules and rationale that should govern democratic practice but simply to pragmatically verify the agency of the poor, it follows that Rancière's view of the political is characterized by an extreme emptiness or negativity. Indeed he is fiercely opposed to the Arendtian and Schmittian trends in democratic theory that elevate a certain form of social being as the quintessence of political activity and ultimate expression of human freedom. In his view, the political cannot be given enduring content of any sort; it is simply a moment of rupture or polemical clash between two worlds – between those who belong and those who do not – that reminds us of the truly radical nature of the premise of universal equality and also throws into question the legitimacy of the established political community. From this anti-ontological perspective, many of the things that other theorists would count as political do not count as such for Rancière. Furthermore, since the political resides only in the moment of disagreement itself, this means that it is by its very nature ephemeral and evanescent; its emergence is unpredictable, its existence is unsustainable and its occurrence, especially in the contemporary world, is rare.

At first sight, then, to accuse Rancière of socially weightless thinking seems to miss the point of his work entirely, since the emancipatory force of the political resides precisely in the extent to which it is not encumbered by pre-existing social content. Nonetheless, given its intrinsic emptiness, the question remains whether Rancière's idea of the political has much to offer thought on radical democracy other than a romantic rereading of the past as a lost history of genuine political disagreement. Given its stringent negativity, a number of radical democrats have indeed concluded that his idea of the political is little more than a provocative but, ultimately, empty gesture. This is perhaps too hasty a judgement, and I argue here that Rancière's idiosyncratic brand of socially weightless theory offers insight into the tacit normalizations set in play by models of democracy that present as universal and impartial procedures what are, in fact, particular modes of social being. His thought also offers reworked accounts of the discourses of recognition and rights that free them from reductive ontological baggage and thereby accord them a renewed significance for emancipatory political struggle. At the most general level, Rancière's work throws critical light on the tendentious nature of ontological models of the political and suggests instead that an approach of disclosing critique might be a more fruitful way of thinking for radical democrats.

In certain respects, Rancière's attack on political ontology crosses over with the critique made by thinkers of social suffering about the exclusionary effects of certain types of universalism in political theory. Rancière would emphatically reject any such comparison because he associates the work of thinkers such as Bourdieu with an intellectual elitism that over-predicts the powerlessness of the poor and thereby denies their agency. But it is with regard to the issue of agency that the limitations of Rancière's socially weightless idea of the political become apparent, as does also the importance of an attentiveness to power for disclosing critique to be meaningful. Lacking a developed account of power and sociality, Rancière adopts an 'all or nothing' logic with regard to agency which is both theoretically naïve and politically ineffective. He disregards the complex dynamics of disempowerment which mean that, contra his assertion, the poor are often unable to act for themselves, at least in the first instance. In the context of his evanescent notion of the political, the presumption of agency turns out to be not so much an act of verification but rather a naïve statement of faith that romanticizes the perpetual marginality of the poor and ultimately comes close to replicating the depoliticized analysis that he denounces in other thinkers.

HIERARCHY AND EQUALITY

On the face of it, Rancière's attempt to isolate the distinctive and autonomous essence of the political seems to be in keeping with the Schmittian and Arendtian tendencies that inform the work of other radical democrats. The identification of a political logic irreducible to that which governs social life is intended to shine a light on the apparent inevitability of an established order so as to denaturalize it and engender a renewed sense of the possibilities for radical democratic practice. This apparent similarity is, however, misleading for, unlike the approach of most other radical democrats, Rancière's idea of the political cannot be enshrined in enduring institutional arrangements, demarcated spaces or rationales, or substantive ethical predispositions. Indeed, in his view, any attempt to prescribe in advance the form that the political should take is deeply mistaken because it reduces its radically contingent nature and disruptive force to a particular set of already existing and known social practices. Differently put, it domesticates the unruly forces of the political. For Rancière, then, the political is necessarily an anti-ontological category; it has no 'proper' content; it is a relation of pure negativity or conflict that, by its very nature, is fleeting, unpredictable and unsustainable.

The principle of negativity that the political encapsulates is a consequence of Rancière's construal of the relation it has with the social order as one of absolute discontinuity. The two orders are not only mutually irreducible but also fundamentally disruptive of each other in that they express antithetical dynamics. The social is governed by a logic of hierarchy, whereas the political is governed by the presupposition of the universal equality of all individuals. The social is the realm where sensible being is distributed and arranged according to the hierarchical principles that govern any given community. Following Foucault, Rancière calls this the order of the police (*la police*), a form of social organization that 'distributes bodies within the space of their visibility or invisibility and aligns ways of doing, ways of being and ways of saying appropriate to each' (Rancière 1999: 28). In this Foucauldian sense, the police is a neutral, non-pejorative term that designates a particular way of organizing and governing a realm of instituted being. It is a 'distribution of the sensible' that is always simultaneously an order of hierarchy and domination, of inequality and injustice (Rancière 1999: 29). The nature of hierarchies varies over time and across cultures, but any social order will always organize sensible existence around distinctions between the ruler and the ruled, the dominant and the dominated or, in Rancière's terms, those who have a part and those who have no part.

In contrast to the social, the political encapsulates a principle that is fundamentally subversive of this hierarchical police logic, namely the assumption of radical equality. Equality, on Rancière's understanding, is an axiomatic presumption that should not be confused with a substantive political goal or legal norm. It has no social essence; rather, it is an unspoken supposition constitutive of all order which is practically re-enacted only in instances of genuine democratic conflict: 'Equality is not a given that politics then presses into service, an essence embodied in the law or a goal politics sets itself the task of attaining. It is a mere assumption that needs to be discerned within the practices implementing it . . .' (Rancière 1999: 18). The presupposition of equality has this constitutive status in so far as it is the hidden grounds upon which any inegalitarian order rests. Any hierarchy presumes that there are those who command and those who obey, but, underpinning this is a suppressed moment of equality that Rancière calls the fundamental equality of speaking beings, namely the presumption that those who obey are capable, in the first place, of both understanding their orders and carrying them out:

> There is order in society because some people command and others obey, but in order to obey at least two things are required: you must understand the order and you must understand that you must obey it. And to do that, you must already be the equal of the person who is ordering you. It is this equality that gnaws away at any natural order. ... In the final analysis, inequality is only possible through equality. (1999: 16)

Although equality of understanding forms the necessary foundation of any structured order, this can never be fully acknowledged, for it would expose the arbitrary nature of social hierarchy. Nonetheless, like the repressed forces of the unconscious, the phantasm of equality always haunts an established order, returning momentarily in instances of political conflict to throw its asymmetrical social relations into disarray. Like the unconscious, the universal supposition of the ultimate equality of all human beings with each other – 'of anyone and everyone' – both founds the social and is totally foreign to it; it is the point from which the contingency of any established order is exposed and its inequalities are challenged.

Politics occurs when the heterogeneous logics of hierarchy and equality clash, resulting in a reconfiguration of the established order such that something that was previously invisible – the part of those who have no part – becomes visible. It is by invoking the idea of universal equality that the dominated and excluded – emblematically represented in the figure of the 'poor' – claim inclusion within an order. But, in doing so and thereby exposing tacit mechanisms of exclusion, they also call into question the legitimacy of the prevailing order:

> Political activity is always a mode of expression that undoes the perceptible divisions of the police order by implementing a basically heterogeneous assumption, that of a part of those who have no part, an assumption that, at the end of the day, itself demonstrates the sheer contingency of the order, the equality of any speaking being with any other speaking being. (Rancière 1999: 30)

Such moments of political challenge occur only when a specific social oppression is transfigured by being framed not as a claim about a particular injustice but as a claim about the universal equality of all beings. It is this universalizing element that gives some struggles a truly subversive political force that is lacking in others because of the way they are limited to certain specific social ends. Indeed, many struggles which are commonly regarded as political are in fact, in Rancière's view, anti-political in nature because they are confined to the assertion of a particular group's demands. A strike, for example, is not political when it restricts itself to denouncing the greed of employers, but becomes political when it questions wage disparity in the name of a deeper equality that throws the legitimacy of the prevailing capitalist order into question (Rancière 1999: 32). Struggles may emanate from a particular social injustice, but it is only when they are presented as claims about the equality of anyone and everyone that they become fully political: 'Nothing is political in itself for the political only happens by means of a principle that does not belong to it: equality' (Rancière 1999: 33). Indeed, it is Rancière's insistence on the immanence of the assertion of universal equality within any singular struggle that means that politics, in his sense, is an exceptional event rather than a normal practice – 'Politics doesn't always happen – it actually happens very little or rarely' (1999: 17).

In short, the emancipatory force of Rancière's idea of the political resides precisely in the extent to which it is entirely distinct from the order of social being. The political is characterized by an extreme emptiness or negativity; it is a *sui generis* moment of pure disruption fleetingly embodied in the demands of the poor and excluded; a 'provisional accident in the history of forms of domination' (Rancière 2001: thesis 6). Beyond the transcendental claim to equality, this moment of political rupture may take any form and emerge in any manner and at any point: 'It is not predictable to any degree but erupts randomly at any time and at anyone's intervention' (Rancière 1999: 60). There is nothing proper to the political; it does not occupy a particular space, it does not have an immanent rationality or necessary procedural logic, nor can it be accompanied by any form of democratic ethics. The political – or, democracy, a term that Rancière uses synonymously – is anti-ontological, a polemical relation of contradictory elements lacking any essential foundations: it is 'always distorted by the refraction of equality in freedom. Is never pure, never based on some essence proper to the community and the law' (1999: 61). The confrontation of the incommensurable orders of the police and equality, in the arguing of a wrong, interrupts the established community and challenges its legitimacy by making visible previously suppressed, excluded groups. Given its destabilizing effects, politics is therefore also an exceptional event and one whose effects are unsustainable in so far as the moment of its institutionalization is also the moment when it becomes its other: that is, it comes to form part of a new police order: 'Every politics . . . works on the verge of its radical demise, which is embodiment as the police, the realization of the political subject as social body' (Rancière 1999: 91). The political must necessarily be socially weightless, as unencumbered as possible by any social content in order to have its ruptural, radically egalitarian impact.

At first sight, Rancière's negative formulation of the political through ideas of rupture, indeterminacy and contingency seems to echo the thematic concerns of other theories of radical democracy. Such negative formulations are a way of remaining theoretically open to agency from below, which may assume diverse and unexpected forms. Prescription of the form that political action should take or the site it should occupy runs the risk of setting up an exclusive theoretical framework which valorizes certain types of political practice whilst discounting, even outlawing, others. This concern with the agency of the oppressed is one of the catalysing insights driving Rancière's thought. What he objects to in many philosophical and sociological treatments of 'the poor' is the way in which the agency of powerless groups is denied, thereby keeping them in a position of subordination or, as he phrases it, reinforcing 'the rule imposed upon shoemakers to do nothing else than make shoes' (Rancière 2003: 165). In his view, the central role of the intellectual is not to tell the poor how to achieve emancipation or to speak on their behalf, since they are able to do these things for themselves. Rather, the task of the intellectual is to affirm the agency of the oppressed. Such an affirmation partly takes the form of a process of historical reconstruction of their neglected voices, a verification which recalls forgotten instances of the egalitarian demand (Rancière 2012). But framing the political in such thin, negative terms is also part of this attestation, a way of avoiding theoretical legislation and of potentially being more receptive than prescriptive theory to the myriad forms that popular agency may take.

Despite this shared underlying concern with popular agency, the negativity of Rancière's formulation of the political is, however, far more extreme than those of other radical democrats. Indeed, he would discern in the work of Arendtian and Schmittian democrats the tendency to derive a concept of the political from the properties of a specific order of being and, by reifying it as a necessary rationale, compound the exclusion of the 'poor'. On a superficial reading, Arendt's idea of the political seems to resemble Rancière's in so far as it is famously 'empty' and devoid of determinate social content. However, unlike his evanescent moment of rupture, she still accords political practice an enduring and essential logic, namely that of inaugural collective action. In doing this, she mistakenly associates the political with a specific way of living and substantive notion of the good, and, in Rancière's view, remains caught within a police logic. Her idea of the political represents nothing more than yet another attempt to partition the sensible realm in such a way that certain determinate modes of being are prioritized over others: 'The supposed purification of the political, freed from domestic and social necessity, comes down to nothing more (or less) than the reduction of the political to the state' (Rancière 2001: thesis 1). In a similar way, there seems to be an initial resemblance between Rancière's and Mouffe's negative formulation of agonistic democracy in terms of the constitutive nature of conflict for political being and the ongoing confrontation between a hegemonic order and those whom it excludes (e.g. Tambakaki 2009). But, again, as in the case of Arendt, Mouffe's idea of the political diverges from Rancière's in so far as she substantializes it by allocating it a specific end (the acquisition of power or hegemony) and an immanent rationality (the conversion of antagonism into agonism). In Rancière's view, such regulated dissensus would amount to a false conflation of the litigious structure of political conflict with empirical disagreement. The political cannot be reduced to the mere divergence of opinion amongst social actors who, beneath the appearance of agonism, are all members of the same established community. In this respect, the radical negativity of Rancière's idea of the political serves to highlight a fundamental and unresolved tension in Mouffe's work between, on the one side, her claim that democratic action properly understood is a radically heterogeneous ensemble of diverse practices and, on the other, her insistence that all political action should conform to the homogenizing logic of antagonism-agonism. Ultimately, then, even though her idea of democracy is grounded in a negative ontology, in Rancière's view, she nonetheless commits the error of attributing to it some kind of social essence and thereby diminishes the radical and singular force of the moment of political disagreement, which always dramatically exceeds any so-called 'necessary logic'.

Rancière's anti-ontological leanings not only set his work apart from other negative concepts of democracy, but they also belie the way his work has been appropriated by thinkers of a post-anarchist politics of multiplicity and becoming (e.g. May 2008; Newman 2011). Although he might share the anarchist rejection of a formalized political sphere as the proper site for radical action, he surely would not endorse the subsequent sociological reduction of the political that equates it with a multiplicity of counter-hegemonic citizen practices. From his perspective, this would involve an improper dilution of the polemical force of political disagreement by eliding it with the substantive logic of social plurality. In short, his idea of the political resists assimilation into the dynamics of hegemony and affinity that are the defining terms of much radical democratic debate.

In the light of this extreme de-substantialization or social weightlessness, the question arises about the nature of the contribution that Rancière's idea of the political makes to radical democratic thought. Other than providing a historical account of popular assertions of equality, a number of commentators have concluded that his idea of the political is theoretically insignificant. Alain Badiou, for example, remarks that Rancière is unable to reach any firm conclusions given the evanescent and self-cancelling nature of his idea of the political (Badiou 2005: 111). Peter Hallward describes his work as an 'inconsequential account of democracy' (2009: 157), and Slavoj Žižek, more trenchantly calls it an 'hysterical provocation' (1999: 237). These sceptical views are not without grounds, and, in the end, I would agree with them in so far as Rancière's express task of affirming the agency of the oppressed is in fact undermined by his abstract negativism. But, contra his more hostile critics, it is possible to appreciate that Rancière does make a substantial contribution to radical democratic thought in several respects. He offers a reconfigured understanding of the politics of recognition that confounds distinctions between the just and the good, the universal and particular, in which it is conventionally construed. He thereby accords a new political salience to recognition issues and the discourse of rights in struggles for democratic equality. At the most general level, his work represents a different way of going about the task of political theory, one that eschews the preoccupation with political ontology and models of democracy and instead takes the approach of disclosing critique.

RECOGNITION AND DISCLOSURE

It is not just theorists of radical democracy who commit the error of conflating the political with the social; rather, for Rancière, most political philosophy is founded on such a mistaken elision. The problem with contemporary political philosophy, in his view, is not that it is too abstract and engaged in an unhelpful flight from reality, but rather the opposite: that it is too determinate in content. Idealization, for instance, serves as a smokescreen that conceals the running together of the political with a particular form of social being. Indeed, from this view, there is no ultimate difference between so-called 'ideal' and 'real' forms of political thinking; the latter simply performs explicitly what the former does implicitly: that is, both annihilate the 'traumatic kernel' of politics by assimilating it to pre-given social logic: 'The "philosophical" return of politics and its sociological "end" are one and the same' (Rancière 1999: 93). Rancière casts his net widely since he discerns variants of this reduction of the political to the social not just in contemporary political philosophy but also in the work of virtually every Western thinker from Plato and Aristotle through to present-day consensus theorists of democracy.

Habermas's consensus theory of democracy epitomizes for Rancière the substantializing 'para-political' logic that depoliticizes struggle by reducing it to fixed rules and procedures. It might seem, at first glance, that there is a similarity between Rancière's idea of the foundational equality of speaking beings and Habermas's idea of mutual understanding as constitutive of democratic equality. Both seem to link the normative primacy of political equality to a universal capacity for understanding. But, in fact, on Rancière's account, Habermas's horizontal order of democratic deliberation obscures the truly hierarchical and polemical structure of disagreement in order to preserve the illusory end of consensus. On the deliberative scenario, deep differences may be overcome and political agreement reached if individuals debate over matters of justice according to the rules of rational discourse. For Rancière, this emphasis on the transparent, rational nature of political communication effaces the fraught structure of political dispute. The arguing of a political wrong is never just a question of expressing different views in shared terms or giving all individuals an equal chance to deliberate. Rather, what is at stake in political disagreement is the violent clash of incommensurable views of the world held by subjects who occupy completely unequal social positions: 'The "discussion" of a wrong is never an exchange – not even a violent one – between constituent partners. It concerns the speech situation itself and its performers. Politics does not exist because men, through the privilege of speech, place their interests in common' (Rancière 1999: 27). Disagreement is not an orderly process of each individual having her say about a certain state of affairs; rather, it involves the more fundamental matter of whether certain individuals get heard at all.

In the end, the Habermasian notion of universal pragmatics, that human beings are equal because of their common capacity for speech, is, in Rancière's words, a 'reasonable-unreasonable' idea. Unreasonable because the assertion of a shared community of discourse fails to confront the asymmetrical nature of all social orders, which necessarily privilege certain types of speech over others, that place some individuals outside of the 'order of saying, the order of doing, and the order of being' (Rancière 1999: 55). There are always some groups, the 'poor', those who have no part, whose speech is not only not listened to, but is also not understood at all, is persistently discounted as noise or the 'inarticulate lowing' of nameless beings. Political dialogue, then, has a double specificity: it involves both speech but also the account that is made of that speech. Who counts as a speaking being is what is at stake in political contention as much as, if not more than, what is being said: 'Politics exists because the logos is never simply speech, because it is always indissolubly the account that is made of this speech: the account by which a sonorous emission is understood as speech, capable of enunciating what is just, whereas some other emission is perceived as noise signalling pleasure or pain, consent or revolt' (Rancière 1999: 28). Consequently, political dispute cannot follow the 'simple rationality of a dialogue of interests' but is inevitably a confrontational process, a 'polemical scene' where the oppressed demand, even usurp, the right to be heard by those who do not hear them. In asserting their wrongs, they radically challenge the supposed inclusiveness and legitimacy of the discursive political community, revealing it instead to be a '"community" of the just and the unjust' (Rancière 1999: 9). In so far as Habermas reduces political disagreement to a measured exchange, he joins the ranks of those 'tired apologists who assure us lukewarmly that we should love democracy "reasonably", meaning "moderately"' and, therefore, perhaps not at all (Rancière 1999: 10).

Although he would emphatically reject such a comparison, Rancière's critique of consensus democracy as a domestication of political disagreement resonates in a significant respect with the critique of deliberation made by thinkers of social suffering, such as Bourdieu and Honneth (see chapter 1). Rancière would vehemently deny any such resemblance because of the deployment by the latter of meta-political reasoning that locates the hidden 'truth' of disagreement in the underlying social reality of domination. Nonetheless there is an interesting cross-over between his work and the critique of deliberative universalism in as much as both highlight how the idea of mutual exchange conceals the hierarchical structure of disagreement where the arguments of some speakers (the dominant) count far more than those of others (the dominated). Differently put, what Rancière views as the inegalitarian partitioning constitutive of any political community, Bourdieu describes as its latent relations of symbolic violence. Consensus theorists fail to see that exclusion is not something external to the deliberative community that can be overcome through inclusion but rather that exclusion is internal to the community itself, a product of its supposedly neutral *modus operandi*: 'The "fight against exclusion" is also the paradoxical conceptual place where exclusion emerges as just another name for consensus' (Rancière 1999: 115). The presentation of deliberation as a neutral procedure (formal competence) that is in theory accessible to all conceals the fact that some speakers, in virtue of tacitly endowed symbolic authority, are vastly more privileged than others (women, the working classes, people of colour) who are often not taken seriously or even not heard at all. It is not a question therefore of trying to incorporate into a pre-given community those who are left out; rather, it is a question of challenging the legitimacy of the community itself.

> Consensus thinking conveniently represents what it calls 'exclusion' in the simple relationship between an inside and an outside. But what is at stake under the name of exclusion is not being-outside. It is the mode of division according to which an inside and an outside can be joined. . . . It is the very invisibility of the partition, the effacing of any marks that might allow the relationship between community and noncommunity to be argued about. (Rancière 1999: 115–16)

If the excluded are to make their demands heard in the first place, this often means shattering the rules of the game, challenging the democratic legitimacy of the established community and possibly instituting a new game. Undoing injustice cannot be regarded simply as a process of bringing excluded and invisible subjects into citizenship practices that are already 'up and running and presumed to be reasonably decent' (Allen 2005: 55). Any model of democracy – consensual, Arendtian or otherwise – reifies itself when it assumes a universal and inclusive status vis-à-vis radical political challenge that is somehow permanently assured into the future. The political cannot be given a fixed form once and for all but must be rethought in the light of what emerges from the unpredictable singularity of struggle.

This is, however, where any similarity between Rancière and Bourdieu ends, for the latter would be much more sceptical of the ability of the dominated to initiate a moment of political rupture in the way envisaged by the former. Furthermore, both thinkers radically diverge in the manner that they pursue their denaturalizing critique of the political: one taking the dramatic form of an instantaneous verification of equality, the other a more laborious form of an analysis of power or 'historical realpolitik'.

POLITICS OF RECOGNITION

Another point of cross-over between Rancière and thinkers of social suffering is the renewed significance that the politics of recognition acquires in the light of the critique of political community. Like Honneth, Rancière re-establishes an intrinsic connection between issues of recognition and those of justice whilst, at the same time, eschewing the dualisms that often organize thought on the matter. Matters of identity recognition are conventionally associated with what are deemed to be substantive, non-generalizable issues of the good that underpin, but are separable from, the universal norms of the just. Honneth, as we have seen, rejects this ethical particularism, arguing that the demand for recognition cannot be compartmentalized in such a way for, in actuality, it goes to the heart of claims about social injustice and the inegalitarian nature of the prevailing order. How just can an order be that does not recognize the demands of people of colour, women, gays, refugees, the poor, and so on? The difficulty with Honneth's challenge to this procedural side-lining is that he deploys a psychologically reductive account of recognition. He establishes its supposed universal import through the contentious claim that it represents a fundamental psychological need that is crucial to healthy self-development. This enables him to recast recognition as the universal structure of ethical life. The framing of recognition in psychological terms, however, is problematic in so far as it has depoliticizing and reductive effects on an understanding of political struggle, which is always somehow motivated by concerns with authenticity and personal integrity (also McNay 2009). It is questionable whether the need for recognition is in fact a universal psychological trait when, for example, 'those occupying advantaged positions in the status order, such as men and heterosexuals, usually shun recognition of their (gender and sexual) distinctiveness, claiming not specificity but universality' (Fraser 2001: 31). In this light, thinkers such as Nancy Fraser argue that recognition should be understood as touching on matters of social injustice and not as the satisfaction of a 'generic human need', which obscures the context of power in which its demands are always situated.

Rancière's performative account of recognition offers a way beyond the depoliticizing entailments of a psychological expressivism by reconnecting it to the context of asymmetrical power relations. On his view, recognition has nothing to do with the expression and acknowledgement of a fundamental need, for this would be to reduce the political to the social subject. Rather, it is the moment when the subject claims an identity that it does not have as an ontological subject and thereby forces entry into the political sphere (Rancière 1999: 146). Phrased differently, the political subject does not pre-exist conflict; rather, it is through conflict itself that it is constituted as such. The demand for recognition forms the political subject by bringing together things that have previously had nothing to do with each other. The yoking of the empty assertion of the equality of anyone and everyone to the particular claims of an excluded group creates a new political subject; it forms a 'body and capacity for enunciation not previously identifiable within a given field of experience' (Rancière 1999: 35). This, in turn, forces a repartition of the social order along new lines. The political subject, then, has an intrinsically contradictory structure; it is what Jean-Philippe Deranty (2003) terms 'suspensive' in nature – it is defined as both dominated and democratically equal. The identities of women, for example, have a self-evident referential quality in the social realm, 'anyone can tell who is meant', yet, in the political realm, this determinate obviousness is disrupted by the claim to inequality. In politics, woman is the subject of experience that denotes a gap between having 'an acknowledged part' (that of sexual complementarity) and having 'no part' (e.g. equal treatement as a worker). Politics is, then, essentially a matter of subjectification: that is, a process of disidentification that removes the social subject from the apparent naturalness of a given place and opens up a new subject space where anyone can be counted. Political conflict is the moment when 'the ontological gap/void becomes palpable, as a gesture that undermines the positive order of Being' (Žižek 1999: 232).

Rancière's redefinition of recognition in performative terms unyokes it from problematic ideas of psychological integrity and authenticity that have such reductive and depoliticizing consequences in the work of theorists such as Honneth, Taylor and others. Defining it instead in terms of power and justice accentuates that 'the recognition needs of subordinated actors differ from those of dominant actors and that only those claims that promote parity of participation are morally justified' (Fraser 2001: 31). At the same time, however, the de-substantialized account also works against the procedural marginalization of recognition, as an ethical particularism or 'merely cultural' issue, and places it instead at the heart of democratic politics, *qua* the demand for equality. Indeed, Rancière's understanding of the polemical nature of struggles for recognition throws into question the very plausibility of the procedural conviction that the following of certain rules will ensure the delivery of justice. In sum, his idea of the political can be understood, according to Deranty, as a 'type of ethics of recognition, but one that also deals seriously with the phenomena of domination and exploitation' (2003: 150).

Whilst it may confound overdrawn dichotomies between the universal and the particular, the just and the good, there remains the question of where, if anywhere, Rancière's reworked account of recognition leads in terms of a more comprehensive political worldview. Here comparison with the work of Fraser may be instructive. Like Rancière, she formulates recognition in non-essentialist terms in order to rescue it from ethical particularism, on the one side, and a potentially exclusionary proceduralism, on the other. Unlike Rancière, however, she works with an expanded notion of justice that encompasses recognition and redistribution as two mutually irreducible dimensions constitutive of the deontological norm of participatory parity. Justice in the sense of participatory parity might require sometimes 'recognizing distinctiveness over and above common humanity' and may involve the scrutiny of patterns of cultural value as well as material distributive inequities. The effect of this reframing of recognition is that many cases that, at first sight, appear to require ethical solutions in fact can actually be solved by a deontological justice approach, or, to quote Fraser: 'The initial effect will be to recuperate the politics of recognition for *Moralität* and thus to resist the turn to ethics' (2001: 23). Rancière would not endorse such an approach on a number of grounds. Although Fraser's idea of participatory parity is relatively thin, it nonetheless installs a regulative framework that sets up criteria for judging whether certain egalitarian conditions for citizenship have been met. In so far as it promotes an analysis of the social conditions that hinder participatory parity, it falls into a meta-political mode of thinking preoccupied with uncovering hidden truths. This concern with 'finding or constructing the hidden' is, in Rancière's view, yet another version of intellectual mastery where the scholar presumes to speak for others on the basis of his superior insight into the nature of social being (2004b: 49). In a manner that recalls statements of Foucault and Deleuze about the indignity of speaking for others, Rancière rejects this legislative role for the intellectual and steadfastly refuses the demand to elaborate his normative worldview beyond the method of the verification of equality.

In the light of this reluctance to systematically pursue the political and normative consequences of his ideas, it seems difficult to demur from the judgement of Badiou and others that Rancière's idea of democratic disagreement is inconsequential. However, it is possible to see that his thought offers us a different way of conceiving of the normative structure of political theory which is closer to one of disclosing critique rather than a prescriptive form of democratic reasoning. Like the method of genealogy, the verification of equality involves a way of telling history so as to estrange us from the present moment in order that we might view it afresh. It is a recounting of the past in such a manner that what had previously seemed inevitable and unavoidable appears as contingent and arbitrary, thus pointing to other possible modes of being. Such disclosure might not take the form of a comprehensive model of democracy, but this does not mean that it lacks normative force. Here again, there is an interesting cross-over with Honneth's work, in that by questioning the primacy accorded to the language of reason in the expression of political demands, both suggest that normativity may take a rhetorical, even aesthetic, form rather than a procedural one. Contra Habermas's marginalization of the rhetorical dimensions of language, Honneth suggests that political critique has a radical disclosive function that is akin to literature and other forms of aesthetic expression in that it makes visible that which was not previously visible. The process of linguistic re-presentation escapes the deliberative strictures of justification through validity because it means to disrupt the 'horizon of accepted meaning' in order to disclose something new (Honneth 2007a: 60). So too, Rancière emphasizes the necessarily aesthetic and disclosing nature of the language of political struggle: 'The *demonstration* proper to politics is always both argument and opening up the world where argument can be received and have an impact' (1999: 56). It is wrong to identify aesthetics with the narrow sphere of 'self-referentiality' that sidetracks the logic of interlocution. On the contrary, aesthetics is what permits the yoking together of utterly opposed elements with radical political consequences; it is what allows 'separate regimes of expression to be pooled' and, thus, the emergence of the new (Rancière 1999: 57). Against Habermas's well-known complaint, in *Philosophical Discourse of Modernity*, that poststructural thought has led to the aestheticization of politics, Rancière asserts that 'politics did not have the misfortune of being aestheticized or spectacularized just the other day'. Rather, the aesthetic is precisely the vehicle through which the settled norms of language are disrupted and challenged and it belongs therefore at the very heart of political dispute, or, as he puts it: 'The modern political animal is first a literary animal, caught in the circuit of literariness that undoes the relationships between the order of words and the order of bodies that determine the place of each' (1999: 37).

Far from being a marginal provocation, then, it is possible to see how Rancière's work on the political, albeit idiosyncratic, stands in an alternative tradition of disclosing critique. It challenges the preoccupation of contemporary democrats with constructing universally applicable models of democracy and also the conflation of the structure of normativity with the formulation of first- or second-order procedures. It also, as we will see in the next section, provides a renewed interpretation of the symbolic impact of rights discourse and, in doing so, obliquely suggests a point of entry for leftists into debates more usually dominated by liberal political theorists. Ultimately, however, any insights that Rancière's work delivers in this regard are undercut by his anti-sociological sentiments, which force him back into a self-cancelling negativism that prevents him from maintaining in any meaningful sense his commitment to verifying the agency of the oppressed.

THE RIGHT TO HAVE RIGHTS

By conceiving of rights discourse as a type of disclosing political challenge, Rancière opens up new potential for it as part of radical democratic agenda where it might play a crucial role in 'anchoring superior levels of universality and equality within a community' (Deranty 2003: 148). On the whole, radical democrats are justifiably cautious of any role that rights talk might play in this regard. This cautiousness has its roots in a fundamental disparity, originally noted by Marx, between the formal and individualist nature of rights discourse, on the one side, and the far-reaching, structural and systemic transformations that are needed for effective emancipation, on the other (see chapter 2). Rights, on this Marxian view, can, at best, only mitigate rather than overcome oppression and, at worst, on a Foucauldian view, may be regarded as a smokescreen for processes of normalization that insidiously accommodate individuals to the dominant order. Rancière, however, turns such leftist views on their head in so far as he maintains that it is precisely the empty formalism of rights discourse that, far from being a central shortcoming, is in fact precisely what gives it a radical, contestatory force. The problem with the leftist critique, in his view, is that it elides the social and political functions of rights discourse, leading to an over-hasty dismissal of the category as invariably normalizing. This forecloses a more radical understanding of rights, not just as tools whose meaning is relative to the political context in which they are engaged, but also as a disruptive symbolic language capable of calling into question the apparently egalitarian nature of any social order.

Rancière elaborates his position via a discussion of Hannah Arendt's famous denunciation in *The Origins of Totalitarianism* of the empty abstraction and consequent political inefficacy of the Rights of Man. Arendt was responding to the plight of the large number of refugees and displaced persons in Europe between the world wars who, because they did not belong to any political or national community, were in effect deprived of rights or any kind of substantive political redress. By losing their place in the world, they were reduced to a state of exception or bare life – beyond oppression, beyond legality. For Arendt, this reduction to bare life exposes the inadequacy of grounding human rights in pre-political ideas of an essential human nature. The condition of statelessness reveals that there is no abstract essence to humanity; rather, humanity is politically defined. Beyond the political, humans do not exist in any meaningful sense; they are reduced to mere particularity, difference and domination. It is only in the political realm, in Arendt's view, that it is possible to live a fully human life, understood in the Aristotelian sense as acting in concert with others, as 'expression within and action upon a common world' (Arendt 1958: 302). Confronted with the inadequacy of human rights in the face of widespread statelessness, Arendt asserts that there can only be one right, the proto-political 'right to have rights': the right to never be excluded from organized political community.

Arendt's assertion of this original right to have rights raises a puzzle, however, with regard to its own foundations, for it seems to rest on precisely the kind of empty essentialism that she elsewhere denounces. As Andrew Schaap says: 'If human rights can be said to exist only in so far as they are the product of political association, what is the ground of the right to have rights?' (2011: 27). This, for Rancière, is where the 'ontological trap' of Arendt's work lies. For, on the one hand, if rights pertain to humans in so far as they are citizens of some constitutional state or another, they are the rights of those who already have rights, which amounts to a tautology. Yet, on the other hand, if the right to have rights pertains to the rightless, then it is by definition meaningless, for on what basis can the unpoliticized person claim such a right? To quote Rancière: 'Either the rights of those who have no rights or the rights of those who have rights' (2004a: 302). For Rancière, then, what Arendt does not recognize in her aporetic formula is another alternative, namely that 'the Rights of Man are the rights of those who have not the rights that they have and have the rights that they have not' (2004: 302). The relation of the individual to rights is not a singular one where an individual claims and uses the rights he or she possesses. Rather, it is a relation of double negation which, in bridging the interval between two forms of existence of those rights, brings the subject into being. Rights have a written form; they are not just predicates of an abstract human nature ('non-existent being') belied by the existence of the rightless. As written rights they form part of a particular social order or partition of the sensible: that is, there is an instituted statement of equality that co-exists with the inequalities of any police order. Rights of Man are the rights of those who make something of that inscription: that is, groups of individuals who call into question the 'open predicates' of equality and freedom in order to 'open up a dispute about what they exactly entail and whom they concern in which cases' (Rancière 2004a: 303). This is the difference between Rancière and Arendt. For the former, the political sphere cannot be designated in advance as a demarcated realm of plurality where equals act in concert; rather, the political only emerges in the encounter between two heterogeneous logics. The subject of rights is not a determinate subject, but comes into existence in the gap between these two conflicting logics of equality and inequality. There is no need for there to be a determinate subject of the Rights of Man because 'the strength of those rights lies in the back-and-forth movement between the first inscription of the right and the dissensual stage on which it is put to the test' (Rancière 2004: 305).

At first blush, Rancière's reading of the gap between the social and political instantiations of rights discourse could seem to resemble the conventional Marxist critique of human rights. There is a gap between the appearance of equality and freedom and the actuality of social and economic inequality that prevents individuals from enjoying rights in a meaningful fashion. This would be to misread Rancière, however, in so far as his understanding of the gap is not the same as that which sustains the materialist critique where the truth of rights discourse is found in the underlying actuality of social existence. On this metapolitical logic, rights are denied political efficacy by being regarded as a bourgeois illusion that conceals the reality of exploitation. Instead, for Rancière, the gap is precisely that which gives rights discourse its polemical force in virtue of its structure of double negation, where, as he puts it, the poor act 'as subjects that did not have the rights that they had and had the rights that they had not' (2004: 304). This double negation is captured in the historical struggles of women to be included as peers in the political sphere and public life more generally (Rancière 1999: 41–2). On one hand, the point of their demonstrations is that they do not enjoy, as women, the right to equality that is formally implied in declarations of universal rights ('they did not have the rights that they had'). On the other hand, the demand for such a right is itself a concrete enactment of this implied equality, a pragmatic verification of their equal status as speaking beings in the face of the actuality of their deprivation of legal personhood ('they have the rights that they have not'). They enact the right to have rights when they speak as if they were already equals of the political community from which they have been excluded. In short, the gap between the fiction of rights discourse and the actuality of inequality is generative of a kind of political agency. The unrealized claim to equality promotes a subversive critique of inequality and, in so far as it enables the emergence of a new political subject, has a practical subversive impact. To quote Žižek: 'The "appearance" of *égaliberté*, precisely, is *not* a "mere appearance" but evinces an effectivity of its own, which allows it to set in motion the process of the re-articulation of actual socio-economic relations by way of their progressive "politicization". . . why shouldn't women vote too. . .' (1999: 195).

The leftist tendency to conflate the subject of rights with a determinate social subject obscures the potential potency of rights discourse in the struggle for emancipation. Such a conflation underpins, for example, the Foucauldian critique of rights discourse as normalizing. Rancière shares with Foucault the recognition that to the extent that rights are institutionalized, they form part of a normalizing social apparatus (*la police*) that may work against their political value. Unlike Foucault, however, he sees rights discourse as irreducible to its social instantiation in so far as its subversive political dimension may always be reactivated by new struggles, *qua* the claim about universal equality: 'Political names and political places never become merely void. The void is filled by somebody or something else' (Rancière 2004: 307). In this respect, then, Rancière shows how rights discourse might be invested with renewed political significance for a radical democratic tradition that has conventionally eschewed it. In the main, Foucault is unable to discern this transfiguring, political force of rights discourse because, from his Nietzschean perspective, rights are viewed primarily as institutional configurations which exert a normalizing power or 'truth' effects upon individuals. In this regard, he reduces the political to the police order. Rights discourse only ever has a limited efficacy in galvanizing collective action and, moreover, any potential it may have is offset by its more insidious effects, where it covertly secures the grip of disciplinary bio-power upon social relations. This running together of the political dimension of rights as a discourse about equality with the social dimensions of rights as institutionalized norms is consistent with Foucault's general depiction of modernity, which ignores the role that law and politics may play in checking the erosion of freedoms by governmental techniques (e.g. Habermas 1985: 286–93). This de-differentiated world-view, where distinctions between types of power are collapsed, prevents Foucault from seeing a more radical potential in rights as the reactivation of a destabilizing claim about universal equality. It also leads him to underestimate the extent to which the discourse of rights may in fact be utilized to present a more radical challenge to the encroachments of disciplinary governance. For instance, in response to critiques of rights discourse as essentially protecting property interests, Sonia Correa, Rosalind Petchesky and Richard Parker point out that it has been overwhelmingly used historically to bring to light and challenge injustices visited upon women, workers and other marginalized groups (2008: 162). The recent rise of 'sexual rights' as a prominent part of the human rights agenda illustrates how 'without the radical structure of human rights . . . such translation of bodily claims into social action would be unthinkable' (2008: 155). In this light, worries about normalization are partially allayed because rights are understood as performative tools which give form to a previously unthematized political demand rather than express a pre-given social identity: 'It is the production, within a determined, sensible world, of a given that is heterogeneous to it' (Rancière 2003: 226). As the basis of a political claim, group identity is not a fixed essence but created in the very act of articulating and demanding enforcement of rights and is always, by implication, in the process of 'becoming and transforming' (Correa et al. 2008: 154).

It is another version of the conflation of the political with the social that ultimately limits Arendt's work, for the correlate of her presumption of a determinate subject of rights (refugees) is that there is a determinate body that bestows rights (the state). The plight of refugees who have lost their place in the world demonstrates that it is the nation-state that must give rights to its subjects. By according the role of bestower of rights to the nation-state, she must inevitably ignore, however, those struggles that take place outside of its boundaries, thereby reinscribing a new police order and division of those who are worthy and not worthy of politics.

The conflation of rights discourse with determinate social content is also expressed by Rancière as a reduction of the 'ought' to the 'is', and it is this that motivates the notions of humanitarian ethics that prevail in contemporary thought. Here Rancière has in mind in particular the work of thinkers such as Giorgio Agamben and Jean-François Lyotard who recast human rights as the rights of the Other and ideas of infinite justice: that is, the inability ever to truly discharge our duty to the Other implies a perpetual, indefeasible ethical responsibility for them. For Rancière this 'ethical infinitization' of the relation to the Other is profoundly depoliticizing. The elision of the is with the ought, of fact with law, confines democratic challenge to the parameters of a pre-established ethical code or set of supposedly shared ontological predispositions. In this way, the established political community is shielded from the radical challenge that the demands of the excluded pose to its legitimacy. This fictitious ethical consensus is used to justify the idea of humanitarian action pursued on behalf of a helpless other or 'absolute victim', and rights conflicts are reduced to the status of social problems that can be sorted out 'by learned expertise and a negotiated adjustment of interest' (Rancière 2004: 306). In short, the ethical recasting of rights discourse substitutes ontological destiny for the logic of political wrong: 'Some people see it [ethics] as a return to some founding spirit of the community, sustaining positive laws and political agency. . . . It means to me . . . the erasure of the political in the couple of consensual policy and humanitarian police' (Rancière 2004: 309). Indeed, in Rancière's view, this presentation of democratic states as a 'humanitarian police' acting on behalf of the rights of 'the absolute victim' is symptomatic of the deeply depoliticized and nihilistic spirit of the contemporary post-democratic world (1999: 127).

There is no doubt, then, that Rancière's idea of disclosing critique offers a powerful alternative way of thinking about the discourse of rights that reveals a latent radical potential vis-à-vis the demands of the oppressed. This potential is often underappreciated by radical democrats, who tend to see talk about rights as a way of diluting radical challenge and of accommodating disempowered groups to the status quo. It is Rancière's strict separation of political from social dynamics that enables him to recast rights discourse in such a potentially fruitful way. It is this same separation, however, that is generative of a rigid hierarchy of the political over the social and that prevents him from developing the disclosing aspects of his thought in a meaningful way. On his dichotomous view, the social realm becomes little more than a residual category whose complex, internal relations are persistently obscured under the undiscriminating category of the police order. This failure to develop a more sophisticated account of the social and, by implication, an account of power undermines Rancière's express concern with verifying the agency of the oppressed, rendering it little more than a well-intentioned but naïve statement of faith.

POLICE OR THE MERELY GIVEN

With regard to the mysterious but emphatic line that Rancière draws between the social and political, the comparison with Foucault's idea of the police is instructive. Although Rancière finds in the discourse of rights a subversive force that others fail to identify, this force seems to be largely a rhetorical one limited to those epiphanic but fleeting moments when the poor demand equality. Foucault, by contrast, although sceptical of the radical potential of rights discourse, regarding it, by and large, as a vehicle for normalization, goes further in identifying possible areas in which it might be used as a tool in counter-hegemonic struggle. Arguably this is because he draws on a more nuanced understanding of the police-social order than Rancière, as one whose internal relations are fragile, uneven and generative of tension and possible conflict. For instance, in his genealogical study of neoliberalism, Foucault identifies a potential incompatibility where in fact rights discourse might form a block or hindrance to the pernicious restructuring of social relations around a market logic. He discusses this incompatibility in terms of the clash between the logic of the subject of right, on the one side, and the subject of economic interest, on the other (see McNay 2009). On this view, civil society is not just a laboratory for enhancing normalizing modes of control; it is also the domain of a 'perpetual confrontation' between the 'mechanics of discipline' and the 'principle of right', where the latter often provides the only effective check against the subjugation effects of the former: 'The only existing and apparently solid recourse we have against the usurpations of disciplinary mechanisms ... is precisely a recourse or a return to a right that is organized around sovereignty' (Foucault 1997: 39). Despite Rancière's claim that the idea of the police is derived from Foucault, the latter's conception is considerably more differentiated in so far as it reveals how any order is more fragile and internally contradictory than it may first seem. This, in turn, yields insight into possible sites of political struggle, how rights discourse might be mobilized as a challenge to the dominant order, but in a more modulated fashion than the adversarial mode envisaged by Rancière.

For Foucault, any emancipatory struggle always bears the marks of the power relations in which it is implicated; it is very rarely a moment of pure rupture. Such an insight is borne out, for instance, in Sumi Madhok's (2013) study of the ambiguous effects of rights talk on the subject formation of female development workers (*sathins*) in Northwest India. Madhok documents how these women appropriated the discourse of constitutional rights, which they had been exposed to as part of their training as community workers, to create for themselves new empowered identities as citizens. This rights-enabled subjectivity enhanced their sense of autonomy and also gave them greater awareness of how to deploy their newly acquired legal knowledge to improve the lives of less privileged women in their communities. In a way that echoes Rancière, Madhok shows how the language of rights permits these *sathins* to appear as political subjects for the first time and, in doing so, to contest the patriarchal norms and practices that so stringently circumscribed the lives of women in Rajasthan. But, in a manner that departs from Rancière, Madhok also finds that the women's acquisition of rights-enabled identity unleashed new forms of coercion and constraint against them. Despite their commitment to women's entry into the public sphere, very few of the *sathins* stood for public office of any kind. The paradoxical consequence of their new visibility as political subjects was that it rendered them vulnerable to intense forms of intimidation and threat from those in their communities who opposed women playing an equal role in public life. Madhok concludes that rights-enabled subjectivities are always conflictual, that the creation of new forms of agency, especially in social conditions already marked by considerable oppression, is invariably accompanied by new forms of coercion.

It is difficult to see how Rancière could reach such a considered assessment of the ambivalent effects of rights discourse in the struggle for emancipation, given that his logic of political rupture is unsupported by an account of power. This lack of an account of power prompts a number of further questions about his work, not least the basis on which he makes judgements such as whether a demand is truly universal and hence political (i.e. made in the name of anyone and everyone), or whether it is more limited in its aspirations and remains simply an assertion of a particular social identity. If the universal character of a particular disagreement is not self-evident, how is it possible to distinguish between the genuinely political demand and the more parochial one? What characteristics does Rancière look for in making this determination? For instance, a common assessment of the early suffragette demands for rights was that in certain respects they were less radical than the sexual politics of late twentieth-century feminism because they were couched largely within inclusionary terms that did not challenge other aspects of the dominant patriarchal order. Rancière, however, would appear not to concur with such a judgement in so far as he frequently holds up these early feminist assertions as examples of political dissensus in a way that he does not with later feminism that belongs to the post-political era of consensus democracy. It is not that his views are necessarily unjustifiable, but it remains unclear on what basis he chooses to lionize certain events as genuine instances of political disagreement and discount others. On the basis of what criteria is he able to confidently assert the radical status of certain events if that status remains, if not obscure to others, at least open to question? As Michael Dillon puts it: 'How to account for the incarnation in time by historical bodies of a principle that is neither temporal nor carnate . . . how to tell whether or not the incarnation of politics has ever truly taken place at all' (2003: para. 10).

Similar questions of judgement arise in relation to a host of political issues which can be deemed radical or not, depending on what criteria are in play. Take, for instance, that of same-sex marriage, which some regard as an important and radical claim about equal rights and others as a capitulation to a dominant heteronormativity. To be counted as a genuinely political challenge, is it sufficient for groups to merely deploy the universal rhetoric of human rights, even when their aims are in fact more sectarian and limited? Or does it necessarily involve a more spontaneous, sincere invocation of the universal, and, if so, how do we ascertain the authenticity of the demand? In all likelihood there are no definitive answers to these questions of judgement, but Rancière nonetheless repeatedly invokes the rigid separation of the properly political demand from the particular identity claim as if these properties were somehow self-evident and do not require further clarification or justification. The fetish of the singular moment of challenge means that he summarily relegates types of intermediate practice and struggle as belonging to the police order that, in a particular social context, might arguably be said to possess a radical political force. For instance, the politics of recognition is not, for Rancière, about the assertion of a shared minority identity, but turns around a process of disidentification that places the subject in the interval between different identities. Yet many political movements do not operate according to such stark alternatives. Queer politics, for instance, questions the nature and strategic usefulness of identity categories, but, at the same time, has been unable to move beyond them in any kind of straightforward fashion (Davis 2010). Even the demand for the inclusion of gays into marriage and other family rights, which some activists regard as essentially conservative and assimilative, might, in certain contexts, have more of a subversive force than Rancière is prepared to allow. To quote Oliver Davis: 'In a qualified and context-specific way, such interventions can interrupt and reconfigure the police order by changing the relationship between the visible and the invisible and by bringing new subjects, new relationships and new understandings into political and social existence' (2010: 89).

The troubling emptiness of Rancière's notion of the political is propelled by his worry about ontology, about diminishing the radical impact of the disincorporated demand for equality by conflating it with some particular species of social being. But is this anxiety justified, or is it in fact a chimera generated by Rancière's own hierarchical paradigm and, above all, the inadequate way in which he conceptualizes the social order? Put differently, there seems to be an intrinsic connection between his flattened-out view of the social order as one of an invariant positivity and his rarefied and unsustainable idea of the political. Some commentators dispute such a view, arguing that Rancière's idea of the political is not as pure and empty as it seems, since the moment of disagreement always takes place in the police order (Chambers 2011). But given Rancière's etiolated account of the social realm, it is unclear how this disruption emerges in the first place other than *ex nihilo*, as a kind of *deus ex machina*. It is precisely this undifferentiated account of the social that, in Žižek's view, pushes Rancière into the trap of a marginal politics based on an improbable logic of 'momentary outbursts of an "impossible" radicalization that contains the seeds of its own failure and has to recede in the face of the existing order' (Žižek 1999: 232). In his view, the police order cannot possibly be as self-sufficient and internally cohesive – a 'flat domain of visibility' – as Rancière maintains, for otherwise where do the demands of the poor originate? The social order must already be riven by internal tensions and latent conflict in order for 'the part of no part' to emerge in the first place. Prior to the moment of the *Political* proper, there is a suppressed *political* element, a disruptive inconsistency within the police order that permits the radical demand to emerge.

It is of course in the nature of the Police to disavow the immanent tensions, negative forces and tacit exclusions that form the conditions of possibility of its own existence. Indeed, such disavowal is, in Žižek's view, the constitutive mechanism of the positive order of police. To maintain any kind of legitimacy, even the worst tyrant must pretend to work for the good of the people whilst covertly pursuing his own wealth and power: 'The order of the police is never simply a positive order: to function at all, it has to cheat, to misname, and so on – in short, to engage in politics, to do what its subversive opponents are supposed to do' (Žižek 1999: 235). This logic of the constitutive exterior locates conflict as an immanent tension at the heart of the social and this, in Žižek's view, engenders a more persuasive account of the political than Rancière's epiphanic demand for equality that is always betrayed by its every instantiation in the police order.

Ultimately, as we have seen, Žižek regards Rancière's self-cancelling notion of the Political as symptomatic of a 'leftist irresponsibility' that focuses on a radical but unsustainable Universal and perpetually postpones the task of thinking how equality might be instantiated in concrete political measures. Attacking the Maoist legacy in the thought of Rancière, Badiou and others, he avers that 'they want a true revolution, yet they shirk the actual price to be paid for it, and thus prefer to adopt the attitude of a Beautiful Soul and keep their hands clean' (Žižek 1999: 236). Such formulations of the Political are caught in a game of hysterical provocation, whereas the 'true' radical turns her attention to thinking how counter-hegemonic challenge might be converted into a new enduring positive order:

> The fear of the impending 'ontologization' of the proper political act, of its catastrophic transposition into the positive order of Being, is a false fear that results from a kind of perspective illusion: it puts too much trust in the substantial power of the positive order of Being, overlooking the fact that the order of Being is never simply given, but is itself grounded in some preceding Act. (Žižek 1999: 238)

Žižek is undoubtedly right to draw attention to Rancière's inadequate treatment of the social realm as the merely given, as a domain that lacks any internal complexity or unevenness or tension. Whether Žižek's psychoanalytic rendering of the social provides a compelling alternative remains moot, however. The logic of disavowal gives a depth and internal complexity to social relations that is lacking in Rancière, but it is ultimately derived from the invariant psychic dynamic that is ahistorically played out between symbolization and lack. On this Lacanian view, complexity is not intrinsic to the social realm and phenomenal existence but comes to it by virtue of a quasi-transcendental, dehistoricizing logic that Rancière dismisses elsewhere as the 'law of the psychic apparatus' (2007: 134). In other words, what Žižek gives with one hand, he appears to take back with the other.

Whatever the shortcomings of the Lacanian paradigm, it is nonetheless the case that Rancière's elevation of the disruptive moment of the political leads him to regard the social as a determinate residue, a secondary realm, devoid of intrinsic depth or complexity. As in the work of other radical democrats, this is in keeping with the Arendtian tendency to treat the social as a kind of alien 'blob', as an ultimately uninteresting positivity. Rancière is not oblivious to such problems: he comments, for instance, on the difficulty of Arendt's excessively stringent separation of the political from the social, which reduces the latter to what she famously called 'the dark background of mere givenness' (quoted in Rancière 2004: 299). Despite this, his conception of the social as a depthless order of instituted hierarchy comes close to replicating the same weaknesses of Arendt's dismissive conceptualization. Rancière maintains that his concept of the police is not without nuance; it is not a 'dim leveller in which everything looks the same, everything is equivalent ("at night all cows are grey")' (1999: 30). The police order is not invariantly one of domination and control; it may generate 'all sorts of good' and there are, therefore, better or worse police orders: 'the better one, incidentally, not being the one that adheres to the supposedly natural order of society . . . but the one that all the breaking and entering perpetrated by egalitarian logic has most often jolted out of its "natural" logic' (Rancière 1999: 31). But that is as far as Rancière goes in making any kind of discriminations because, ultimately, for him, it is irrelevant whether or not an instituted order is 'sweet and kind'; it does not make it any less the opposite of what he understands as politics.

But, in the end, perhaps it does matter, more than Rancière thinks, the precise ways in which a given social order may be deemed to be more sweet and kind than any other. Rancière's disingenuousness on this issue is problematic, because, as we will see in the next section, it locks him into a zero-sum, all-or-nothing logic that leaves him unable to develop in any meaningful sense the animating insight of his work: that ordinary people are capable of acting on their own behalf. The pragmatic verification of equality is more meaningfully fulfilled not through protestations of faith in the agency of the poor, but by paying attention to the specific power relations that construct differing kinds of oppression.

EMANCIPATION AND THE POOR

The figure of Pierre Bourdieu represents for Rancière the paradigm of the intellectual whose analysis of domination is tantamount to a practical denial of the ability of the dominated to act on their own behalf. The concept of habitus is the mechanism through which this denial of agency is achieved. In Bourdieu's view, the oppressed are accommodated to their oppression through a manipulation of their corporeal being so insidious that it happens, so to speak, behind their backs. Only the sociologist-king is able to recognize the hidden complicity that sustains inequality but that is misrecognized by everyone else as the inevitable and legitimate order of things: 'If the social machine captures us, it is because we do not know how it captures us. And if we do not know how it captures us even though it is right before our eyes, it is because we do not want to know it. All recognition is a misrecognition, all unveiling a veiling' (Rancière 2003: 170). Bourdieu's work exemplifies meta-political reasoning that unremittingly locates the truth of the political in the social 'reality' that subtends it (Rancière 1999: 82ff.). The ultimate irony is that Bourdieu's recognition of what is otherwise misrecognized by everyone else preserves the very hierarchy that he ostensibly condemns. In the same moment as he denounces elitism, the sociologist's revelation of invisible mechanisms of control reaffirms an order based on his superior powers of discernment and analysis: 'granting science a position of eternal denunciator of its eternal repudiation' (quoted in Pelletier 2009: 140). At the same time, the postulation of a hidden violence visible to the sociologist alone ascribes to the poor a passivity that leaves them even more unable to climb out of their state of dispossession: 'There remain the lowly ranked. We now know that they can expect nothing from emancipatory pedagogy' (Rancière 2003: 179). Sociological miserabilism is, then, a variation of the ethical fixation with suffering humanity that replaces the political subject with that of universal victim.

Rancière counters this miserabilist reification of inequality with his understanding of political agency as a kind of spontaneous vitalism from below. Bourdieu assumes inequality as his starting point, and, on this view, emancipation becomes an endlessly deferred endpoint towards which the poor must strive, but inevitably always fail, to reach. Against the foundational presupposition of inequality, Rancière argues that the only way emancipation can be achieved is to assume equality as one's starting point rather than one's goal and then to set about systematically verifying and affirming its existence (1991: 138). The radical implications of this axiomatic assumption of equality are illustrated by Rancière in his discussion of the pedagogical methods of the eighteenth-century teacher Joseph Jacotot in *The Ignorant Schoolmaster*. The French-speaking Jacotot found in his new teaching position in Flemish-speaking Louvain that, because of the language barrier, he was unable to fulfil the conventional role of the schoolmaster imparting knowledge and enlightenment to pupils. Instead he had to adopt a bottom-up method where the students had to continuously review their own and each other's progress and impart to him what they were learning from their joint study of a bi-lingual edition of Fénelon's novel *Télémaque*. Expecting work of a poor quality, Jacotot was surprised to discover that it was of a much higher standard, despite the fact that, from a conventional perspective, he had taught his pupils nothing. This unexpected outcome forced him to radically revise his ideas about pedagogical method, moving from one based in a hierarchical relation of explication to one based in an egalitarian relation of emancipation. Intellectual emancipation ensues not from the bestowing of knowledge by an expert upon the ignorant, but from assuming a foundational equality of intelligence between human beings: 'The same intelligence is at work in all acts of the human spirit' (Rancière 1991: 18). Knowledge is not the gift of master to student; indeed, the very presumption that it is amounts to a 'method of stultification' in so far as the 'ignorant' also then assume that they are not capable of learning without instruction. Thus the 'circle of powerlessness' is endlessly reinforced: 'Those excluded from the world of intelligence themselves subscribe to the verdict of their exclusion' (Rancière 1991: 16). Against this, Rancière asserts that knowledge is there for the taking and individuals are capable of accessing it themselves, although, in fact, very few choose to recognize the universal presence of this 'method of emancipation': 'The "method" ... is the oldest in the world, and it never stops being verified every day, in all the circumstances where an individual must learn something without any means of having it explained to him' (1991: 16).

There is no doubt that Rancière's desire to avoid over-predicting the powerlessness of the 'poor' is attractive, as is the method that construes emancipation as the verification of a foundational equality. Yet the appealing simplicity and altruism of such a theoretical position conceal its troubling limitations with regard to a critique of inequality in a way that recalls Gayatri Spivak's (1987) well-known response to Foucault and Deleuze's statement about the fundamental indignity of speaking for others. Spivak points out that underlying this seemingly self-abnegating gesture of solidarity on the part of the intellectual is the problematic attribution to the oppressed of full self-presence and an untrammelled capacity for expression. Her concern is for those subaltern groups who are unable to speak for themselves or make themselves heard, because of the opaque nature of the mechanisms of power – material and symbolic – that ensure their subjection. Exploitation in advanced capitalism is often complex, indirect and insidious, and consequently not always easily identifiable, especially from a position of subordination and disempowerment within those relations. In such cases, there is no 'naturally articulate subject of oppression', and, in assuming that there is, the intellectual refuses the responsibility of her privileged position to track and challenge the dynamics of oppression on behalf of those who do not have such a possibility. Spivak's concerns remain relevant to Rancière in so far as his refusal to pursue the issue of power beyond the romantic verification of equality disregards important distinctions between the different types of oppression that influence the emergence of agency. Political agency is not a capacity that is evenly distributed across all subordinated groups. In fact, by failing to take up the issue of power in a more nuanced way, Rancière's all-or-nothing logic perpetuates the powerlessness of the disempowered by confining them to perpetual marginality.

The theoretical imposition involved in speaking for others is not necessarily the same as speaking about others, as in the analysis of subordination (e.g. Alcoff 1991). The two are undoubtedly bound up with each other, but it is unnecessarily obscurantist to run them together in order to naïvely denounce *tout court* any systematic inquiry into the dynamics of oppression. The flip-side of Bourdieu's alleged miserabilism is, after all, to force us to think more seriously about the obstacles – many of them internalized – that confront oppressed groups and prevent them from being effective agents of their own interests. By bracketing off such issues of mobilization and empowerment, indeed by condemning them as the miserabilist concerns of meta-political reasoning, Rancière's commitment to affirming the agency of the powerless seems to amount to little more than a somewhat romantic assertion of faith. The underlying all-or-nothing logic of the *'sans part'* is not very helpful, for instance, in unpacking the variety of ways in which oppression is perpetuated and the different forms of oppositional agency that it may or may not engender. To describe the dominated as the 'part who

All or Nothing 163

have no part' is, as Hallward observes, an 'unnecessarily simplistic articulation', for 'there are many who have a very small part, a share that is minimal or marginal but that is nonetheless something rather than nothing' (2009: 157). The figure of the *sans part* fetishizes the position of marginality and substitutes a model of absolute exclusion for a more complex and nuanced account of the varying dynamics of inequality. Some types of inequality may be captured in the straightforward idea of exclusion but, in other cases, types of symbolic exclusion are interwoven with formal inclusion, recognition with misrecognition (second-class citizens, for instance), being heard but de-authorized, and so on (e.g. Allen 2005; Davis 2010: 92). It is important to attend to the logic of different asymmetrical relations because it may generate, *inter alia*, a heightened awareness of obstacles to be overcome and forms of empowerment necessary to facilitate the emergence of effective political agency. Such specificities are irrelevant, however, to Rancière's idea of political agency, which arises mysteriously from the asymmetrical order of the police, although somehow its own internal logic owes nothing to these conditions of emergence.

Differently put, Rancière moves too swiftly from the presumption of equality to the presumption of agency. It does not necessarily follow from the assertion of a foundational equality that one must also maintain that the poor are always able to speak and act on their own behalf. Indeed, Rancière's rendering of agency as a spontaneous, unproblematic given results in him adopting a troublingly quietist, even dismissive, attitude when it comes to an analysis of present-day political struggle. A pernicious feature of neoliberalism is, as Foucault, Bourdieu and others note, that its mode of individualizing governance erodes precisely the collective social conditions necessary for the emergence of the types of radical demand that Rancière holds up as examples of the truly political. The poor, for example, often no longer live in conditions that promote political solidarity, and there are many other types of social marginality and vulnerability whose inherent fragmentation and division block democratic mobilization. Rancière has no response to this problem; he simply disregards it, in keeping with his dismissal of the contemporary era as one of post-democratic nihilism where opportunities for genuine politics are increasingly rare. In other words, he brushes aside some of the most pressing difficulties facing contemporary societies in favour of a backward-looking celebration of moments of worker solidarity and revolt taken mostly from the nineteenth century. But this abandonment of the present day as the depoliticized era of post-democracy is troubling for it forecloses an understanding of the pathologies that distort contemporary societies and what might be done politically to combat them. Ironically, this disregard intensifies in Rancière's own work the very same tendencies to depoliticization that he deplores in others. He fails to see that politics is not some cataclysmic rupture of the social order but is always already being played out in a manifold of different ways in the present moment (e.g. Day 2005). The reply that these forms of struggle are not political but belong to the police order and that we are by and large living in a post-political order is, as Jodi Dean remarks, 'childishly petulant. It's like the left is saying . . . If the game isn't played on our terms, we aren't going to play at all. We aren't even going to recognize that a game is being played' (2009: 23).

In response to such criticisms, Rancière maintains that it is not his intention simply to discredit organized, strategic political practice and to valorize explosive scenes (see Bensaid 2009: 26). But the all-or-nothing logic that governs his paradigm proves to be a theoretical straitjacket that prevents him from developing this claim in any meaningful and sustained sense. He reduces politics to the confrontation between those who assert equality and those who deny it, and, whether he intends it or not, this has the *de facto* effect of excluding many other types of democratic struggle that he does not consider to be proper stagings of disagreement. To be considered properly political, democratic agency must arise *ex nihilo* from the blanket fixity of the police order, in a fashion that cannot be predicted or facilitated and with radical but unsustainable disruptive effects. Such a notion of political agency may be romantically appealing, but it is problematic, not least because, as Ernesto Laclau (2005) remarks, it involves a naïve faith that the impulses of the people are always necessarily democratic. In the end, although he might avoid miserablism, Rancière does not avoid the moment of theoretical imposition – a naïve intellectual conceit in any case – it simply takes a covert form in his thought. He retreats into eschatological rarefaction that keeps the poor in a state of perpetual marginality. As Nick Hewlett says: 'How could the *sans part* . . . ever play a full and positive role in a democratically organized society if the very existence of democracy depends on their playing a marginal role and being in an apparently constant state of revolt?' (2007: 111). It is undeniable that some forms of radical agency do seem to explode as if from nowhere, but it is also often the case that the mystification of an act as a singular spontaneity conceals the long, often arduous, political labour that precedes it, enabling its emergence.[1]

Ultimately, Rancière's notion of the political seems best suited to explaining a certain type of radical agency, a revolutionary clash that erupts in the face of strong oppression. In this respect, his idea of the political resembles Sheldon Wolin's notion of fugitive democracy. Wolin (1994) understands the political moment of democracy as an extraordinary commonality that, in the normal run of events, remains latent in the ordinary practices of everyday life. This catalysing vision of a shared destiny becomes evident only at moments of extraordinary struggle, where it inspires ordinary individuals to break with the passively shared 'community of misery' and temporarily challenge the established order of things. Like Rancière, Wolin does not associate his idea of the political with the ongoing struggles that constitute daily politics, but reserves it for moments of dramatic transformation, for example the Solidarity movement in Poland. Stephen K. White queries, however, whether Wolin's model of radical political action necessarily presupposes the kind of extreme forms of repression that characterized daily life in Communist Poland. As he puts it: 'The extremity of injustice called forth an extraordinary response.' White doubts that the same response could emerge from Poland nowadays, where, poverty notwithstanding, conditions more closely resemble the constitutional democracies of many other European countries. White's point is that the logic of radical political rupture only makes sense in the context of explicit repression: 'It presumes, first, something like a relatively monolithic source of injustice that can become a clear and steady target or foe; and second, an intensity of suffering that can initiate . . . a cognitive and affective transformation toward solidarity' (2001: 178). In other words, it is possible to discern in Wolin the same all-or-nothing logic that animates Rancière's *sans part*. While it has a certain messianic appeal, it is not really suited to explaining many aspects of late modernity, where the conditions of existence are more complicated than that of a confrontation between a huge *demos* and a small repressive elite. This is not to say that in modern societies there are no longer extreme, unendurable forms of oppression, but where they do exist, they are often perpetuated in an indirect, systemic manner through governance at a distance not through direct repression and explicit denial of rights.

Rancière would surely respond to such criticisms by reaffirming his idea that such issues of governance and resistance properly belong to the police order and that, in his view, genuine examples of political struggle are rare in contemporary post-democracies. But in a sense he wants to have his cake and eat it. For, on the one hand, the axiomatic assumption of equality implies a claim about a universal capacity for agency – that the *sans part* may assert their demands in any way and at any time. Yet, on the other hand, his obscure, heroic model of action denies the radical potentiality of many other types of political practice, consigning them to the inert order of the police. This throws into question the plausibility of thinking about emancipatory change through the invariant opposition of the cold routines of social order versus the hot revolutions of political disagreement. Arguably, some of the most radical political changes emerge gradually through grassroots activism that is submerged in a network of community relations. These do not necessarily make themselves visible through symbolic assertions of equality but rather reveal themselves less dramatically and more slowly through the enactment and entrenchment of pathways to more progressive forms of living (e.g. Cooper 2004). Rancière's quasi-mystical notion of the political has no sense of the importance of working from within the system to create conditions for greater equality, nor of how to sustain counter-hegemonic political challenge beyond the initial moment of demand. His work, then, poses a counter-intuitive paradox for leftist democrats, where radical egalitarian politics is placed 'in opposition to the end state of fairer distribution' (Davis 2010: 93). In the end, one is left wondering whether what Rancière stipulates as the radical political assertion of equality can ever be more than a dramatic but self-cancelling rhetorical gesture.

CONCLUSION

There is an obvious circularity to the argument in this chapter in so far as to criticize Rancière for socially weightless thinking is, in some sense, no criticism at all since he himself would claim that this is the very point of his idea of the political. Political disagreement can never be substantialized into actual group conflict and concrete social demands without diminishing the radical force of the assertion of equality. In accordance with this logic, it is undoubtedly correct that Rancière finishes by stipulating the emptiness of his notion of the political. Indeed, the rigorousness with which he insists on its social weightlessness serves to shine critical light on the way in which, despite claims to neutrality and inclusiveness, consensus theories of democracy may tacitly maintain the status quo. The very insubstantiality of the political exposes the surreptitious move where the supposedly de-ontological is derived from the ontological, the purportedly transcendental from what is in fact a mode of being that more closely mirrors the interests of those who have a part rather than those who have no part. Rancière's ultimate point is that radical political action will always exceed the parameters of any pre-given political community and therefore it is futile to try, as so many political theorists currently do, to come up with a universally valid model of democracy. No model of democracy – deliberative or otherwise – can guarantee in advance its ability to respond to radical challenge, especially when this may involve the overturning of its own procedures.

Whilst other historically or pragmatically minded democratic theorists might agree with this critique of strong universalism, they might not be so willing to follow Rancière to his stark conclusions about the pure nature of the political. This is because the all-or-nothing logic that governs his thought shrouds the idea of the political in obscurity and leaves him unable to advance beyond a series of false antinomies and paradoxes. It is an account of radical democracy that asserts an absolute sympathy with the voices of the excluded but dismisses out of hand most real-world attempts to make those voices heard. It is a radical historicism that claims that the truly political moment is born out of the unpredictable singularity of struggles, and yet measures the progressive import of these struggles against a mysterious, quasi-theological notion of egalitarian rupture. It is a democratic theory that denounces the depoliticizing tendencies in the contemporary world but that itself falls back into a depoliticized analysis of that same world. It has become a commonplace of a certain type of radical political theory to assert that the essence of democracy lies in paradox and in the attempt not to overcome it but to live productively within its terms. The case of Rancière, however, might make us question this truism a little and wonder whether, sometimes, it might not be more productive to question the validity of the paradox itself and the flaws of the underlying reasoning that has produced it.

5

Pluralism and Practice: The Existential Agonism of Connolly and Tully

INTRODUCTION

The theories of radical democracy considered in previous chapters have been variously grounded in what might be loosely understood as negative political ontologies. Ideas of non-identity – foundational lack or limitless indeterminacy – are used to convey the contingency of social existence and the myriad of possible forms that, as a consequence, political freedom may assume. A difficulty with such negative formulations is that they deprive social existence of autonomous significance, reducing it to a weak ontic reflection of prior ontological dynamics. The models of radical democratic action that flow from this style of socially weightless reasoning seem to have little relevance to crucial underlying issues of domination and disempowerment. There is another strand of thought on radical democracy, however, that expresses the open and generative nature of political action not through negative ontological premises, but rather through according a primary significance to the logic of social practice. These approaches hold that the activities of ordinary citizens are characterized by a spontaneous creativity and diversity that do not follow determining first principles. This bottom-up, practice-centred approach abandons the idea that political action may be routed through a formal space of democratic agonism and instead sees it as a potential immanent in the radical plurality of everyday practices and struggles.

Two leading exponents of this practice-centred approach to radical democracy are William F. Connolly and James Tully. On the face of it, both Connolly and Tully go some way to overcoming tendencies towards social weightlessness in radical democratic theory because of the primary they accord ordinary practice, rather than abstract dynamics, in sustaining political life. Connolly does indeed start from ontology but, contra other radical democrats, it is a positive one of abundance that stresses the endless possibilities for a radical micro-politics immanent in the logic of emergent becoming that governs social existence. Eschewing explicit ontological claims, Tully proceeds from a Foucauldian emphasis on practices of freedom, which leads him to an account of radical democracy as the diversity of citizen struggles against normalizing forms of governance. Following on from the primacy he accords practice over theory, he also offers a methodological reformulation of radical democratic theory as itself a practical intervention on behalf of the subaltern. In short, both thinkers conceive of democratic action as an unpredictable and unbounded generative force.

Despite the insights their work offers, I argue that their theories also have tendencies to social weightlessness in so far as they are both committed to an underlying view of social pluralism that is insufficiently integrated with an account of structural inequality. This is evident in their respective accounts of agency, which exaggerate the pluri-potentiality of social life by focusing on citizens who are already engaged in counter-hegemonic practice whilst paying insufficient attention to those whose conditions of existence render them unable to do so. Although both emphasize the situated and embodied nature of agency, they give scant regard, in fact, to the lived reality of deprivation and disempowerment that may lead to deep dispositional reluctances on the part of individuals to participate in political activity. Ultimately they finish in naïvely celebratory accounts of agonist contestation that pass over the negative aspects of social experience. What in the end seems to matter for both Connolly and Tully is the plurality of struggles *per se* rather than a consideration of how some struggles may go further than others in challenging deep-seated asymmetries of power. In short, they assume too easily that the generative logic of social action somehow assures progressive social transformation.

LACK, PLENITUDE, AGENCY

During the course of his writing, Connolly has used various terms to describe his multi-faceted vision of socio-political life: a philosophy of abundance, an immanent naturalism, an ethics of generosity, a multidimensional pluralism, a 'protean care for the world', and so on. More recently, his work has been associated with the emerging, interdisciplinary school of thought known as vitalist or speculative materialisms and Actor Network Theory (e.g. Bryant et al. 2011; Coole and Frost 2010). These terms all express the same core idea that a vitalist energy infuses the material world, giving rise to a manifold dynamism, richness of being and limitless alterity. The world is radically contingent in the sense that there are no necessary social forms, but this contingency proceeds not from a constitutive lack – as it does in other theories of radical democracy – but from a constitutive plenitude. The instituted forms or 'hegemonic assemblages' of established social orders repress and constrain these 'diverse energies and strange vitalities', imposing on them the logic of identity and regularity. But a substrate of 'energetic uncertainty' always eludes these constraints, with the consequence that there is always 'more to reality than actuality', although this 'more' cannot be explained by any conventional theory of determination, first principles, regularity or any other foundational logic. Social relations are complex assemblages of the human and non-human, dense, visceral networks of embodied practices and affective registers, operating on multiple levels and too protean to be mapped according to a single unifying logic. As Connolly puts it: 'Emergent causality – the dicey process by which new entities and processes periodically surge into being – is irreducible to efficient causality' (2010: 179). This partially suppressed superabundance of being makes itself felt in fugitive experiences of the uncanny, of otherness, and in the unforeseen emergence of new modes of being that characterize everyday existence.

Connolly, along with other new materialists, makes the ambitious claim that these vitalist suppositions overturn established modes of intellectual inquiry and engender innovative new ways of understanding the world and some of the most pressing problems that face us today. They displace, for instance, conventional, anthropocentric accounts of the world as in some sense passively there for humanity and, in highlighting the complex interactions of human and non-human elements ('vibrant matter'), point towards new hybrid forms of agentic capacity (e.g. Bennett 2010). They also throw into question the uni-directional constructivism that, since the linguistic turn, has dominated cultural, social and political theory and views the world essentially as an inert entity that receives its meaning and significance from the symbolic representations we make of it. From the vitalist perspective, material being has its own intricate internal dynamics that escape the exogeneous logic of constructivism: 'New materialists are rediscovering a materiality that materializes, evincing immanent modes of self-transformation that compel us to think of causation in far more complex terms' (Coole and Frost 2010: 9). Finally, vitalist materialism is non-dualist; it rejects the conceptual oppositions that structure much Western thought: mind versus body, reason versus emotion, culture versus nature, and so on. It uses instead ideas such as Deleuze's notion of the rhizome to capture the capacity of material being to generate radically new forms of existence. These emerge not according to dialectics or other dualist schemata, but in an irregular and unpredictable manner: 'Radical difference operates within contingently defined networks that are capable of synthesising existing differences into something radically new' (Tønder and Thomasen 2006b: 6).

Of all its theoretical entailments, Connolly places perhaps most emphasis on the reconfigured account of agency that can be derived from an ontology of abundance. Its anti-dualist premises lead to an understanding of action as incarnate, non-teleological practice governed by a dynamic of creative emergence. At first sight, this doesn't appear to be that different from the way agency has been conceptualized by any number of strands of radical thought – poststructuralism, feminism, psychoanalysis, and so on – that have taken issue with conventional notions of the asocial, sovereign subject. From a vitalist perspective, however, while these approaches may overturn a rationalist voluntarism, they still operate largely within the dualist, top-down logic of constructivism. Corporeal being is understood as materialized through the external imposition of power upon the passive body, and this delivers an etiolated, negative notion of agency. A vitalist conception replaces this uni-directional determinism with a generative dynamic of becoming that is understood to constantly push against and disrupt the limits of instituted being. By being attentive to the dynamic potentiality of embodied being, we arrive at what is claimed to be a fundamentally more creative and spontaneous notion of agency.

Connolly's main concern is to use this reworked conception of agency to shine a critical light on conventional democratic theory and, in so doing, to offer an alternative radicalized notion of a micro-politics of becoming. In an immediate sense, it is easy to see how this ontology of plenitude seems to overcome the social weightlessness that hampers other radical democratic accounts of agency. Grounded in a negative ontology that views social being as poised over a radical lack, these theories are often only able to think about agency in the most formulaic and empty of terms. An animating insight of radical democracy is that the source of political renewal comes from below, from the practices of engaged citizens. Yet, negative theories are often unable to develop this insight in a substantive manner because all social practice is regarded as merely another empirical manifestation of a foundational indeterminacy. Put differently, concrete practice has no autonomous significance; it acquires meaning only in the extent to which it affirms or disavows the prior principle of the Political. Negative accounts of democracy remain stranded in a socially weightless universalism which, 'caught by the spectre of structuralism ... does not appreciate the complexity or depth of social life but instead reduces the experience of difference to the question of failure' (Tønder and Thomassen 2006b: 6). In contrast to these one-dimensional accounts, Connolly's materialism strives to add depth and stature to sociality and the flows of everyday experience. Consequently, he redirects radical democratic theory away from the abstract logic of hegemony, antagonism and undecidability to the logic of practice and ethics. This, in turn, yields an expanded account of democratic agency and of sites for political mobilization and resistance. In particular, as we will see in the next section, Connolly's work throws into question distinctions between the procedural and the substantive, the political and the ethical, that conventionally structure thought about democratic citizen practice.

ETHICS AND POLITICS

The relation between politics and ethics is a vexed one for democratic theorists. In recent years, partly as a reaction to the preoccupation with proceduralism, a number of theorists have turned their attention to thinking through the ethical underpinnings of radical democracy (Garber et al. 2000; White 2009). Yet, for many on the left, this ethical turn is far from straightforward because it is felt to be fundamentally undermining of radical politics. On this view, the political is the vantage point from which social relations and practices may be denaturalized and contested on the grounds of their inegalitarian and oppressive nature. The affirmation of certain ethical dispositions and practices as necessary democratic virtues seems to stand in tension with this critical political perspective in so far as it appears to shield them from scrutiny and challenge. Consequently, the move from politics to ethics, from contestation to affirmation, is regarded by a number of theorists as essentially a regressive one of depoliticization. To quote Raymond Guess: 'Ethics is usually dead politics: the hand of a victor in some past conflict reaching out to try to extend its grip to the present and the future' (2009: 43). Even amongst thinkers who have taken an ethical turn, such as Judith Butler, these misgivings about the occlusion of power by morals are not easily set aside: 'I've worried that the return to ethics has constituted an escape from politics, and I've also worried that it has meant a certain heightening of moralism and this has made me cry out, as Nietzsche cried out about Hegel, "Bad air! Bad air!"' (2000b: 15).

The anxiety about ethical decontestation means that some radical democrats condemn outright as an anti-political move the effort to formulate a democratic ethics. For Rancière (2006), as we have seen, democratic politics proper has the structure of radical disagreement, and any attempt to render its litigious logic compatible with a background of shared ethical dispositions – respect for the other, presumptive generosity, critical self-awareness, and so forth – blunts its emancipatory edge. The demand on the part of excluded groups for political recognition is not just a demand for inclusion within an already established order but amounts to a fundamental challenge to the legitimacy of the prevailing order itself. The containment of democratic struggle within the parameters of certain shared ethical codes serves to shield the community from the radical import of this challenge. While not adopting such a stringent line, other radical democrats are nonetheless suspicious of the part played by ethics in democratic politics, arguing that its role should be curtailed or that it should be turned to only in the last resort when other modes of political framing and judgement have been exhausted. The strategy of curtailment is famously the one adopted by thinkers such as Habermas and Rawls, who, in their different ways, seek to demarcate the ethical from the political by separating non-universalizable issues of the good from transcendental norms of the just. The strategy of last resort is the one favoured by thinkers such as Nancy Fraser (2001), who maintains that many of the issues that are commonly treated as ethical are in fact better understood as political and should be dealt with in the former terms only when deontological justice approaches fail.

In the light of this widespread concern amongst democratic theorists, Connolly's work stands out, for, rather than trying to delimit the precise relation that should pertain between ethics and the politics, he abandons any attempt to separate the two realms. Instead, he proposes a single domain of ethico-political being. Indeed, according to him, any attempt to distinguish between properly political matters and ethical ones is untenable because it rests on a misrecognition of the grounding role played by the latter in daily social existence. On the procedural view, ethical beliefs are depicted as freely chosen, spiritual and intellectual orientations towards the good. Following Foucault, however, Connolly understands them not just as symbolic representations or metaphysical convictions but as incarnate, lived practices that embed individuals in the world and profoundly shape their relations with others. They are ineluctably woven into the fabric of daily practice, as 'contingent routines, traumas, joys, and conversion experiences' (Connolly 1999: 9). The tendency in procedural theory to empty ethics of this phenomenal significance is exemplified by the secular nature of their frameworks, which rests, in his view, on an underestimation of the centrality of religious practices in daily life. When religious belief is understood as a practice of self-formation rather than as doctrinal conviction, it becomes difficult to maintain the arbitrary and 'shallow' distinction between private faith and public reason, where the former can be set aside in deference to the supposedly impartial demands of the latter.

Ethical belief has a foundational existential import and, in Connolly's view, this is downplayed by Rawls, in his 'stingy, cramped and defensive' idea of reasonable value pluralism (Connolly 1993a: 28). Rawls is only able to ensure a stable foundation for the idea of overlapping consensus by a conceptual sleight of hand where persons and generic facts about them are understood to be relatively static and 'flat'. This 'drive to stillness' robs ethical beliefs and practices of their depth and vibrancy, relegating them to the secondary, peripheral status of private, individual choices. Connolly maintains that Habermas goes further than Rawls in recognizing the existential grounding role of ethical practice, but his rationalism ultimately also imposes a limit on the type of practice he is willing to encompass in his supposedly more inclusive idea of deliberation. His construal of deliberation as the formalization of validity claims means that he dismisses those beliefs and claims that, for whatever reason, might not be amenable to purely rational reconstruction. Echoing communitarian critics, Connolly maintains that it is implausible to think that persons would be willing to lay aside their thick metaphysical world-views in order to give precedence, in their role as citizens, to the thin procedural norms that govern public political life. More than that, he suspects, along with other critics, that the neo-Kantian appeal to impartial procedures is in fact ultimately 'a rhetorical gesture that conceals the particular interests of the dominant segments of late modern society' (Wenman 2008: 161).

In place of unsatisfactory attempts to segregate ethical from political life, Connollly proposes a singular, capacious category of ethico-political being from which he derives his idea of a micropolitics of becoming. Political agency is not something that can be defined from the transcendental perspective of democratic theory in terms of the particular duties and role of citizens. Rather, it is immanent within a layer of experience that falls below the threshold of 'the coarse practice of justice' and manifests itself in a radical plurality of practices – a politics of becoming: 'The task of politics is to challenge the collective hegemony of creeds of transcendence so that the voices of immanence can assume a more active presence in public life, so that the depth grammar of public life itself becomes more actively pluralised' (Connolly 2006: 250). Social space is not, for Connolly, a realm of fixed interests and pre-given tendencies; rather, it is a dense network of heterogeneous, dynamic intersections, a space of radical immanence. It is from this energetic space that new political identities and counter-hegemonic types of agency emerge 'formed out of unexpected energies and institutionally congealed injuries', and which, in their confrontation with the established world, change 'the shape and contour of already entrenched identities' (Connolly 1999: 57). The failure to grasp the diversity of ethico-political being limits the ability of procedural justice approaches to identify not only emergent forms of agency but also types of suffering and oppression that fall below the register of established political discourse. It follows from the dynamic nature of social being that some types of social suffering are diffuse and inchoate, rendering them inaccessible to the 'determinate set of categories' of the justice perspective (Connolly 1999: 47). There is, for instance, a register of religious suffering that is not confined to specific forms of group misrecognition but is diffuse and polycultural in nature and therefore often not identified as a problem in theory oriented to specific justice claims. Operating as it does around the dualism of public and private, democratic proceduralism is frequently not attuned to these unthematized experiences; it is, as Connolly describes it, 'tone deaf to the multiple modes of suffering below the register of justice' (1999: 9). In this respect, Connolly's argument echoes Honneth's critique of discourse ethics as unable to respond to types of unthematized suffering that are not revealed as violations of moral norms.

Indispensable to this micro-political receptivity to the dynamic texture of ordinary existence is what Connolly terms an ethos of generosity. This denotes the sensibility that should typify democratic interaction between partisans in a world of 'multidimensional plurality'. At first sight, this ethos seems to resemble liberal notions of tolerance, but, according to Connolly, it is, in fact, far more pro-active, entailing not just passive acceptance of the 'private' other but a presumptively generous and self-critical type of public engagement. Such engagement requires agonistic respect where parties set aside prejudice and over-drawn distinctions, between, say, the secular and religious, private faith and public reason, and so forth, and interact with each other with modesty and forbearance. Only when appropriate would they bring into discussion 'chunks' of their respective faiths into the public realm as part of 'a positive ethos of engagement' (Connolly 2006: 250–1). The aim of such an engagement is not the attainment of consensus, in a deliberative sense, nor does it involve the acceptance of perpetual disagreement and conflict, contra some forms of agonism. Rather, the desired outcome is the fostering of 'ethically sensitive, negotiated settlements' (Connolly 1999: 33). Agonistic respect in this sense encompasses only horizontal relations of diversity between already recognized democratic constituencies, so a second crucial component of a presumptively generous sensibility is the explicit recognition of vertical social relations. A genuinely inclusive ethos must also cultivate a sensitivity to disempowered groups who face the prejudice of not being recognized as legitimate partners in political debate: 'Critical responsiveness is a presumptive generosity to new constituencies struggling to move from a place of subsistence below the reach of established recognition, justice, or legitimacy onto one of those registers' (Connolly 2004: 177). Finally, agonist respect also requires the cultivation of a relational sensibility where all parties accept the contestability of their own views, no matter how deeply held their convictions may be; each party must acknowledge 'that its highest and most entrenched faith is legitimately contestable by others' (Connolly 2005: 47).

The cultivation of these democratic virtues would result not in an uncritical relativism but a multidimensional pluralism that does not shy away from making difficult judgements. Connolly acknowledges that the development of these virtues is by no means a straightforward matter. It takes courage to bear the 'agony of diversity' (Connolly 2005: 81), and it requires intense work on one's basic affective responses and deepest convictions: 'Agonistic respect and critical responsiveness are civic virtues that require cultivation and negotiation. They involve tactical work on the lower affective registers of being that filter into the higher intellect but are unsusceptible to its direct regulation' (Connolly 2004: 177). Nonetheless, this ethical self-discipline is necessary and unavoidable if radical democratic politics are to take root and capture the imagination and loyalties of citizens: 'Radical democracy has the best chance to progress if . . . a significant minority of citizens are to come to terms with the abundance of life' (Connolly 2006: 251).

Connolly explicitly positions his ethics of generosity as an extension of formalist accounts of radical democracy advanced by thinkers such as Laclau and Mouffe. Like Mouffe, he maintains that one of the central aims of a progressive democratic order is to channel potentially destructive social antagonisms into the safer political form of agonistic contestation – 'to transmute cultural antagonisms . . . into debates marked by agonistic respect between the partisans' (Connolly 2005: 47). But Connolly is able to go much further than Mouffe in advancing this insight, because agonism for him does not have the formal structure of ineradicable antagonism but is grounded in the lived experience of openness and care towards an other (e.g. Glover 2012; Kioupkiolis 2011).

Although Connolly claims a radical status for his micro-politics of becoming, he pulls his punches somewhat in clarifying in precisely which respects it overturns political creeds of transcendence (e.g. Howarth 2008: 183–4). He suggests, on the one hand, that his radical ethical sensibility represents not so much an outright rejection of procedural approaches as a supplement to them, giving them an enriched appreciation of the complexity of ethico-political practice and thereby extending their normative reach (Connolly 1998: 93). Yet, in so far as he rejects the conceptual dualisms of proceduralism, he suggests, on the other hand, that the radical thrust of agonist pluralism cannot be contained within a single overarching model of the political, no matter how seemingly inclusive. This equivocation is reflected in the views of his commentators, some of whom see his micro-politics of becoming as aligned with a hegemonic project of radical democracy, others of whom see it leading to a neo-anarchist politics that rejects an autonomous space of the political in favour of a plurality of sites of resistance (e.g. Glover 2012; Newman 2008; Wenman 2003).

This equivocation is significant because, as I will argue in the following sections, it is symptomatic of a deeper limitation in Connolly's thought, namely, its failure to interrogate sufficiently how the 'abundance of life over identity' is mediated through entrenched asymmetries of power and enduring inequalities (2006: 253). An unreflective commitment to a one-dimensional and glamorized idea of cultural pluralism undermines his ability to advance the type of critique of power that is necessary for the idea of a micro-politics of becoming to have radical bite.

ONTOLOGY AND POWER

The difficulties with deriving a supposedly radical micro-politics from what are deemed to be foundational characteristics of social being have been addressed to some extent in the debate amongst political theorists about 'weak ontologies' (see *Hedgehog Review* 2005). The issue, as far as Connolly's work is concerned, is whether an ethos grounded in an immanent capacity for openness and creative becoming lacks sufficient critical force to sustain the type of discriminations necessary for an emancipatory politics. Is affirmation an insufficiently politicized way of conceptualizing democratic agency? Jodi Dean argues, for instance, that whilst, in principle, an ethos of affirmation is not incompatible with radical democratic concerns, it tends to result in a politics of avoidance. Crucial issues of political judgement are endlessly deflected by casting intersubjective social relations in terms of underlying capacities and tendencies, instead of in terms of hierarchies of power. This results in a therapeutic politics based on the self-referential idea of ethical cultivation rather than a macro-politics of progressive structural social change: 'Its interiorized micropolitical emphasis on cultivating an affirmative sensibility avoids addressing the choices, gaps, and exclusions constituting the space of politics' (Dean 2005: 6). In a similar vein, Stephen K. White (2005) argues that a commitment to pluralism and existentially figured notions of generosity and contestation are too underdetermined to support the strong normative judgements necessary for a progressive politics. Others, like Richard Flathman (2005), argue that the idea of an ethics of generosity would tend to promote indecision and tentativeness amongst citizens rather than the deep commitments and strong 'will to believe' that he believes are necessary democratic virtues. In short, ontologized ideas of ethics encourage a pusillanimous affirmation of the prevailing order of things and consequently reinforce a reformist politics that insists on living 'generously' within that order rather than a politics of radical challenge and emancipation (see also Myers 2013).

These criticisms have much force, but there are several responses that Connolly might make to rebut them. First, ontological presuppositions – weak or otherwise – cannot be bypassed entirely. Even the most deontological types of political theory are necessarily based in some kind of loose figuration or pre-understanding of basic human tendencies and capacities, even though these may not be explicitly acknowledged. The virtue of Connolly's work in this regard is that he makes these presuppositions explicit and attempts to develop them in a self-consciously reflexive manner, acknowledging their ultimate contestability and moving back and forth between the levels of ontological and sociological reflection. The way to rescue openness is, as Alexandros Kioupkiolis points out, not to mistakenly forgo ontology, but to heighten reflexivity and explicitly distinguish between different planes of ontological, ethico-political and epistemic affirmation (2011: 692).

Connolly himself is aware of the depoliticizing potential of defining radical agency in terms of ontological capacities rather than in terms of power, and, consequently, he repeatedly emphasizes the politicized nature of his agonistic ethics. He insists, for instance, that a micro-politics of becoming must be accompanied by systematic attempts to rectify social inequalities. The 'majority assemblage' must work, as he puts it, to reduce inequalities, to ensure that every citizen can participate in public life with dignity (Connolly 2006: 253). At other points, he asserts that his politics of deep pluralism presupposes a programme of progressive economic redistribution; the ethos of engagement is intended to apply pressure to capitalist institutions. He also stresses that an ethics of generosity is emphatically not one of uncritical acceptance. It signifies an initial ethical gesture in democratic encounters that would enable powerless groups to acquire political voice in the first place, but it is not intended as a perpetual deferral of the moment of political judgement. Moreover, it is undoubtedly the case that a vitalist ontology of becoming is, at least on the face of it, not as conceptually constraining in terms of an account of power as other ontologically grounded approaches to politics. Unlike, for instance, ideas of democracy grounded in negative ontologies, Connolly's model attributes a complexity and depth to patterns of sociality that are, in principle, compatible with a differentiated account of power. Social being has an intrinsic dynamism that exceeds explanations such as, say, Mouffe's, where the necessary logic of antagonism governs practice in an invariant fashion. An ontology of abundance is also, in theory, less constraining than, say, Axel Honneth's strong ontology of recognition, which turns around the single explanatory principle of modern societies as imperfectly realized recognition orders. Its normative monism deprives social and political struggles of heterogeneity by viewing them as, at base, expressions of a foundational need for recognition. In contrast, Connolly's notion of emergent causality explicitly rejects notions of necessary causality or determining logic and offers, in theory, a more open and potentially radical account of social relations and agency. From this generative perspective, these other ontologically grounded accounts of politics fall into the error of over-determination or 'efficient causality' that denies the character of social relations as dense, multi-layered networks of embodied practices. On the face of it, then, what saves Connolly's ontology of abundance from depoliticization is the extent to which its attentiveness to the myriad dynamics of social practice leaves open the possibility of formulating a multidimensional account of power.

Differently put, it is not ontological argument in itself that is depoliticizing but the way in which the move from an ontological to a sociological register is articulated. Ontological assertions may become problematic when social dynamics of power are derived in a relatively reductive and direct fashion from foundational presuppositions. Given this, a lot hangs on the success with which Connolly manages to reflexively integrate his vitalist ontology with a differentiated account of power for it ensures the radical bite of his micro-politics of becoming. But it is precisely here that the central failing of his thought lies. For despite repeated assertions of the protean and complex nature of social being, Connolly falls back on a one-sided depiction of everyday life as a spontaneous process of minoritarian becoming that ignores negative aspects of the lived reality of inequality. This naïve vision is compounded by being theorized through a series of over-drawn dualisms between being and becoming, linearity and duration, domination and resistance, transcendence and immanence that stand in for a more mediated account of power. These dualisms express, in one way or another, the self-same dynamic where the perpetual flux of everyday life is pitted against the stasis of instituted forms. Without wanting to deny that embodied practice does indeed have spontaneous and creative aspects, it is nonetheless hard to see what relevance Connolly's exoticized idea of becoming has to the conditions of existence of many individuals which are also marked by isolation, boredom, routinization, vulnerability, disempowerment, and so forth.

EMBODIMENT, POWER AND TIME

A key claim of Connolly's, as we have seen, is that the ontology of abundance generates an acute sensitivity to the nuances and dynamics of embodied social existence and therefore an awareness of unexpected forms of political agency. He repeatedly stresses the importance of paying close attention to the 'visceral texture' of daily life in order to discern these emergent modes of being, or, as he phrases it, to identify' 'new breezes blowing softly through the subterranean tissues of life' (Connolly 2005: 130). Yet, it is precisely in this supposedly textured account of embodied existence that what in fact becomes evident is Connolly's reliance on a series of formulaic dualisms, in lieu of a more differentiated account of power. These structuring dualisms impart to the account of embodied being a curiously generalized quality where it is understood in terms of vague cultural tendencies rather than the specificities of social location.

Take, for instance, Connolly's treatment of the temporality of embodied being through the dualism of linear versus durational time. Echoing Weber and others, Connolly maintains that industrialized societies are dominated by linear, causal notions of clock time that emerge with the increasing rationalization of social and economic life. Running beneath this tendency to standardization is another temporal register of duration, first identified by Henri Bergson, and that pertains to the level of embodied, perceptual existence or the 'affectively imbued experience of duration'. Duration is time as it is experienced at the level of incorporated being, a level that does not correspond to linear, teleological schemata because it is, in essence, a dissonant, heterogeneous and fugitive type of experience. It encompasses, for example, mundane experiences of temporal disjunction where past, present and future collide; where memories might flood present consciousness; where five minutes of clock time is felt to be endless; where an unexpected conjunction of events might abruptly alter the temporal flow of daily life. It is a 'continuous pulse of time, with each element shading into the others and melting into them in turn' (Connolly 2005: 100). In a more fluid and mutable contemporary world, the unsettling implications of durational time have been intensified, and this throws up increasingly pluralized and indeterminate modes of experience and identity. Reasoning mainly through analogy, Connolly associates durational time with the unpredictable process of 'multiple becomings' that 'exceeds human explanation or control' (2005: 103, 104). Then, in another syncopated move, he links it to a synergetic ethical perspective that is destabilizing of conventional concepts of meaning and morality which are too closely tied to uni-linear, Kantian notions of time as progress, 'the endless progress of our goodness toward conformity to the law' (Connolly 2005: 115). Teleological concepts of moral reasoning are ill equipped to deal with the unexpected shifts or 'swerves' in time that may lead to the emergence of the radically new when a new cultural identity 'surges into being'.

For example, by disrupting conventional habits of perception and recasting them in an unorthodox and fluid way, visual media such as film, TV, exhibitions, and so forth, have created the grounds for a radical micro-politics of perception (Connolly 2010). In short, it is not 'closed morality' but agonistic ethics, with its presumptive generosity and acceptance of contestability, that is able to identify the pluri-potentiality of durational experience and unexpected possibilities for agency to which it gives rise. In a final analogical leap, durational time is understood as the register through which 'historically specific suffering' may emerge from a 'netherworld' to 'shake up something' in the established world: 'The politics of becoming ... emerges out of historically specific suffering, previously untapped energies, and emerging lines of possibility eluding the attention of dominant constituencies' (Connolly 2005: 121–2).

If Connolly's tendency to argue through analogy is resisted, however, one might consider the sociological plausibility of such a depiction of embodied temporality. Put simply, what kind of lives does this describe and whose social reality is this? Above all, the yoking of 'social suffering' to an existential flux of duration-becoming seems questionable. There are many types of dispossession and suffering that do not have the 'untapped energies' or immanent vitality to 'surge' into being in the romanticized fashion described by Connolly. Lawrence Langer (1996), for instance, uses a very different notion of durational temporality associated with the 'frozen experiences of atrocity' to examine the inability of Holocaust survivors to speak of their experiences. To be sure, Connolly acknowledges in passing that the logic of temporal becoming does not always 'generate positive things'. Moreover, he claims that his general idea of embodiment is deeply informed by a Foucauldian notion of disciplinary power as 'coded into perception' and is consequently alive to the insidious dynamics of normalization that take hold of the body. Yet, in the end, what he offers is a one-sided depiction of embodiment as minoritarian becoming that floats free from any grounding in concrete social relations.

It is instructive to contrast Connolly's analysis of embodiment with the way Bourdieu understands it through an ontology of complicity or mutual possession between body and the world that, *inter alia*, emphasizes how the experience of time – lived temporality – is closely tied to social location. From this perspective, the dualism of linear versus durational time does not capture anything significant about the nature of suffering and dispossession. Take, for example, the temporal reality of the long-term unemployed as powerfully described in Simon Charlesworth's *A Phenomenology of Working-*

Class Experience (2000). With Connolly, we might see that such experiences escape the regularities of linear clock time since the world has lost a sense of purpose and progress for the chronically unemployed. But it can hardly be said to correspond to the generative dynamism of duration that Connolly associates with the temporality of daily existences. Temporal dispossession in this case is more aptly captured, following Bourdieu, as the experience of time as empty or 'negated time' that follows from the absence of work, one of the primary foundations of a meaningful and purposive life. In Bourdieu's words:

> Employment is the support, if not the source, of most interests, expectations, demands, hopes and investments in the present, and also in the future or the past that it implies, in short one of the major foundations of illusion in the sense of involvement in the game of life, in the present, the primordial investment which ... creates time and indeed is time itself. (2000: 222)

In short, time and power are connected, and this connection is mediated, to some degree or another, through the dynamics peculiar to a given social position.

Not only is it difficult to characterize this type of suffering as one of minoritarian becoming, but it also cannot really be said to be generative of alternative types of agency. In fact it could be said to undermine the capacity to act, it 'drives out the human' (Charlesworth 2000: 24). The emotions that often accompany this dead time are, as Charlesworth shows, those of despair, boredom, hopelessness, rage, fear of rejection, and these dispositions have profound implications for the capacity for political agency for they distort the most basic sense of purposive being in the world. The confidence in one's ability to shape the future according to one's desires is shaped in an immediate sense by power in the present. As Bourdieu puts it: 'Capital in its various forms is a set of pre-emptive rights over the future' (2000: 225). If dispositions and the practical sense of how to go on are, in part, the result of the internalization of the tendencies of the world into the body, then when that familiar world falls away, when it no longer has meaning or purpose for the individual, the capacity for practical action may also be undermined. Such disempowerment is illustrated, for example, in Thomas Luhrmann's (2006) use of the term 'subjectivity of social defeat' to capture the basic demeanour of homeless women, whose relation to the world is defined by the daily experience of humiliation. The practical, tacit sense of knowing how to go on can be eroded by the 'pointless pain of boredom', or a 'growing inertia to experience itself'. It is not of course that these individuals cannot act, but in alien circumstances, where the world presents itself as indifferent, if not hostile, a fear of rejection can paralyse action: 'In this situation of withdrawal, it is as if the world now stands out from them as a series of practices they are exempted from. . . . They experience a radical discontinuity . . . a sense of the loss of meaning of their lives and yet which makes the meaninglessness of the world in which they live more explicit' (Charlesworth 2000: 79).

Such negative experiences are of course not universal, yet they remind us that domination is not a purely external relation but, at its most effective, an internal one of symbolic violence. Domination is taken into the body and lived in the naturalized form of deep-seated, often debilitating, dispositions. Economic deprivation is not just brute material lack but may be lived as a lack of second-order agency, as feelings of vulnerability and powerlessness that often leave subordinated individuals unable to control their lives or do anything other than endure their oppression. On Connolly's model, domination seems to remain a largely exogenous force that is imposed from above, that represses the vitalist substrate of embodied being but somehow never fully penetrates it, deforming its very essence. The symbolic and material dispossession of the homeless and long-term unemployed is, of course, not representative of all types of inequality and, needless to say, it is important not to exaggerate the powerlessness of subordinated groups and fall into a countervailing miserabilism. It is the case, nonetheless, that Connolly's depiction of embodied being as one of abundance, spontaneity and becoming is one-sided in its failure to consider in any detail at all the more negative aspects of social experience. This gap is especially surprising given the supposed 'fine-tuning' of his theory to the sufferings of marginal and disempowered groups. Instead, he falls back on an exoticized account of social being that exaggerates its fluid and 'enchanted' aspects and is entirely disconnected from any but the most notional social context. By bracketing off issues of power, durational time is presented as a general existential category, as a universal experiential substrate that is true for all individuals. To be sure, an emphasis on social location would not necessarily rule out a priori the type of vitalist agency posited by Connolly, but it undoubtedly would be more attuned to the ways in which embodied being is mediated through the relations of power that traverse and define specific social spaces. Ultimately such a perspective would generate a more complicated and uneven picture of the possibilities of minoritarian becoming than the one that Connolly gives us. Instead, he treats embodiment through simplified oppositions that, in one way or another, uncritically valorize the flux and mobility of becoming. To quote Leslie Thiele, Connolly flees 'the hard choices of politics by means of literary fabrication coupled with a flippant iconoclasm of rootlessness' (1992: 778).

PLURALISM AND INEQUALITY

The shortcomings in Connolly's account of embodied existence are symptomatic of a deeper underlying difficulty, namely, the extent to which his reliance on an account of power as pluralization blocks a sufficient understanding of the dynamics of inequality. Overemphasis on the logic of becoming confines him to a superficial and quasi-naturalist account of power that fails to penetrate the surface commotion of cultural difference to explore the asymmetrical structures that persist beneath. Throughout his work, Connolly emphasizes the fluid nature of the logic of social pluralization and its unpredictable, transformative effects on all levels of social being, from the local to the global; as he puts it, the future is not contained in the present. Thus, he understands neoliberal capitalism as part of what he calls a 'global resonance machine', an open system composed of multiple elements (markets, states, environment, populations, etc.) whose interactions with each other perpetually throw up new antagonisms, crises and forms of minoritarian becoming. It is 'an expressive machine, composed of heterogeneous constituencies that interpenetrate and exacerbate each other' (Connolly 2011: 141). The idea of the machine is intended to convey an 'irreductionist' world-view that displaces 'reductive' explanations of reality that position capitalism at their centre. Capitalism is just one element in an open and complex system where entities and systems (human and non-human) act upon one another with unpredictable and dynamic effects. This global resonance machine has both negative and positive effects, but one of its main consequences is a widespread temporal disequilibrium or acceleration of time that in turn intensifies process of minoritarian becoming.

Connolly depicts the complex and unpredictable social effects of these destabilizing tendencies through the use of terms such as molten lava, loose play, energetic uncertainty, radical immanence and even litter. The use of these quasi-organic terms to portray the logic of pluralization leads ultimately to a depoliticized account of social conflict and the emergence of counter-hegemonic challenge.

For instance, the difficult and often fraught process through which subordinated groups become effective political agents is presented as some kind of spontaneous emergence from below where they spring up as fully formed counter-hegemons from the substrate of everyday practice. To be sure, Connolly acknowledges in passing the difficulties that oppressed groups have in getting their experiences and claims registered within public discussions, but he assumes by and large that, given the right conditions of presumptive generosity, new cultural and social groups and identities will 'surge' into being as pre-given unities. Many oppressed groups, however, do not exist as coherent, pre-political constituencies in the way Connolly's model implies. They do not necessarily have the internal unity, shared identity and common voice that he seems to presuppose as unproblematic givens. One might call to mind, for instance, Frantz Fanon's (2001) description of the way in which the structural violence of colonial exploitation is taken into the bodies and psyches of its subjects with brutalizing, pathological and deeply disempowering effects. Fanon's contentious conclusion is that the only effective way to cast off these psychic distortions is through a cleansing counter-violence. Such issues of violence, counter-violence, structural dispossession and ideological oppression simply do not figure in Connolly's domesticated account of group conflict. According to Mark Wenman, for example, Connolly's response to fundamentalism is woefully inadequate; it 'identifies and spirits away the problem of fundamentalism all in one breath' (2008: 172–3). Groups may lack internal cohesion and often also a shared language in which to express themselves and their demands. Take, for instance, Loïc Wacquant's study of the 'advanced marginality' that has emerged over the last thirty years in the major cities of established democracies and that is typified by unprecedented forms of material fragmentation and psychological destitution. Structural dynamics of dispossession crystallize around a socio-spatial logic of ostracization or 'territorial stigmatization', creating isolated and bounded regions that are perceived by those both within and outside as 'leprous badlands . . . where only the refuse of society would agree to dwell' (Wacquant 2008: 237). The experience of living in these areas is not one that can be depicted, *pace* Connolly, as suppressed abundance, as immanently meaningful for its inhabitants, even though such meaning is imperceptible to those on the outside. It would be difficult to characterize such 'neighbourhoods of relegation' as counter-hegemonic communities that create a sustaining alternative reality to the oppressive relations of the wider world. Rather, the experience of living in these 'social purgatories' is too often one of negativity, meaninglessness and alienation from agencies of representation and mobilization. There is a fixity to such social positions, often accompanied by feelings of entrapment, that is too swiftly passed over by Connolly in his glamorization of cultural becoming and social flux. Territorial stigmatization gives rise, on the part of its inhabitants, to a loss of a sense of place in the world, 'the loss of a humanized, culturally familiar and socially filtered locale with which marginalized populations identify and in which they feel "at home" and in relative security' (Connolly 2008: 243). Membership of some groups does not endow individuals with a shared identity or aim; rather, it is simply a stigmatized position from which they may want to escape: for example, membership of the precariat, which, in Wacquant's words, 'is a sort of stillborn group, whose gestation is necessarily unfinished since one can work . . . only to help its members flee from it, either by finding a haven in stable wage labour or by escaping from the world of work altogether' (2008: 247). These dynamics of fragmentation – the negative side of what Connolly presents as the positive process of pluralization – demonstrate that the sharing of the same social space is not enough to ensure the kind of common bonds or unity of purpose that the idea of minoritarian becoming too swiftly presumes.

In so far as he fails to articulate the logic of pluralization with that of social inequality, Connolly falls back on a cultural expressivism that moves him closer to conventional notions of multicultural difference than he would care to acknowledge. He claims to replace standard accounts of multicultural pluralism based on the toleration of minority groups by a stable majority, with a more radical notion of multidimensional minoritization: 'The national image of a centred majority surrounded by minorities eventually becomes transfigured into an image of interdependent minorities of different types connected through multiple lines of affiliation' (Connolly 2005: 61–2). Against the emphasis placed by 'mosaic' multiculturalism on the bounded and internally coherent nature of cultural identities, Connolly highlights instead the contingency and contestability of all identities. Yet, whilst he may problematize essentialist notions of identity on one dimension, he reinstalls them on another through the quasi-naturalist idea of minoritarian becoming, which presents political mobilization as a spontaneous, unproblematic inevitability. The ungrounded idea of cultural hybridization shares little sense of the depth and systematic basis of social inequalities captured in Iris Marion Young's politics of positional difference, which 'calls attention to relations and processes of exploitation, marginalization, and normalization that keep many people in a subordinate position' (2007: 79). There is no mention, for instance, of dynamics of racialization that systematically traverse group differences and are more adequately analysed through ideas of segregation, exploitation and subordination than those of unconstrained cultural plurality. As Anthony Appiah puts it, against such an air-brushed cultural vision 'it is not black culture that the racist [disdains], but blacks. . . . Culture is not the problem and it is not the solution' (quoted in Mills 2007: 95). Similarly, if we are really to be sensitive to the emergent practices of subordinate groups, then it might also be necessary to bring into play a stronger sense of those structural inequalities of gender that lie beneath social dynamics of becoming and render women vulnerable to domination and deprivation in most societies in the world (Young 2007: 88).

Connolly's response to such socially negative critique has been to denounce it as a left-wing miserabilism that wilfully over-predicts the powerlessness of the oppressed. In his view, persistent dwelling on the negative and a failure to develop an 'exquisite sensitivity to life' is a leftist form of 'self-indulgence' that immobilizes progressive politics and 'fails to contribute positive energy to a counter-resonance machine' (2008: 333). But there is more at stake in the emphasis on suffering and inequality than the swapping of an optimistic for a pessimistic perspective. The claim is that extrapolation from an ontology of abundance leads Connolly to fundamentally misunderstand the nature of power under neoliberal capitalism. The one-sided focus on pluralization, disequilibrium and seemingly limitless becoming occludes the recognition of persistent structural dynamics of power, leaving him with an underdeveloped sense of the entrenched nature of certain inequalities and types of social misery. Ultimately, as I argue in the next section, this skewed vision throws into question the radical import of his ethics of generosity and his claim that 'ontological affirmation, the democratic left, and political militancy belong together in the late-modern era' (Connolly 2010: 197).

GENEROSITY OR QUIESCENCE?

The suspension of a sense of how pluralized social existence may be distorted by inequality inevitably limits the radical subversive potential of Connolly's ethics. Take, for example, his proposal of the adoption of a warrior ethos as a way of progressively reorienting some of the destructive tendencies of global capitalism. An effect of living in a world of pluralized becoming is the multiplication of social roles. This may have negative effects on the individual because of the pressure to manage the often 'rapid shifts' between role assignments. But it may also be positive in so far as it engenders a 'pluri-potentiality' of forms of resistance or ways of 'turning the machine in a different direction'. To this end, Connolly suggests that individuals might infuse their daily performance of differing roles with a 'warrior ethic', understood as a 'militant, visible, creative and inspirational' way of being that yields 'new experiences that might alter our relational sensibilities' and establishes connections with 'noble role warriors in other regions' (2011: 144–5).

If the effects of neoliberal capitalism were simply those of pluralization or increased diversity on a horizontal social plane, then this warrior ethos might be seen to represent a viable micro-political response. But, as a number of thinkers, including Foucault, have pointed out, social pluralization is only one side of the story. The other side is one of deepening social inequality. The dispersal of power under neoliberal governance is articulated through an economic logic that attempts to refashion social relations according to a market model (Foucault 2008). The remodelling of social bonds as market relations may indeed have pluralizing effects, at one level, but, at another, it interacts with, reinforces and reshapes enduring structural inequalities such as class, race and gender. The growth of the 'precariat', for instance, exemplifies how the move to seeming flexibility and differentiation in labour practices intensifies deep-seated social inequalities, creating new forms of vulnerability and social insecurity. Precariousness, on this view, is not, as Connolly might have it, an existential embrace of the energetic uncertainty of life, 'the capacity to dwell sensitively in historically significant, forking moments' (2011: 165). It is an experience characterized not so much by mobility and dynamism but rather by the less glamorous struggle to survive. In the light of widespread social precariousness, Connolly's idea of a warrior ethos to progressively reorient globalized consumerism seems naïve at best and, at worst, ineffective in so far as it compounds the very structures it claims to alter. The celebratory emphasis on the supposedly counter-hegemonic powers of an informed consumerism renders theoretically invisible its complicity in the intensification and restructuring of poverty.

From this perspective of the repressed context of power, even the sensibility of responsiveness and generosity central to Connolly's ethos is questionable in terms of its supposedly radical entailments. The vision of agonistic contestation as 'restrained partnership' fails to interrogate its own social conditions of possibility and, consequently, to consider how it might propound an ethical disposition more suited to the empowered than the disempowered. In keeping with other agonistic thinkers, Connolly stipulates that all participants acknowledge the contestability of their own beliefs and claims and express them with forbearance and generosity: 'We pursue restrained terms of contestation and collaboration between multiple, overlapping traditions . . . to acknowledge the contestability of its own presumptions and to allow that acknowledgement to infuse restraint, agonistic respect, and responsiveness' (2000: 168–9). Yet what are the social conditions that have to be already in place in order to render this stipulation of contestability and self-restraint feasible? Connolly expects all participants, regardless of their histories and social positions, to accept the terms of agonistic debate. But it might be said that this is really only a plausible scenario from the perspective of a cultural vitalism that empties struggle of political urgency by detaching it from its context of inequality. For many oppressed groups and minorities who have undergone prolonged experiences of misrecognition, oppression or exploitation, their demands for justice and reparation have an immediacy and moral force that is not felt to be contestable or contingent in any meaningful sense. It is not clear, for example, how fear of persecution is supposed to engender a presumptive generosity, rather than deep wariness or desperation. As Robert Glover phrases it: 'To claim that receptivity will emerge out of fear without carefully specifying the means by which to achieve this transformation is an extremely risky assertion' (2012: 97). Nor is it clear how the negative identities and self-images that individuals often internalize as a result of being exposed to prejudice and denigration can be subject to a process where 'fixed identities . . . are pressed periodically to come to terms with their constructed characters' (Connolly 1993b: 265).

Indeed, the discourse of 'restrained contestation and collaboration', presumptive generosity, and so forth, could arguably be seen to belong to the linguistic habitus of more empowered groups who, because of the relative privilege of their social position, are accustomed to expressing themselves in the mode of forbearance prescribed by Connolly. It is an ethos that appears to be more suited to those who already have a political voice, who are confident of being listened to, and also for whom there is less at stake than there is for those who, from positions of often gross inequality and injustice, seek to radically challenge – or, in Connolly's tellingly quietist vocabulary, 'disturb' – the dominant order. Ultimately, then, by failing to scrutinize more fully its own repressed social conditions of possibility, Connolly's ethos of generosity is in fact far less inclusive than it purports to be. As Kioupkiolis puts it: 'Connolly does not face up to this [the] limit of his approach. ... The self-critical recognition of doubt proceeds in a manner that neutralizes reflectiveness ... converting it into an imperious, quasi-neutral prescription for plural democracies' (2011: 704). The ethos of restrained partisanship is intended as a corrective to the inability of procedural justice approaches to respond to the suffering of oppressed groups, but in the end it replicates rather than rectifies this shortcoming. The tacit exclusions set in play by the rationalism of the deliberative community are reproduced in a different fashion in the requirements of moderation and self-directed contestation. Such prescriptions have the effect of outlawing the confrontational types of speech and protest that, historically, marginal groups have had to use to force entry into the democratic game and for their demands to be taken seriously at all. Ultimately, there is a serious incompleteness in Connolly's domesticated model of agonistic contestation because it cannot really incorporate radical democratic challenge and transformative action within its circumscribed limits. In so far as it seeks abstractly to lessen the conflictual nature of politics, and to transform it into more benign forms of interaction, then it can be seen as diminishing the sense of crisis and urgency that often propels radical political transformations. Agonistic respect, on this view, is little more than 'a release valve for the built-in tensions of contemporary capitalist-liberal democratic politics' (Vazquez-Arroyo 2004: 9). Democratic transformation of inegalitarian practices and structures often requires 'a more powerful challenge to the socio-economic structures of late capitalism, something that ... involves more than ... a practice of forbearance, especially when the latter includes those in charge of the oppressive structures that are in place' (Vazquez-Arroyo 2004: 12). Ultimately, in so far as it suspends these underlying questions of power, agonistic respect is arguably more compatible with a politics of reform than with radical social transformation.

In short, despite its claimed sensitivity to the visceral texture and nuances of social experience, Connolly's idea of ethico-political practice is in fact marked by a pervasive social weightlessness. In so far as it emphasizes individualized, existential dynamics detached from a systemic account of power, his ethical *modus vivendi* invokes 'a reified and ephemeral moment of equality' (Vazquez-Arroyo 2004: 11). This seems to confirm the view of Nancy Fraser (2001) and others that the turn to ethics should be postponed for as long as possible because of its erroneous construal of matters of inequality as matters of value and personal development. Connolly complains that one of the limitations of the academic left is that it fails to 'fold an existential dimension into its political appeals', and this leads to a dogmatic prescriptivism that is tone deaf to the affectual resonances that galvanize counter-hegemonic practices. One might refute this by saying that the left does indeed have a sense of the existential dimensions of being but, unlike Connolly's, it is an explicitly politicized one that understands personal experience as shaped, to some degree, by impersonal social structures. The difficulty with Connolly's ideas of the existential, the visceral, the affectual, is that they are not firmly enough grounded in an account of power and social location. Consequently, the ethos that is presented in generic psychological terms is in fact more likely to represent the perspective and experiences of relatively privileged social groups. Indeed, when Connolly talks about the experience of suffering, he does not present it in terms of deprivation and inequality, but prefers to use a language of generalized misery and 'existential resentment' (2005: 33). His justification for using these depoliticized and uncomfortably Nietzschean terms is that feelings of resentment and generosity do not coincide with social position: 'The distribution of ressentiment and gratitude for being . . . does not correspond neatly to any distribution of social positions' (Connolly 2005: 39). In a general, existential sense, this might be the case: all individuals undergo experiences of loss, vulnerability and hardship. But it is also unarguably the case that many other types of *social* suffering are not evenly distributed and afflict some groups far more than others. Deprivation of symbolic and material resources make it more difficult for certain groups of people to imbue their lives with meaning and purpose and to be able to transcend misfortune when it arises. It should surely be challenging and overcoming the latter that should be the central concern of a radical micro-politics, rather than the development of an ethics of self-cultivation that speaks mainly to those already in a position of privilege.

SUBALTERN POLITICAL PHILOSOPHY

Like Connolly, James Tully emphatically rejects the proceduralism that prevails in 'elite political theory' and proposes instead a practice-oriented mode of political thinking that is attuned to the everyday struggles of citizens against inequality and injustice. Following Foucault, Tully argues that, from Kant to Habermas, the 'universal intellectual' has envisaged her main task to be abstraction from 'specific juridical practices of morality and politics' in order to produce a discourse of 'universal norms and procedures definitive of the de-centred world view' (2008a: 104). This tradition is politically ineffective not just because of its formal nature but, in Tully's view, because it misrepresents 'other, non-juristic forms of knowledge, relations of power and practices of ethics in which we are constituted and governed as subjects' (2008: 104). The very practices that renew democratic politics, giving them relevance and direction, are too often disregarded by the juridical tradition as secondary, unimportant activities. The primary purpose of political theory is not to develop a comprehensive set of democratic procedures, because such top-down approaches finish by valuing the integrity of abstract models over concrete political action. Prioritization of theory over practice – what Wittgenstein describes as the 'craving for generality' – leads to the reification of the former, where the most important task for the theorist is upholding the validity of the model regardless of whether or not the logic of concrete struggle supports it. In this way, models of the political acquire a quasi-transcendental status that renders them immune from radical critique and revision. For Tully, political thinking must resist the drive to theoretical imperialism and, if it is to arrive at general conclusions at all, should try to derive them from close study of the practices and struggles of ordinary citizens against the 'practices of governance in the present that are experienced as oppressive in some way' (2008a: 16). In so far as it is possible, theory should aim to follow practice rather than vice versa.

Unlike Connolly, Tully develops his concern with the primacy of subaltern struggle not through ontological claims, but through a praxeological emphasis on the multiplicity of ordinary citizen practices or 'games of freedom' that make up social life. This entails neither a straightforwardly descriptive approach to concrete practices nor a simple inversion of the theory–practice hierarchy that asserts the validity of experience over formal knowledge. Rather, in so far as 'engaged public philosophy' grants primacy to practice over theory, it is necessarily a form of interpretative critique that scrutinizes prevailing norms and practices for potentially oppressive and inegalitarian entailments. Critical historical investigation into seemingly established modes of social being serves to denaturalize them and to suggest ways in which they might be progressively transformed or replaced by other, more emancipatory types of practice. The ultimate aim of such genealogical redescription is to contribute to a general process of citizen empowerment, to enable citizens to see 'possibilities of governing themselves differently' (Tully 2008a: 16). In this respect, critique has a practical allegiance to citizen struggles and is explicitly partisan: it is 'an interlocutory intervention on the side of the oppressed' (Tully 2008a: 17). This 'subaltern school' of public philosophy understands itself as a practical political intervention that aims to have a progressive impact both on how debates are pursued in political theory and on wider civic struggles. It is addressed to 'citizens who are engaged in ... struggles and seek assistance from university research. This is a communicative relationship of reciprocal elucidation and mutual benefit between public philosophy and public affairs' (Tully 2008a: 37).

Tully's formulation of public political philosophy not as disengaged reflection but as praxis, as a practical move in the struggle for freedom, has, for good reasons, been influential. He is one of few contemporary theorists who eschew the current concerns of the 'universal-juridical' tradition in favour of an open-ended, practice-oriented mode of theorizing. In David Armitage's words: 'At a moment when almost every major political philosopher of our time seems to be producing definitive, comprehensive accounts of justice *contra* Rawls, Tully's imposing project is distinctive for refusing to make justice its central focus' (2011: 125). Amongst other things, Tully's understanding of theory as situated practice suggests a revised account of the normative aims of political thought. Instead of impartial prescription, normativity takes the orthogonal approach of disclosure, of revealing other possible ways of being, the political relevance of which is established only through ongoing dialogue with others. The rejection of a legislative model also entails that theorists undertake a form of normative self-critique where the tacit norms and presuppositions that shape their own world-view are subject to critical scrutiny. As Tully puts it: 'The first and often overlooked step into any enquiry into justice ... [is] ... to investigate if the language in which the enquiry proceeds is itself just: that is, capable of rendering the speakers their due' (1995: 34). There is never a point at which this kind of inquiry is complete; rather, it constitutes the ongoing task of political theory as a perpetually unfinished process of practical engagement and critique.

Despite its interesting entailments for radical democratic thought, there is a significant sense in which Tully fails to enact this methodological insight about self-reflexive critique with regard to the project of subaltern political philosophy. Although he is rightly alert to the crypto-normative effects of supposedly neutral theoretical models on an understanding of political struggle, he in fact re-creates this problem in his own uncritical use of the idea of games of freedom. Following on from his earlier work on multiculturalism, Tully choses to thematize the idea of games of freedom through a reconfigured account of struggles for recognition. Even in this revised form, however, the idea of recognition is in fact more limiting than Tully acknowledges in that, as with Connolly, it commits him to a pluralistic model of power that misframes issues of social inequality as those of difference. As a result, there is an unresolved tension between Tully's avowed commitment to a subaltern politics, on the one side, and his investment in the general idea of games of freedom, on the other. In the end, the latter seems to suggest that what matters most is the plurality of games per se rather than a consideration of how some games are more effective than others in challenging inequalities.

GAMES OF FREEDOM AND RECOGNITION

Tully thematizes the idea of games of freedom partly following Wittgenstein's practice-based reworking of rationality and partly following Foucault's work on governmentality and practices of the self. Like other thinkers of democratic agonism, he rejects a formal account of citizenship that sees it as guaranteed by the possession of rights and duties, by agreement on comprehensive common goods and constitutional essentials or by consensus on universal norms. Such arrangements constitute the background framework for democratic participation, but citizenship must be understood primarily as a type of praxis where, in their engagement with authority, citizens modify or challenge the rules and norms through which they are governed. Tully depicts this praxis as game playing, action whose intrinsic creativity means that it is never completely rule-bound and always has the potential to exceed any institutional framework. These games of freedom should not be restricted to a sphere of properly political activity, as Arendt does, for instance. Rather, Tully takes from Foucault a broader, unbounded idea of contestatory citizen activity as a 'permanent provocation' that might take place anywhere, in any form and whose aim is to unsettle and challenge the normalizing games of truth through which individuals are governed (Tully 2008a: 144–5). Indeed, at the limit, the radical possibility always exists that games of freedom will initiate entirely new ways of speaking and acting. By contesting the legitimacy of the rules of the game itself, citizens may finish by overthrowing the established order: 'Accompanying the agonistic free play in any game of power, by which the rules of the game are continuously modified, is always the possibility of insubordination, of challenging the relation of power itself by escape or confrontation' (Tully 2008a: 125). These games or practices of liberty are constitutive of freedom itself. Freedom, as Foucault has it, is not an end state guaranteed by institutional or moral arrangements but an ongoing practice of contestation, a ceaseless questioning of the given, the ultimate aim of which is to open up spaces to 'think and act differently'.

The idea of citizen practice as permanent provocation means that for Tully there is little point in stipulating a priori either a specific zone or style of political engagement, as Mouffe does, or a necessary ethical predisposition, as Connolly does, for, likely as not, this will serve to set up tacit barriers to genuinely radical challenge. At one point, for example, Tully includes armed struggle in the possible forms that agonistic contestation may assume, something which Connolly's idea of restrained partisanship would find difficult to incorporate. If democratic freedom resides in the possibility of citizens being able to question the legitimacy of any given order or practice in any way whatsoever, then it follows that theory should strive to grant as much primacy as possible to the diverse, often unpredictable logic of concrete struggles. Clearly theorists cannot divest themselves entirely of theoretical and normative presuppositions and retreat into thick ethnographic description. Nonetheless this does not absolve her of the responsibility to resist the tendency to place herself above the *demos* in order to produce an authoritative theoretical solution to real-world practices. As a situated practice itself, public philosophy should itself engage in a process of critical contestation analogous to that of wider citizen practices and constantly scrutinize its urge to set up schematic and tacitly normalizing models of the political. Given these stipulations, it is curious that Tully choses to interpret citizen practices through a monist notion of struggles for recognition, which, despite significant revisions, is ultimately a normalizing construct. Although he is methodologically committed to an anti-universal, anti-systematic and fallibilist mode of political theorizing, he resorts to a model that ultimately explains all struggles according to dynamics of reciprocity, mutuality and dialogue. This misframing displaces from view systematically produced inequalities and consequently curtails the genealogical scrutiny of power that is supposedly the key feature of subaltern political philosophy.

To be sure, Tully is critical of conventional 'monological' models of recognition and revises the idea so as to render it compatible with ideas of democratic contingency and contestation. He replaces problematic notions of authenticity that underpin essentialist accounts of identity recognition, such as, say, Charles Taylor's, with an open-ended, constructivist account of identity formation. Recognition struggles are reconfigured as multidimensional; they exceed a dyadic structure, they may serve multiple political aims and they are never settled once and for all: 'It is not a game ... that aims at an end state or final goal but, rather, at the free activity of citizen dialogues ... over time and generations (Tully 2008a: 152). Tully also acknowledges more explicitly than other thinkers – Honneth, for example – that the act of recognition itself can be normalizing and that is why struggles for recognition must be understood as ongoing rather than as a single moment of acknowledgement. Recognition struggles are never just about issues of cultural identity but have a far wider political relevance. All struggles, even ones that appear to be only about matters of economic redistribution, have a recognition dimension in the sense that, in one way or another, they can be seen as struggles over the 'norms of mutual recognition through which the members ... of any system of action coordination (or practice of governance) are recognised and governed' (2008a: 293). Like Honneth, then, Tully universalizes recognition in so far as it is constitutive of the 'dialogical civic freedom of ... agents' (2008a: 292).

In the same moment, then, that Tully ostensibly de-essentializes the recognition paradigm, he also over-generalizes it as the single explanatory paradigm for all political struggle. Given his views on the practice sensitivity of theory, there is no obvious reason why Tully should prefer a uni-dimensional explanation to a multidimensional one that discriminates in some way between different types of struggle, as, for example, Fraser's distinction between redistribution and recognition does. Indeed, his inclusion of armed struggle as a type of dialogic negotiation exemplifies the loss of analytical precision that comes from stretching the idea of recognition so thinly. The question remains, as Armitage points out: 'How can his philosophy take account of widespread armed struggles driven by greed or grievance rather than directed strategically toward peaceful negotiation?' (2011: 127). Part of the problem is that, like other theorists of multicultural recognition, Tully's focus on the struggles of indigenous groups leads him to generalize this as the paradigm of conflict (2008a: 169). However, as a number of critics have pointed out, there is no easy translatability of one type of group struggle into another without running the risk of effacing specificity and misunderstanding the dynamics at play. Above all, systemically produced inequalities cannot be properly conceptualized through a fragmenting model of group difference and recognition. Armitage captures this dilemma as follows: 'How ... might Tully's public philosophy need to be reshaped or extended if the plight of the bottom billion were as close to the heart of its concerns as those of the 250 million or so Indigeneous peoples around the world?' (Armitage 2011: 127).

In short, recognition monism has reductive implications for Tully's understanding of power and inequality. There are certain forms of injustice and inequality whose essential dynamics are just not very well captured in the idea of the recognition for ultimately they have little to do with the norms that structure identity. Gender inequality, for instance, is often inaccurately presented as an issue of misrecognition when, in fact, this is fairly tangential to understanding the structural dynamics of distribution and lack of bargaining power that cause it. In many cases, 'revaluing' or recognizing women's work will not alter gender inequality; the focus on cultural valuation, in fact, tends to obscure the systemic mechanisms (low pay etc.) through which the injustice is perpetuated. Indeed some thinkers claim that the best way for women to escape a low-pay trap is to 'train up and marry down', and in this regard the 'recognition' and revaluation of women's labour may in fact be a hindrance in so far as it dulls the incentive for young women to adopt this strategy (Heath 2008: 202). In other words, framing gender inequality as, at some level, about the 'intersubjective negotiation of identity' captures little of significance about its essential dynamics or ways in which it may be overcome.

A key difficulty with Tully's depiction of political practice as games of freedom is that it passes over too quickly those individuals who are unable to participate in these games. The model seems to be intrinsically oriented to identifying those citizens who are already empowered and engaged in formal or informal processes of political contestation but not to those disempowered and dispossessed groups who are excluded from the game from the outset. In principle, such issues of domination and exclusion are central concerns for Tully, whose critical genealogy is attuned to exposing the difficulties that certain individuals have in making themselves heard within the prevailing norms of political discourse. He argues, for example, in a critique of Habermas and the language of constitutionalism, that even the most ostensibly inclusive and consensual forms of political dialogue often establish tacit norms that serve to deprive relatively disempowered actors of a political voice (Tully 1995, 2008a; also Owen 1999). Yet, despite this, there is an important sense in which Tully fails to consider sufficiently the adequacy of his own analysis of domination and the obstacles it presents to citizen participation in games of freedom.

Tully approaches the problem of domination through a distinction between citizens and subjects. When individuals are unable to participate in games of freedom, because, for instance, they experience political association as alien or imposed, then they must be defined as subjects rather than citizens, even though they may have the formal status of the latter. In such cases of domination, Tully maintains that subjects resort to other '*loci* of democratic participation that are available to them and in these forums they debate how they can reform the larger political association so they can get in or how they can secede from it. The larger political association tends to instability and disintegration, and it is held together by force and fraud' (2008a: 147). The problem with thinking about domination in this manner is that it is based on a notion of power as primarily an external, repressive force – in Tully's terminology, a 'straightjacket' (2008a: 216). Exogeneously imposed barriers prevent certain individuals participating as political equals, and this repression eventually forces them to challenge and possibly disrupt the prevailing order. Whilst this repressive logic might explain the lack of political voice in certain limit cases, it does not really explain other, indirect dynamics through which groups who are formally included within a political system are nonetheless persistently disregarded. Tully occasionally gestures towards these dynamics of symbolic violence, but in general he seems to fall back on a domination–resistance 'pressure cooker' model of power where sustained lack of recognition is held to eventually provoke a counter-mobilization on the part of minority groups (e.g. 2008a: 165–6). Many oppressed groups do not have the internal unity or common purpose, however, that enables them to mobilize in this fashion. Disempowered individuals often do not belong to a coherent subaltern community that acts as a haven and source of counter-hegemonic identity and mobilization.

By failing to seriously consider anything but the most obviously repressive dynamics of disempowerment, Tully, like Connolly, presupposes a certain degree of political agency on the part of oppressed groups that may not in fact be there. He claims, for instance, that when they are excluded from the dominant political speech community,

> Subjects turn to other communities of democratic discussion and dialogue available to them, centred on their language, culture, ethnicity. . . . As a result of being in on these local discussions,

> they identify with *this* community rather than the larger political association. In these forums they debate how they can reform the larger political association so they can 'get in' or how they can 'secede' from it'. (2008a: 165)

Whilst this might capture certain dynamics of group discrimination, it is not necessarily the case for other groups. There are forms of oppression and inequality that are fragmenting and isolating in their effects and consequently present significant, even insuperable, barriers to the kind of counter-hegemonic group mobilization that Tully presents as an almost inevitable countervailing effect of domination. Because of their internal divisions, many groups do not share a common language or vision in which to express their demands. Some types of chronic deprivation are difficult to give words to precisely because of their ongoing, diffuse nature. Long-term unemployment, for instance, 'persists as the context of the individual occurrences of their lives, almost as an "unconscious"; it over-shadows, poisons the sensuous living of their present. ... And it is this that makes it very difficult for the unemployed to know, and hence to speak about, what is happening to them' (Charlesworth 2000: 81). Difficulties with giving voice to oppression may be compounded by the sense of de-authorization that is often a characteristic of the linguistic habitus of members of dominated classes and groups. Lacking access to certain symbolically distinguished 'vocabularies of self-articulation', oppressed groups are often aware that they express themselves in a socially devalued manner, that they lack authority when they speak in a public or semi-formal situation. To quote Bourdieu: 'The sense of the value of one's own linguistic products is a fundamental dimension of the sense of knowing the place which one occupies in the social space' (1991: 82). It is perhaps ironic, then, that despite his avowed commitment to prioritizing the logic of practice, Tully leaves hanging such basic issues pertaining to the underlying social conditions necessary for equal and effective participation. As Robin Celikates says: 'The question how the diverse socio-economic and political conditions and the forms of structural violence to which people are differentially subjected on a global scale affect their political agency, their capacity to seize the always existing possibility of transformation and resistance, still remains' (2011: 266).

This shortcoming in Tully's account of power and agency points to a further problematic consequence of the recognition model of struggle, namely, a rather naïve faith in the reconciliatory and emancipatory properties of the 'open practice of dialogue'. He frequently presents political dialogue as the antidote to violence, as well as coercive and asymmetrical social relations, claiming, for instance, that 'dialogue is the form of human relationship in which mutual understanding and agreement can be reached and, hence, consent can replace coercion and confrontation' (Tully 2008a: 239). His faith in the redemptive force of dialogue has led a number of commentators to note that his work is perhaps closer than he cares to acknowledge to the ideas of deliberation that he explicitly opposes. Certainly, Tully is critical of the normalizing tendencies of rationalist models of deliberation which ultimately legitimate 'what is already known' rather than exploring possibilities for 'thinking and acting differently' (2008a: 95). In place of the reconstruction of validity claims, he works with an expanded, open-ended idea of political dialogue as the language of 'diverse citizenship', which encompasses a broader range of speech acts, including non-linguistic practices or the 'singular civic activities and improvisations of the governed' (Tully 2008b: 248). Despite these modifications, he continues to tacitly endorse a dialogic model of speech that, *inter alia*, underplays the effects of structural violence on disempowered groups. Bonnie Honig and Marc Stears (2011) note, for instance, that in his discussion of early intercultural dialogue between Euro-Canadians and Canadian aboriginals, Tully sees not only domination and genocide but also dynamics of mutuality and generosity that have subsequently been obliterated in the writing of history from the colonial perspective. It is undoubtedly admirable that Tully's construction of a counter-history recovers from these early treaties instances of a forgotten politics of equality and common interest that may prove instructive for contemporary democrats. Yet these treaties were also overwhelmingly instruments of domination and, in directing our attention away from this indubitable historical fact, he is in danger of underplaying the very issues of oppression and inequality which he claims are his main concern. There is the risk of sanitizing reality in order to render it compatible with a somewhat unjustified belief in the panacean force of dialogue. To quote Honig and Stears: 'Tully seems ... to assume as a condition of negotiation the very thing we cannot assume in real politics: the mutual respect whose absence is the reason we need negotiation in the first place. ... When Tully says that with recognition and then dialogue "consent can *replace* coercion and confrontation", he seems to be a bit dazzled by his own ideal' (2011: 198–9).

FREEDOM AND EQUALITY

Ultimately, Tully's 'romantic belief in the irenic force of dialogue' (Celikates 2011: 266) is symptomatic of a deeper problem, namely, whether he ingenuously over-estimates the transformative properties of games of freedom. Are the games of freedom played by ordinary citizens really sufficient to produce the far-reaching democratic transformations in the name of the oppressed that he claims? Is it not naïve to think that relatively disempowered groups have the capacity, as free subjects, not only to contest the rules of the game but ultimately to fundamentally challenge and transform the political game itself? To hold out this type of radical change as an ever-present possibility of ordinary citizen practice seems somewhat disingenuous as, arguably, it considerably under-estimates the barriers that prevailing institutions and established social inequalities pose to those groups mounting counter-hegemonic challenge. What really needs explaining is how a dispersed set of practices add up in a way that is sufficient to initiate genuinely transformative political action.

In the final analysis, the exaggerated radical force that Tully imputes to games of freedom is a consequence of his reliance on a one-dimensional account of power as pluralization. Like Connolly, he over-emphasizes an idea of social life as governed by a logic of pluralized difference, the intersection of which with entrenched forms of disempowerment and inequality remains largely unaddressed. This disconnection is exemplified in Tully's one-sided account of neoliberalism as a dispersed and de-centred mode of governance that is 'no longer . . . gathered together only or predominantly under the auspices of the formal governmental institutions' (2008a: 156). Neoliberal governance 'at a distance' operates through a process of disciplinary individualization where citizen behaviour is indirectly controlled through the proliferation of differences and apparent freedoms. Tully does not examine, however, how this pluralization of individual freedoms at one level takes place within a consumerist framework that inevitably intensifies inequalities between the affluent and the poor at another. Instead, he one-sidedly focuses on how the dispersion of modes of governance gives rise to a countervailing proliferation of possible sites of citizen resistance: 'Citizens have responded to the dispersion of practices of governance by participating directly at specific sites of struggle in order to democratise the global process that the formal democratic institutions fail to govern' (Tully 2008a: 157). The multiplication of possible ways of thinking and acting differently is not enough on its own to sustain a radical democratic politics oriented to the interests of subaltern and disempowered groups. Nor is adherence to a pluralistic world-view sufficient to guarantee a commitment to challenging inequality. Tully maintains, for instance, that 'nothing has changed more ... than the identities of men and women ... over the last twenty years as a result of their participation in ... negotiation for and against diverse forms of citizen participation' (2008a: 152–3). Whilst it is important not to under-estimate the significance of the civil and political liberties acquired by women in past decades, there is also much evidence to suggest that emergent forms of female autonomy have been accompanied by the deepening of old and new forms of gender subordination. Many feminists might suggest a more complicated picture than Tully where despite the formal freedoms and rights given to women and an apparent mitigation of sexual stereotypes, there has been little deep change in the gender division of labour, inequality in wages, the glass ceiling, violence against women, the over-representation of women as members of the global poor, and so on. The shift that Tully notes in gender identities is rendered more doubtful if we recall Fraser's claim that progressive ways of thinking about identity have been co-opted and, to varying degrees, de-radicalized by the rise of the recuperative new 'neoliberal' spirit of globalized capital. For Fraser this underscores the importance, in any assessment of gender equity, of connecting struggles against personalized subjection to a critique of the capitalist system, and it is such connections that Tully's pluralized model of power fails to make.

The descriptive inadequacy of Tully's pluralized conception of power flows from the normative skewing of his framework towards an over-emphasis on a vague notion of freedom unconnected to the critique of inequality. If an abstract value could be said to guide Tully's political thought, it is, on his own admission, a concern with freedom rather than justice: 'Questions of politics are approached as questions of freedom. . . . What are the possible practices of freedom in which free and equal subjects could speak and exchange reasons more freely over how to criticize, negotiate and modify their always imperfect practices?' (2008a: 38). In the immediate sense, this lexical ordering of 'freedom before justice' speaks to a methodological lapse on Tully's part in so far as it suggests the kind of a priori theoretical imposition that subaltern philosophy ostensibly rejects. Indeed, this failure of methodological self-reflexivity might in fact be regarded as an indication of a general underlying difficulty with his formulation of a practice-led form of political theory. Theory, by definition, can never be purely practice-led; the granting of primacy to practice is not an act of simple reflection but inevitably an interpretation guided by normative presuppositions, whether they be explicit or implicit. In Rainer Forst's words: 'If the task of critical public philosophy is . . . to be internally connected to emancipatory social movements, then it needs to have certain normative criteria for what counts as "emancipatory", what "injustice and oppression" mean, and how such phenomena can be identified' (2011: 119). Tully acknowledges the interpretative nature of his project, in principle, but fails, in practice, to pursue sufficiently the implications that the intrinsic connection between fact and norm have for his theoretical endeavours. As a result he often lapses into oversimplified dualisms of theory versus practice, resistance versus domination, subject versus citizen, that belie a far more complex social and political reality.

Behind this methodological lapse stands the issue of whether Tully's freedom before justice approach provides sufficient normative resources for a theory committed to the interests of the subaltern. At the most fundamental level, there seems to be a normative incompatibility between a political philosophy that speaks for the 'oppressed and exploited' and Tully's general paradigmatic investment in the idea of games of freedom. Holding up the possibility of thinking and acting differently as a political end in itself seems to impute an inherent emancipatory quality to the practice of game playing per se. It is not acting differently in itself, however, that ensures substantive freedom, but rather acting in a way that challenges and dismantles the entrenched asymmetries of power that exist between citizens, rendering some more free than others. Not all citizen practices are going to possess an equally progressive import in this regard; indeed, some may ultimately be compatible with normalizing modes of governance rather than disruptive of them. It is crucial, then, to discriminate between those games that challenge inequality and domination and those that do not. On what basis otherwise would it be possible to ensure, for instance, that the 'multiplicity of practices of governance' do not themselves become 'closed structures of domination'? The normative thrust of Tully's theory is clearly egalitarian, but it is undercut by his investment in the paradigm of games of freedom, which, developed through a limiting recognition monism, fails to focus sharply enough on issues of inequality. Tully may be reluctant to prioritize the abstract value of equality at the outset because, for him, it represents the kind of aprioristic imposition typical of the elite theory that he opposes. It is not necessary, however, to set out in advance a comprehensive 'positive' account of equality to ground his subaltern theory; a stronger, 'negative' sense of inequality would be sufficient to give him a systematic perspective in which to ground judgements. Without this, he comes dangerously close to proposing a freedom-centred theory that upholds the negative liberty of playing the game regardless of the positive emancipatory ends it serves: 'It values the *struggle* over recognition above the end to which the struggle aspires' (Fraser 2008: 332). A primary concern of radical democrats must be with equality, and, in Fraser's view, this necessitates the replacement of a 'freedom-theoretic' notion of struggle with a 'justice-theoretic' version: that is, one that interrogates the underlying asymmetries of power that form the backdrop to such struggles: 'A struggle over recognition cannot be considered a bona fide expression of freedom unless the antagonists are equally empowered to exercise their freedom in and through it' (2008: 332–3). To the extent that he fails to develop a stronger critique of power, Tully's freedom-theoretic view is in fact parasitic on the justice-theoretic view: 'The view of recognition as freedom maintains its critical-theoretical bona fides only insofar as it presupposes the view of recognition as a dimension of justice in the sense of participatory parity' (Fraser 2008: 333). This is a surely a judgement that Tully should strive to overturn in his otherwise important attempt to develop a subaltern political philosophy.

CONCLUSION

In conclusion, there is a paradoxical quality about the political theories of Connolly and Tully, for although, in a certain sense, they grant primacy to concrete practice and struggle, they are marked, in another, by a social weightlessness. They rely too heavily on a limited idea of power as pluralization that is insufficiently integrated with an account of power as structural inequality. As a result they place an exaggerated emphasis on the intrinsic vibrancy, flux and creativity of social life. Missing from these celebratory visions are some of the negative aspects of embodied being associated with the experience of domination and oppression that, in the end, may prevent individuals from acting in the innovative and dynamic manner Connolly and Tully envisage. In short, both presume too easily the existence of ready-made political agents.

The shortcomings in Connolly's account of power stem from too hasty a move from ontology to sociology. There is no doubt that an ontology of plenitude enables him to attribute a greater *prima facie* significance to the practices of everyday life than other agonist accounts of democracy grounded in ontologies of lack. But like these other theorists, he effects an ontological reduction where the logic of social action is extrapolated more or less directly from these supposedly prior foundational dynamics. Daily life is, however, not just a ceaseless flow of emergent being but also the place where individuals endure, often at great cost to their embodied well-being, the negative impact of social constraints. Put differently, the reliance on a paradigm of limitless plurality vitiates Connolly's commitment to progressive social transformation. The shortcomings in Tully's account of power stem not from ontology but from the model of games of freedom, which confines him to an account of power attuned to group rather than structural dynamics. The skewing of the model towards those already playing the political game, and not to those disempowered and dominated groups who, for a variety of reasons, are unable to do so, weakens the express commitment of his theory to the subaltern. Nonetheless, Tully's idea of subaltern political philosophy is methodologically significant because it represents one of few attempts to conceptualize radical democratic theory beyond the parameters of the current preoccupation with political ontology. Tully maintains, rightly in my view, that given its central concern with unmasking inequality, radical democratic theory should start from observation of social life rather than attempts to come up with definitive models of the political. From this starting point flow other entailments for radical democratic theory, including that it is interpretative and dialogic in nature, and that it operates through the indirect means of disclosing critique rather than explicit theoretical prescription. It is to such issues about the nature of radical democratic theory that I will now turn by way of conclusion.

Conclusion

Political Theory as Critique: Reconsidering the Negative

This book has made a case for the importance of strong links between radical democratic theory and a critical phenomenology of negative experience, exemplified in the idea of social suffering. Where it lacks such links, radical democratic theory is unable to substantiate in a meaningful fashion the claim that it is centrally concerned with the unmasking and overcoming of domination. It relies instead on abstruse accounts of radical action that are governed by an abstract, self-perpetuating logic and that fail to connect to the embodied existence of oppressed groups. It ends up trading in socially weightless ideas of the political that disregard key features of the experience of inequality; in particular, the way in which internalized structures of oppression may undermine the capacity for autonomous agency. When they are reproduced in the body, chronic inequalities may be realized as a habitus of disempowerment, as feelings of resignation, despair and vulnerability, which make it difficult for some individuals to act as autonomous political agents in their own interests. It would be unrealistic, of course, to expect the democratic theorist to provide a comprehensive model of political agency that anticipates all such negative social circumstances and possible barriers to action. But the type of symbolic violence that is the central focus of this book, namely, the internalization of objective asymmetries of power as subjective dispositions of powerlessness, is not a randomly distributed or particularly unusual feature of social existence. Arguably, the 'non-event of quiescence' is a relatively common and predictable existential feature associated with living in impoverished and oppressive social circumstances. Indeed, a number of commentators would argue that such sorts of disempowerment are intensifying in the contemporary world with the emergence of new forms of social marginality and precariousness that have been unleashed by neoliberal governance. Given this, it is surprising that radical democrats do not attend more closely to the depoliticizing effects of symbolic violence and instead take political agency as an unproblematic given (Shapiro 2007: 46). This presumption of agency is then compounded by the troubling tendency to conceive of agency through formal dynamics of plurality, contestation and flux regardless of how meaningfully they relate to the negative conditions that mark the lives of oppressed groups. A hiatus exists between the theoretical exhortation to embrace the apparently limitless possibilities of 'becoming' and the experiences of fixity, monotony and entrapment that often accompany subordination.

A root cause of this social weightlessness is, on my reading, the 'ontological' turn taken by a number of radical democrats in the belief that reflection on essential political dynamics – in the manner of Schmitt and Arendt — will engender a revivified understanding of possibilities for democratic action. The shared feature of these diverse political ontologies is a thorough-going anti-foundationalism; a radical indeterminacy is found to underpin social being, and the theoretical acknowledgement of this engenders a new perspective from which to challenge the supposedly fixed and inevitable features of existing democratic orders, no matter how seemingly inclusive. What Jean-Luc Nancy (2001) terms the 'coincidence of the political with the ontological' is understood to be key to unleashing a far-reaching expansion of the democratic imagination. There is no doubt that the premise of radical contingency has engendered significant new ways of thinking about democracy, particularly with regard to its agonistic aspects, but the shift to this ontological mode of conceptualizing the political also has troubling entailments. It sets radical democrats off on a misguided theoretical path that culminates in the effective detachment of political dynamics from social relations of power. The consequences of this separation are an unvindicated privileging of political over social life, a valorization of impersonal dynamics over experiential ones and the construal of radical agency as an empty process of flux and contestation rather than as embodied practice in the world. Essential questions of oppression, powerlessness and inequality that purportedly motivate radical democratic theory are treated as secondary, merely empirical issues or, worse, drop out of the picture altogether. In the end, the quest for a purified space of the political that would re-energize democratic thought and action is, in my view, misguided.

It is not that radical democrats should not seek to dislodge settled ways of thinking about the world and thereby disclose innovative new possibilities for political action. But whether ontology is the most theoretically convincing way of achieving this is moot. Ultimately, it is a task that may be more effectively undertaken through an examination of the social relations within which the political is always ineluctably entangled. Addressing such underlying issues of power is crucial to the realization of radical democracy as a project of intervention in the world rather than as a promissory note of transformative change always to come.

What, then, should the democratic theorist do in the face of such a negative critique as mine, given that the theoretical enterprise, by its very nature, involves abstraction away from concrete relations of power and consequently always runs the potential risk of their occlusion? Does a focus on embodied inequality necessarily undermine the theoretical enterprise of normatively informed and constructive generalization? Is the only alternative for the political theorist to restrict herself to a descriptive and potentially moralistic mapping of hidden forms of suffering and other unarticulated negative experiences? This supposed choice between positive theoretical construction and the negative critique of power is, from the Critical Theory perspective that informs this book, a false antithesis that obscures the inherent connection between fact and norm. Following thinkers such as Adorno and Honneth, I maintain that a focus on negative social experience, *qua* suffering, is an intrinsic part of political theory understood as disclosing critique. The idea of disclosure flows from the guiding principle of Critical Theory, namely, to produce an account of society that has the practical aim of unmasking domination and, in doing so, revealing possible paths to emancipation. Its founding premise is that capitalism is an exploitative and deeply irrational system and consequently has alienating, even pathological, effects upon the bodies and minds of its subjects. The job of the political theorist is to try to expose these insidious distortions as part of the attempt to overcome them, and it is in this regard that the notion of critique plays a central role. Disclosing critique aims to penetrate various types of domination, the ways in which symbolic forms are used to naturalize and legitimate exploitative and unequal social relations and, above all, to manufacture political quiescence. A central problem for critique is how a social system that can produce unjustifiable inequalities and degraded, heteronomous forms of life ensures the apparent passive consent of its subjects. It is by revealing these mechanisms of subjection that pathways to emancipation can begin, in part, to be thought about. On this view, then, suffering is not a moralistic or existential category denoting the finitude and general vulnerability of the human condition. Rather, it is a political category, where certain generic types of social suffering are understood to be the outcome of asymmetrical relations of power and, in so far as they are socially caused, are unjustified. As Adorno puts it: 'The need to lend a voice to suffering is a condition of all truth. For suffering is objectivity that weighs upon the subject; its most subjective experience, its expression, is objectively conveyed' (2005: 17–18).

The intertwining of fact and norm presumed in disclosing critique is distinct from the oppositional manner in which the relation is frequently construed in the ideal–real debate that currently preoccupies political theorists. On the one hand, in contrast to the ideal view of norms as, to some degree or another, independent of facts, disclosing critique stresses the ineluctably situated nature of normative judgements. Far from obscuring the search for moral principles, situatedness is its very condition of possibility; the negative moment of injustice is necessarily prior to and grounds the positive moment of justice. Sociological critique is always, then, inextricably interwoven with the positive moment of normative thought in so far as it holds that the kernel of emancipation lies within existing unfreedoms. On the other hand, against the realist view, the fact–norm dialectic serves as a reminder that the critique of power itself proceeds from a normatively informed account of the world. In this hermeneutic formulation, the world is always already pre-interpreted; there is no neutral, value-free standpoint on social 'reality'. It is a reflexive awareness of the inherent normativity of its own interpretative perspective that is often lacking in realist political theory. In their critique of the 'ethics-first' approach to democratic theory and countervailing emphasis on struggle and conflict as the ineliminable core of political action, realist thinkers often finish by simply inverting the ideal–real opposition. Consensus theories of democracy ignore the constitutive role of power struggles in political existence and, as a result of this idealization, render themselves irrelevant to the most pressing concerns of political life. The realist criticism is not without force, but it is not always clear what the status of the 'real' is that they appeal to in the attempt to forestall accounts of politics as applied ethics. In Christoph Menke's words: 'Philosophical realism cannot simply take the reality of its subject matter for granted; it must first reclaim and ensure that reality, or even produce it, through the very act of critique' (2010: 144).

This lack of reflexive clarity about the status of the 'real' is attested to in the divergent theories that are often bundled together under the label of realism, as if they all shared a coherent and overlapping account of power when in fact they do not. So, for example, in order to reject explicitly normative ideas of transformative action, Raymond Guess frequently invokes a Hobbesian scenario of 'real' politics as a perpetual struggle to maintain order in the face of the atavistic impulses of humanity. On the face of it, he is too familiar with Adorno's negative dialectics to explicitly resort to a naïve empiricism, but, nonetheless, his account of power remains unjustified and opaque. It is not clear why his bleak vision of the real should be regarded as more persuasive or compelling than any other account. In short, insufficient reflection on the suppositions that inform a particular depiction of reality can often go hand in hand with an 'overcautious conservatism' that blocks the radical reshaping of practices, ideas and institutions that usually form part of a radical democratic agenda (Stears 2005: 327). At the more optimistic end of the spectrum of realist thought, James Tully attacks the systematic moralism of ideal theory on the grounds that it fails to grasp the practical logic that guides political struggle. For Tully, political action is not about the application of pre-established ethical principles to a specific situation, but rather is a form of creative practice whose strategic and normative rationale is determined by the circumstances peculiar to any given fight against normalizing modes of governance. The rejection of rule-following ideas of action means that, for Tully, theory should, as far as possible, track practice and adopt an anti-universalist, non-systematic and fallibilist mode of reasoning. This is an interesting methodological proposition, but the assertion that theory follow practice is as potentially problematic as the idealized approaches it opposes in so far as it reinforces, from the other direction, a real–ideal dichotomy. Theory cannot simply follow or mirror real practices in any straightforward way. There is always an initial, often untheorized, moment of normative pre-judgement on the part of the theorist that influences which citizen practices are selected as examples of progressive 'games of freedom' and which are discounted as democratically 'unreasonable'. Tully does not always think this through sufficiently in relation to his own notion of practice-oriented theorizing. In short, fact and norm are bound up with each other in a way that exceeds the dichotomized separation that frequently seems to motivate debates over real versus ideal theory. To quote Rainer Forst: 'We always live in both worlds, the realm of practice and of reasons, which in fact are not two realms but just two aspects of social reality, and with Wittgenstein we should rid ourselves of the habit of only seeing one aspect at a time. We are . . . "transcending" beings as well as social beings, when we criticize our practices' (Forst 2011: 122).

While disclosing critique would go along some way, therefore, with the realist claim that normatively informed political theory should pay closer attention to social relations of power, it differs in its effort to achieve a greater methodological reflexivity in its reconstruction of 'reality'. It does this by making explicit, at the outset, the normative presuppositions that influence its reconstruction of social reality and also by acknowledging that its validity is open to challenge. It starts from the assertion that capitalism is an irrational and pathological system by virtue of the fact that it gives rise to systematic forms of suffering and injustice that it has the capacity to prevent. Experiences of suffering are not proof of anything in themselves; it is only in so far as they can be connected to the analysis and critique of power that they acquire political significance. As Erik Olin Wright puts it: 'It is not enough to show that people suffer in the world in which we live, or that there are enormous inequalities in the extent to which people live flourishing lives ... emancipatory theory must show that the explanation for this suffering and inequality lies in the specific properties of social institutions and structures' (2010: 7). It is of course possible to disagree with the soundness of this initial premise, and disclosing critique acknowledges the contestability of its world-view and any claims about injustice that might flow from it. A phenomenological emphasis on social suffering may be crucially important in bringing to light hidden types of oppression and unthematized social pathologies, but it does not in itself deliver the self-evident 'truth' of social injustice. By presenting a 'new description of social living conditions', disclosing critique attempts to shift the values and concepts that determine prevailing views of the world by evoking news ways of seeing. It recognizes, however, that the validity of any such redescription is always open to further debate, contestation and revision. Given the essentially rhetorical nature of the attempt to make 'something visible that would otherwise remain hidden in the horizon of accepted meanings', the relation of disclosing critique to truth must be understood, in the final instance, as indirect (Honneth 2007a: 60). It seeks to influence debates not through direct truth claims about the real, but through the 'attempt to change the preconditions under which a society conducts evaluative discourse on the ends of common action' (Honneth 2007a: 58). In this light, methodological reflexivity is especially important to ensure that, as far as possible, disclosing critique itself does not become yet another ideological mode of thinking: that is, one that reproduces the prejudicial beliefs that themselves reinforce or mystify unjust social hierarchies.

There is an undeniable circularity to this dialectic of fact and norm, but it is nonetheless instructive in so far as it confounds not only the schematic separation of ideal from real but also an analogous separation of the positive or constructive elements of theory from its negative ones. Theory as a positive enterprise is understood as the attempt to develop comprehensive models of democracy, whether they be normative in a first- or second-order sense or more thinly procedural in an agonistic sense of enshrining conflict. It is the scope of these models of democracy, the claim to universal applicability, rather than their content, that renders them constructive. As a negative enterprise, theory is used to describe those more 'limited' genealogical approaches that focus on the analysis of asymmetrical power relations. Again, however, this over-schematic division is questionable, not only because the 'negative' position is always invariably informed by normative judgement, but also because of the unfeasible nature of much so-called 'constructive' theory. This applies not just to the more outlandish thought experiments deployed in some ideal theory, but also to the political ontologies examined here whose relevance to the logic of social practice is often highly tenuous. Radical democratic theorists would explicitly reject an over-dichotomized separation of the real from the ideal, the negative from the positive, but, in the final analysis, their ontological formulations of the political push them into a form of abstraction that effectively reinstates such a separation. As Raymond Aron once put it:

> The term 'constructive' is applied even to projects that are unrealizable, and the term 'negative' to analyses which tend to delimit what is possible and to form political judgment – a judgment which is essentially historical in nature and must focus on the real or set itself an attainable objective. One is sometimes tempted to invert the hierarchy of values and to take the term 'negative' as a compliment. (quoted in Anderson 1998: 108)

If we pursue Aron's suggestion not just to invert the hierarchy of positive and negative but to deconstruct it, we might see that a negative approach does indeed have a constructive element, even though it does not necessarily take the form of a universally applicable model of democracy. It throws into question whether we really even need a fully fleshed-out constructive framework to orient ourselves politically in the world, suggesting instead that this might be achieved through the more minimal, so-called 'negative' identification of inequality and suffering. In other words, in so far as it complicates a simplified positive–negative distinction, it suggests a reconfigured approach to the structure of normativity. There is, as David Owen (2011) points out, a well-established, if diverse, intellectual tradition that regards political normativity in this more modest way, as a movement from the 'attained to the attainable' rather than as a 'teleological orientation' to an abstract or ideal model of some kind or another. On this view, the constructive element of political theory resides in the extent to which it inspires individuals to intervene in the world to change conditions of collective existence for the better. In this respect, a negative and limited focus on particular instances of inequality and oppression may be as persuasive and action guiding as other, supposedly more positive types of democratic theory.

What other features might a radical democratic theory possess that takes seriously the critique of social suffering? It may be more fruitful to adopt an approach that, at least in the first instance, is problem- rather than model-oriented. Radical democrats might do better to develop principles from an initial focus on specific issues of social inequality, rather than embark at the outset on a quest to distil the essence of the political and from this derive models into which all concrete struggles are subsequently shoehorned. Of course, any problem-oriented approach will unavoidably be 'influenced' by theoretical presuppositions, but it won't necessarily be as 'driven' by the rigid logic of the model that seems to flow from a one-sided focus on political ontology (see Shapiro 2007). It is, after all, a problem-oriented approach that has informed many other types of radical theorizing, such as feminism, and has made them suspicious of the formal abstractions of theory that disregard the distinctiveness of certain group experiences (e.g. Martineau and Squires 2012). Partly because of its established links with activism, feminist theorizing has more often than not been propelled, in the first instance, by particular problems relating to gender inequality and the marginalized experiences of women. Feminist political theorizing about justice, for instance, starts with the problem of the gendered division of labour, and the undervaluing of women's care work. It uses this sociological perspective to expose the conceptual deficiencies of asocial individualism as a device for deriving principles of justice because of the way it obscures human vulnerability and dependency and thereby fails to recognize care as a fundamental element of social justice (Bubeck 1995; Fraser 1997; Kittay 1999). Others feminists think through issues of democratic participation starting from the problem of the underrepresentation of women in established democratic structures, their effective political invisibility, which is a consequence of their vulnerable position as workers in transnational production processes (e.g. Fraser 2008; Phillips 1991).

The hope is that a problem-oriented approach to radical democratic theorizing is less likely to result in the marginalization of the actual and disregard of distinctive group experiences than are approaches oriented to the issue of ontology. The difficulty with the latter approaches is that the strategy of temporarily bracketing off social relations in order to capture the essence of the political turns into a theoretical inability to reintroduce excluded issues of power without violating the pristine foundational logic that they claim to have identified. Consequently, the logic of political ontology is given an unwarranted primacy that effectively occludes the autonomy and specificity of social relations and practices. Differently put, in so far as it lacks a sense of mediation, this political anti-essentialism becomes an essentialism. Thus, Mouffe is unable to address substantive issues about power that have a direct bearing on her model of democratic agonism because of a misplaced fear of falling into an essentialism that would violate her rigid linguistic constructivism. Arendtian ideas of political action as creative inauguration are famously empty, proscribing many issues of subordination and oppression by relegating them to the realm of social necessity and, therefore, privacy. Although his ontology of abundance is more materialist in nature, Connolly finds it hard to incorporate types of social experience or practice that do not conform to his notions of creative becoming and dynamic assemblages. In all these cases, social being is treated in a tokenistic and cipher-like fashion as simply yet another empirical exemplification of foundational dynamics of indeterminacy. Although it is not abstraction per se that causes socially weightless thinking, it may be that radical democratic theory may be better placed to think about oppression by deploying abstractions that are, at least in the first instance, sociological rather than philosophical in nature. The aim of grounding political theory in sociological reconstruction rather than ontological construction would be to, in Charles W. Mills's words, 'reflect the specificities of group experience, thereby potentially generating categories and principles that illuminate rather than obfuscate the reality of different kinds of subordination' (2005: 173; also Honneth 2012: 46–8).

An obvious entailment of the claim that radical democratic theory should be based in an initial process of sociological reconstruction is that it should be interdisciplinary in nature. Critical theorists have long insisted on the interdisciplinary nature of critique, that it is, by its very nature, a '"homeless" form of inquiry', situated somewhere between political and social theory (Kompridis 2004: 342). Some, like Honneth (2007a), even reject any clear demarcation of the two disciplinary domains, preferring to use the term 'critical social philosophy' to designate emancipatory theory. The claim is that when intellectual inquiry is contained within a single discipline unified by received assumptions about how to proceed, there is no imperative for critical self-reflection and it runs the risk of becoming reified. Thought on emancipatory social change is best advanced, therefore, through a dialogue with different modes of inquiry. This engenders a theoretical responsiveness to concrete political struggles and also, in the effort to reach understanding, forces critical reflection upon one's own theoretical and methodological presuppositions. It has not been my purpose to explore in detail the numerous methodological issues that arise in connection to the stipulation that emancipatory theory should be self-consciously interdisciplinary in nature. I do, however make one specific claim in this regard arising from the focus on agency, namely, that it is vital for radical democratic theory to include an interpretative perspective on embodied being. The social conditions necessary for engendering effective agency are not, I maintain, issues of peripheral concern to radical democratic theory, but go to the heart of its critique of power and its belief that the source of democratic renewal lies in the practices and struggles of ordinary citizens. A phenomenology of embodied being is invaluable because it reveals a substrate of 'ordinary violences' and unthematized suffering that often drops below the radar of mainstream political theory and that, given the concern with oppression, is important for radical democrats to take into account. It brings into relief, amongst other things, some of the barriers to agency that arise when enduring inequalities are internalized by oppressed groups as dispositions of disempowerment. Radical democratic theory should not presume the existence of ready-made political agents; indeed, it criticizes other types of normative theory for doing precisely this. It follows therefore that it should be obliged to consider some of the relatively predictable obstacles and barriers that hinder the emergence of effective agency amongst disempowered groups. Indeed, this task numbers among one of the three that Erik Olin Wright lists as fundamental to emancipatory thought, along with elaborating a systematic diagnosis and critique of the world and envisioning viable alternatives. It would be unrealistic to expect any single theory to carry out all three functions, and in different times and places one or another of them may be more pressing than the others, but 'all are necessary for a comprehensive emancipatory theory' (Wright 2010: 10). It is the case that the emphasis here has been not on empowerment but on disempowerment; nonetheless, it is in its contribution, albeit narrow in focus, to this task of 'understanding the obstacles, possibilities, and dilemmas of transformation' (Wright 2010: 10) that the value of a phenomenology of negative social experience is understood to lie.

The eschewal of an interpretative perspective on embodied being is by no means peculiar to the thinkers considered here but reflects a wider scepticism, shared by post-identity political theorists of different stripes, who associate a focus on experience with the shibboleths of essentialism, subjectivism and a reductive identity politics. This conflation of the experiential with a solipsistic suffer-mongering is over-hasty and fails to appreciate the intrinsic connections, theorized by Bourdieu amongst others, between embodied being, social location and power. Lacking such a socio-centric perspective on embodiment, radical democratic theorists proffer ideas of agency which, while they might follow the necessary logic of ontology, do not necessarily have relevance to actual social practice. Their formulations of democratic agency are either so thin or so exoticized that it is hard to see how they relate meaningfully to the experiences of oppressed and marginalized groups. Why, for example, are agonistic strategies of contestation and conflict regarded as particularly productive or even easily accessible for disempowered subjects who might find such ways of proceeding profoundly alienating? Or, for instance, what purchase do ideas of agency as flux and becoming have on the very different logic that governs projects of social empowerment such as, say, the worker-owned Mondragon cooperative in Northern Spain or participatory city budgeting in Porto Alegre, Brazil (e.g. Wright 2010)? There might well be a connection, and such ungrounded ideas of agency may in fact have emancipatory potential, but to make this evident they undoubtedly need to be thought through more carefully according to the tendencies of power in the world rather than those of a socially weightless ontology.

My conclusion is that the radical democratic search for the political is misguided ultimately because there is no single foundational rationality or essence to be uncovered. In this regard I agree with Rancière's anti-ontological assertion that the political is 'never pure, never based on some essence proper to the community and the law' (1999: 61). The difficulty is that, while he exposes the limitations of conceptualizing the political through ontology, he has an insufficient account of power with which to develop his alternative idea beyond an etiolated notion of egalitarian rupture. Once radical democratic theory is informed by a critique of power, then it becomes difficult to subscribe to the quest for a singular political space or underlying rationality. Instead, the political is understood, in a Foucauldian fashion, as a potential immanent in a multiplicity of social practices that may take a variety of forms, is not confined to a single space and does not have a single underlying rationale. This does not necessarily mean a dissolution of political space into social space. Rather, it is to follow a number of other thinkers who advocate multidimensional ideas of the political as divergent, sometimes overlapping networks of formal and informal practice, of strategies of contestation and empowerment, dynamics of struggle and agreement. The idea of disclosing critique does not undermine the enterprise of political theory, but it does undoubtedly suggest a different way of going about the job of theorizing. On my account, it suggests an approach that is dialogical, interdisciplinary, problem- rather than model-centred and includes an interpretative element. Its aim is not to delineate a definitive framework or rationale for emancipatory democratic action but rather is more aptly conceived as a contribution to the ongoing project of challenging oppression. In this light, it might be more productive to envisage the task of radical democratic theory as the sketching of pathways of social empowerment. This idea, used by thinkers in the Real Utopias project, bypasses what Tully calls the 'myth of finalism' that encumbers some types of democratic thought and suggests instead a more open-ended and exploratory approach to theorizing. To quote Wright: 'The best we can do ... is treat the struggle to move on the pathways of social empowerment as an experimental process in which we continually test and retest the limits of possibility' (2010: 270). Political theory, on this view, becomes akin to an ongoing conversation rather than the polemical clash of one model of democracy against another. This is admittedly, on first sight, a less ambitious and decisive way of proceeding than reflection on the putative foundations of political being, but it ultimately might prove to be a more fruitful one for radical democrats.

In response, some might say that the mapping out of pathways of empowerment still requires a general sense of the overall direction of travel, and this is where the value of models of the political could be seen to lie. Given its primarily negative orientation, critique must necessarily be complemented by an overarching framework which gives a purposive significance to concrete political action. I do not deny this, and critique does not ultimately undermine general paradigms as much as insist on them being theorized in conjunction with an account of power. The difficulty with such overarching models is, however, that they can quite easily slip into closed totalities – an imperialism of the political – that oscillate around their own distilled dynamics to the detriment of an engagement with the social world. Moreover, there is the question of the openness of the future; any model of the political cannot possibly encompass in advance the full range and nature of the struggles that might emerge. Models, of course, can be revised in the light of events that throw into question some of their underlying premises; however, usually this does not seem to happen. Too often the model is reasserted and stretched even further to explain all empirical instances. This is especially the case with political ontologies, which, in virtue of their supposedly foundational nature, are particularly amenable to being endlessly expanded in the face of conflicting practices that are thereby consigned to the uninteresting realm of the social and the merely given. So, in conclusion, perhaps the negative moment of disclosing critique might get us further along the road of radical democratic thinking than is generally assumed to be the case. What Bourdieu regards as thinking in accord with the tendencies of the world arguably is a theoretical strategy that has impact and urgency and is more effective in an action-guiding sense than a strategy based on the socially weightless premise of the radical contingency of being. It reminds us, in the words of Adorno, that 'suffering ought not to be, that things should be different' (2005: 203).

Notes

CHAPTER 1 SUFFERING AND SOCIAL WEIGHTLESSNESS

1 The inspiration behind this unpacking of the illusion of 'socially weightless' thought is traced back not to Marx – as one might expect – but to Pascal and, in particular, to his idea that 'true philosophy makes light of philosophy'. Bourdieu finds in Pascal a concern, devoid of populist naïvety, for ordinary people and for their practical activities, which are unencumbered by the delusions of those who misrecognize their positions of social privilege as evidence of their superior capacity for enlightened thought.
2 Bourdieu cites as an example of this Clifford Geertz's description in *The Interpretation of Cultures* of a Balinese cock fight, where Geertz '"generously" credits the Balinese with a hermeneutic and aesthetic gaze which is none other than his own' (Bourdieu 2000: 52).
3 In Bourdieu's view, even the most ritualized and repetitive of actions are necessarily linked to time by their movement and duration. It is the particular temporality of the process of gift exchange, for example, that makes it possible to understand how it operates as a form of symbolic domination. The 'euphemized violence' of the process resides in the contradiction between the experienced truth of the gift as a gratuitous act and its objective truth as a stage in a relation of exchange. It is the interval between the giving of the gift and its reciprocation which establishes hierarchical relations. Over-eagerness in responding can be a sign of dependence; a delayed or non-response can be a sign of subordi-

nation and indebtedness or, conversely, it can be seen as a snub to the giver. The atemporal categories of the scholastic perspective obscure the polysemous temporality of the gift by considering 'monothetically', that is, in simultaneity, a process which unfolds 'polythetically', that is, in succession and discontinuities (Bourdieu 2000: 56).

4 For example, Bourdieu discerns a problematic version of linguistic universalism in Judith Butler's work on the performative, where the material inequalities and economic exclusions constitutive of gender hierarchies are foreclosed by the narrow focus on the symbolic construction of sexual identity: 'It is naïve, even dangerous to suppose and suggest that one only has to "deconstruct" these social artefacts in a purely performative celebration of "resistance" in order to destroy them' (Bourdieu 2000: 108).

5 This, of course, raises the potentially uncomfortable question of the position from which Bourdieu speaks and which, to a degree, draws upon the authority imputed to the impartial perspective of the scholar in order to legitimate itself. Bourdieu recognizes the possibility of such a performative contradiction: 'The sociologist might seem to be threatened with a kind of schizophrenia, in as much as he is condemned to speak of historicity and relativity in a discourse that aspires to universality and objectivity' (2000: 93). This scholastic double-bind can only be circumvented through a thoroughgoing reflexivity understood as a process of historical objectivization which, by uncovering underlying material conditions, relativizes scholastic claims to universal impartiality. (For a more extensive discussion of reflexivity, see Bourdieu 2000: 118–22.)

6 Adorno and Horkheimer (1972) lose this emancipatory foothold in the 'actual' with their 'negativist' turn, where they abandon any hope in the continued relevance of working-class, or indeed any popular, struggle as a harbinger of progressive social change. Although his Critical Theory has more positive implications vis-à-vis the possibility of progressive social change than are to be found in Adorno and Horkheimer, Habermas also loses this grounding in pre-theoretical experience in so far as his theory of communicative ethics takes its cue from abstract linguistic capacities rather than the embodied experience of injustice.

7 Habermas would of course deny this charge and claim that the normative ideal of communicative ethics is grounded in a deep sociological understanding of the power dynamics and inequalities of capitalist democracies. Precisely because it is grounded in reconstructive social theory, Habermas maintains that he

produces a theory of justice which is normatively more robust and encompassing than that, say, of Rawls, which, because it is grounded in the acceptability of logically correct arguments rather than in an account of existing social inequality, overlooks crucial aspects of oppression. As evidence of the weakness of this logical abstraction, Habermas (1998) criticizes Rawls for his unnecessary reliance upon the bracketing device of the original position and the veil of ignorance to structure deliberation about the first principles of a just society. He claims that communicative deliberation is normatively stronger and more inclusive precisely because it does not block off the facts of the 'real world', because it starts from the actuality of conflicting views and deep differences and does not need to resort to such devices of information deprivation in order to achieve consensus. In short, communicative ethics accepts the intertwinement of fact and norm and is firmly embedded in a sociological awareness of empirical inequalities and deep differences between individuals. Despite these claims there are many different ways in which communicative ethics disregards and underplays certain phenomenal realities of oppression that may impede the smooth progress of communicative deliberation (see McNay 2008b).

8 Neoliberalism is not just a set of globalized free market policies but a more insidious political rationality which 'governs the sayable, the intelligible and the truth criteria of these domains' (Brown 2006: 693). It is of course Foucault (2008) who compellingly develops this idea of neoliberalism as a form of political reason or governmentality and focuses in particular on the restructuring of the self around moralized notions of responsible self-management. Foucault calls this neoliberal strategy of governance 'self as enterprise', where, in accordance with its marketized view of social relations, the individual is construed as an 'entrepreneur' of his or her own life, who relates to other individuals as competitors and his own being as a form of human capital. A distinctive feature of self as enterprise is that it operates according to a principle of active self-regulation rather than, on the Frankfurt School's account, one of passive submission that eliminates the capacity for autonomous thought and critique. In this self-relation, individual autonomy is not an obstacle or limit to social control but one of its central technologies. Discipline and freedom are not opposites but intrinsically connected in that biopower indirectly organizes individuals in such a way that their apparent autonomy is not violated but is used as a vehicle of governance at a distance.

CHAPTER 2 THE UNBEARABLE LIGHTNESS OF THEORY: MOUFFE'S DISSOCIATIVE AGONISM

1 Many of these criticisms have been incorporated, to varying degrees, into the deliberative paradigm by thinkers who have sought to more explicitly include expressive and affectual dimensions within an enlarged notion of public debate. In the light of these revisions, critics such as George Crowder argue that Mouffe both exaggerates the rationalist tendencies of liberalism (forgetting, for instance, thinkers such as Mill, who conceives of political practices as experiments in living) and also, in her countervailing assertion of politics as affect, fails to appreciate that the stress on reasoned deliberation enshrines the important insight that individuals are autonomous beings capable of critical reflection upon their beliefs and actions no matter how passionately they adhere to them. Yet Mouffe's critique of rationalism is not so easily dealt with by deliberative thinkers; its implications are more radical than those of simply expanding debate to include non-rational styles of expression or a general theory of citizen virtue.

2 Care, or rather its deficit, is one of the central problems facing both traditional and post-traditional societies, and understanding its complex ramifications involves a multidimensional analysis that connects the affectual and psychological dynamics of care work to a broader account of gender and class inequalities, which themselves must be situated in the context of global trends in migration. An increasing population of elderly, the growing entry of women into the workforce and the neoliberal privatization of types of social provision previously provided by the welfare state are amongst the factors that have led to the emergence of care deficits in Western democracies. These deficits have been filled to a large extent by the migration of female workers from poorer countries, which, whilst providing them with much-needed employment, also compounds certain patterns of gender and race inequality. Migrant labour is cheap and this exerts a downward pressure on an area already characterized by low pay for its predominantly female workers. The privatized nature of many of these migrant solutions also creates new inequalities of class and gender around a distinction between care commanders and care providers. As a result of female migration to rich countries, poorer countries are drained of a supply of emotional labour, leaving them also with a care deficit whose effects are as much psychological as material (see, e.g., Hochschild 2000; Lynch et al. 2009).

3 She levels a similar criticism at other thinkers such as Levinas, Butler and Derrida whose 'postmodern' ethics run the risk of emptying agonism of its antagonistic elements: 'as if once we had been able to take responsibility for the other . . . violence and exclusion could disappear' (Mouffe 2000: 134).

CHAPTER 3 FREEDOM BEYOND THE SUBJECT: FEMINISM, AGENCY AND AGONISM

1 Allen compares Arendt's response to that of Ralph Ellison, who disagreed publicly with her on the Little Rock episode. He argued that not only were the parents' actions heroic but they also exposed, in a stark way, the sacrificial logic that defines the daily experience of being a black American citizen: 'Since democracy claims to secure the good of all citizens, those people who benefit less than others from particular political decisions, but nonetheless accede to those decisions, preserve the stability of political institutions. Their sacrifice makes collective democratic action possible' (Allen 2005: 37). Allen claims that the difference between their respective views is illustrative of a general theoretical difference between understanding inequality through a logic of inclusion and exclusion (Arendt) and through that of domination (Ellison). The latter, in Allen's view, has far greater purchase in explaining the complexities of racial injustice. Arendt's position is troubling because although she thinks inclusion within the political sphere is vital to overcoming inequality, she maintains that it is inappropriate to use the social issue of racial identity to force entry into that sphere. Ellison's interpretation, however, is more nuanced and less condemnatory because it acknowledges a continuity between social and political practices and also the complex way in which dynamics of domination operate on subjects who are already, in some senses, included within a political order. According to Allen, Arendt relies on a simplistic dualism of inside and outside, where undoing injustice is regarded as a process of bringing the excluded and invisible into the political sphere and into citizenship practices that are already 'up and running and presumed to be reasonably decent' (2005: 55). The problem for Allen is that the term 'exclusion':

> (1) works against attending to the agency of the dominated; if anything it reduces their agency; (2) implies that the citizenly

Note to p. 164

habits of people who are inside the public sphere are fundamentally healthy; and (3) encourages, as the best way to deal with a past injustice, prescription of a policy of education, wherein those who have been excluded must be educated in the healthy habits that have been developed with the political sphere and must assimilate those habits. (2005: 60–1)

CHAPTER 4 ALL OR NOTHING: RANCIÈRE'S RUPTURAL AGONISM

1 Remarks made by Karma Nabulsi on the Arab Spring, Bernard Williams Day, University College, Oxford, 16 April 2011.

References

Adorno, T. (2005) *Minima Moralia: Reflections on a Damaged Life*. London: Verso.
Adorno, T. and Horkheimer, M. (1972) *Dialectic of Enlightenment*. New York: Herder and Herder.
Alcoff, L. (1991) 'The Problem of Speaking for Others'. *Cultural Critique* 20, 5–32.
→Alcoff, L. (2006) *Visible Identities: Race, Gender and the Self*. Oxford: Oxford University Press.
→Allen, A. (2008) *The Politics of Our Selves: Power, Autonomy, and Gender in Contemporary Critical Theory*. New York: Columbia University Press.
Allen, D. (2005) 'Invisible Citizens: Political Exclusion and Domination in Arendt and Ellison', in S. Macedo and M. Williams, M. (eds) *Political Exclusion and Domination*. New York: New York University Press.
Anderson, B. (1998) *Raymond Aron: The Recovery of the Political*. Lanham, MD: Rowman and Littlefield.
Arendt, H. (1958) *The Origins of Totalitarianism*. Orlando, FL: Harcourt Brace.
Arendt, H. (1973) *On Revolution*. Harmondsworth: Penguin.
Arendt, H. (1999) *The Human Condition*. Chicago: University of Chicago Press.
Armitage, D. (2011) 'Probing the Foundations of Tully's Public Philosophy', *Political Theory* 39 (1), 124–30.
Bader, V. (2007) 'Misrecognition, Power and Democracy', in B. Van Den Brink and D. Owen (eds) *Recognition and Power: Axel Honneth*

and the Tradition of Critical Social Theory. Cambridge: Cambridge University Press.

Bader, V. and Engelen, E. (2003) 'Taking Pluralism Seriously: Arguing for an Institutional Turn in Political Philosophy', *Philosophy and Social Criticism* 29 (4), 375–406.

→ Badinter, E. (2006) *Dead-End Feminism*. Cambridge: Polity.

Badiou, A. (2005) *Metapolitics*. London: Verso.

Bauman, Z. (2001) *The Individualized Society*. Cambridge: Polity.

Bennett, J. (2010) *Vibrant Matter: A Political Ecology of Things*. Durham, NC: Duke University Press.

Benhabib, S. (2002) *The Claims of Culture: Equality and Diversity in the Global Era*. Princeton: Princeton University Press.

Bensaid, D. (2009) 'Permanent Scandal', in G. Agamben, A. Badiou, D. Bensaid and W. Brown, *Democracy in What State?* New York: Columbia University Press.

Berlant, L. (2000) 'The Subject of True Feeling', in S. Ahmed, J. Kilby, C. Lury, M. McNeil and B. Skeggs (eds) *Transformations: Thinking through Feminism*. London: Routledge.

Bernstein, J.M. (2005) 'Suffering Injustice: Misrecognition as Moral Injury in Critical Theory', *International Journal of Philosophical Studies*, 13 (3), 303–24.

Bickford, S. (1997) 'Anti-Anti-Identity Politics: Feminism, Democracy, and the Complexities of Citizenship', *Hypatia* 12 (4), 111–31.

Boltanski, L. and Chiapello, E. (2007) *The New Spirit of Capitalism*. London: Verso.

Bosteels, B. (2009) 'Thinking, Being, Acting: Or, On the Uses and Disadvantages of Ontology for Politics', in C. Strathausen (ed.) *A Leftist Ontology: Beyond Relativism and Identity Politics*. Minneapolis: University of Minnesota Press.

Bourdieu, P. (1990a) *In Other Words: Essays towards Reflexive Sociology*. Cambridge: Polity.

Bourdieu, P. (1990b) *The Logic of Practice*. Cambridge: Polity.

Bourdieu, P. (1991) *Language and Symbolic Power*. Cambridge: Polity.

Bourdieu, P. (2000) *Pascalian Meditations*. Cambridge: Polity.

Bourdieu, P. (2001) *Masculine Domination*. Cambridge: Polity.

Bourdieu, P. and Wacquant, L. (1992) *An Invitation to Reflexive Sociology*. Cambridge: Polity.

Bourdieu, P. et al. (1999) *The Weight of the World: Social Suffering in Contemporary Society*. Cambridge: Polity.

Brown, W. (1995) *States of Injury: Power and Freedom in Late Modernity*. Princeton: Princeton University Press.

Brown, W. (2001) *Politics out of History*. Princeton: Princeton University Press.
Brown, W. (2002) 'Suffering the Paradoxes of Rights', in W. Brown and J. Halley (eds) *Left Legalism/Left Critique*. Durham, NC: Duke University Press.
Brown, W. (2006) 'American Nightmare: Neoliberalism, Neoconservatism and De-Democratization', *Political Theory* 34 (6), 690–714.
Brown, W. and Halley, J. (eds) (2002) *Left Legalism/Left Critique*. Durham, NC: Duke University Press.
Bryant, L., Srnicek, N. and Hartman, G. (eds) (2011) *The Speculative Turn: Continental Materialism and Realism*. Melbourne: re.press.
Bubeck, D. (1995) *Care, Gender and Justice*. Oxford: Clarendon Press.
Butler, J. (1997) *The Psychic Life of Power*. Stanford: Stanford University Press.
Butler, J. (2000a) *Antigone's Claim: Kinship between Life and Death*. New York: Columbia University Press.
Butler, J. (2000b) 'Ethical Ambivalence', in M. Garber, B. Hanssen and R.L. Walkowitz (eds) *The Turn to Ethics*. London: Routledge.
Butler, J. (2002) 'What is Critique? An Essay on Foucault's Virtue', in D. Ingram (ed.) *The Political*. Oxford: Blackwell.
Butler, J. (2008) 'Taking Another's View: Ambivalent Implications', in A. Honneth, J. Butler, R. Guess, J. Lear and M. Jay, *Reification: A New Look at an Old Idea*. Oxford: Oxford University Press.
Cavell, S. (1990) *Conditions Handsome and Unhandsome: The Constitution of Emersonian Perfectionism*. Chicago: University of Chicago Press.
Celikates, R. (2011) 'Review of Public Philosophy in a New Key', *Constellations* 18 (2), 264–6.
Chambers, S. (2011) 'Jacques Rancière and the Problem of Pure Politics', *European Journal of Political Theory* 10 (3), 303–26.
Charlesworth, S. (2000) *A Phenomenology of Working-Class Experience*. Cambridge: Cambridge University Press.
Cheah, P. (2006) *Inhuman Conditions: On Cosmopolitanism and Human Rights*. Cambridge, MA: Harvard University Press.
Chodorow, N. (1989) 'What is the Relation between Psychoanalytic Feminism and the Psychoanalytic Psychology of Women?', in D.L. Rhode (ed.) *Theoretical Perspectives on Sexual Difference*. New Haven: Yale University Press.
Connolly, W.E. (1993a) *The Augustinian Imperative: A Reflection on the Politics of Morality*. Lanham, MD: Rowman and Littlefield.
Connolly, W.E. (1993b) 'Democracy and Territoriality', in F.M. Dolan and T.I. Dunn (eds) *Rhetorical Republic: Governing Representation*

in American Politics. Cambridge: University of Massachusetts Press.

Connolly, W. E. (1998) 'Rethinking the Ethos of Pluralization', *Philosophy and Social Criticism* 24 (1), 93–102.

Connolly, W.E. (1999) *Why I Am Not a Secularist*. Minneapolis: University of Minnesota Press.

Connolly, W.E. (2000) 'Secularism, Partisanship and the Ambiguity of Justice', in E. Portis, E. Gundersen and R. Shively (eds) *Political Theory and Partisan Politics*. New York: SUNY Press.

Connolly, W.E. (2004) 'The Ethos of Democratization', in S. Critchley and O. Marchart (eds) *Laclau: A Critical Reader*. London: Routledge.

Connolly, W.E. (2005) *Pluralism*. Durham, NC: Duke University Press.

Connolly, W.E. (2006) 'Immanence, Abundance, Democracy?', in L. Tønder and L. Thomassen (eds) *Radical Democracy: Politics between Abundance and Lack*. Manchester: Manchester University Press.

Connolly, W.E. (2008) 'Interview with William Connolly', in D. Campbell and M. Schoolman (eds) *The New Pluralism: William Connolly and the Contemporary Global Condition*. Durham, NC: Duke University Press.

Connolly, W.E. (2010) 'Materialities of Experience', in D. Coole and S. Frost (eds) *New Materialisms: Ontology, Agency and Politics*. Durham, NC: Duke University Press.

Connolly, W.E. (2011) *A World of Becoming*. Durham, NC: Duke University Press.

Connolly, W.E. and Strathausen, C .(2009) *A Leftist Ontology: Beyond Relativism and Identity Politics*. Minneapolis: Minnesota University Press.

Coole, D. (2005) 'Rethinking Agency: A Phenomenological Approach to Embodiment and Agentic Capacities', *Political Studies* 53, 124–42.

Coole, D. and Frost, S. (2010) 'Introducing the New Materialisms', in D. Coole and S. Frost (eds) *New Materialisms: Ontology, Agency and Politics*. Durham, NC: Duke University Press.

Cooper, D. (2004) *Challenging Diversity: Rethinking Equality and the Value of Difference*. Cambridge: Cambridge University Press.

Correa, S., Petchesky, R. and Parker, R. (2008) *Sexuality, Health and Human Rights*. London: Routledge.

Crowder, G. (2006) 'Chantal Mouffe's Agonistic Democracy', *APSA 2006 Conference Proceedings*, 1–29.

Davis, O. (2010) *Jacques Rancière*. Cambridge: Polity.

Day, R. (2005) *Gramsci Is Dead: Anarchist Currents in the Newest Social Movements*. London: Pluto Press.

Dean, J. (2005) 'A Politics of Avoidance: The Limits of Weak Ontology', *The Hedgehog Review: Critical Reflections on Contemporary Culture* 7 (2), 55–65.

Dean, J. (2009) 'Politics without Politics', *Parallax* 15 (3), 20–36.

Deranty, J.-P. (2003) 'Jacques Rancière's Contribution to the Ethics of Recognition', *Political Theory* 31 (1), 136–56.

Deranty, J.-P. (2008) 'Work and the Precarisation of Existence', *European Journal of Social Theory* 11 (4), 443–63.

Deranty, J.-P. and Renault, E. (2008) 'Democratic Agon: Striving for Distinction or Struggle against Domination and Injustice', in A. Schaap (ed.) *Law and Agonistic Politics*. Farnham: Ashgate.

Deveaux, M. (1999) 'Agonism and Pluralism', *Philosophy and Social Criticism* 25 (4), 1–22.

Dietz, M. (2002) *Turning Operations: Feminism, Arendt and Politics*. London: Routledge.

Dillon, M. (2003) '(De)void of Politics? A Response to Jacques Rancière's "Ten Theses on Politics"', *Theory and Event* 6 (4).

Donzelot, J. (1979) *The Policing of Families*. Baltimore: Johns Hopkins University Press.

Erman, E. (2009) 'What Is Wrong with Agonistic Pluralism? Reflections on Conflict in Democratic Theory', *Philosophy and Social Criticism* 35 (9), 1039–62.

Fanon, F. (2001) *The Wretched of the Earth*. London: Penguin.

Farrelly, C. (2007) 'Justice in Ideal Theory: A Refutation', *Political Studies* 55 (4), 844–64.

Flathman, R. (2005) 'Interview with Richard Flathman', *The Hedgehog Review: Critical Reflections on Contemporary Culture* 7 (2), 103–6.

Forst, R. (2011) 'The Power of Critique', *Political Theory* 39 (1), 118–23.

Foucault, M. (1984) 'What is Enlightenment?', in P. Rabinow (ed.) *The Foucault Reader*. London: Penguin.

Foucault, M. (1991) 'Governmentality', in G. Burchell, C. Gordon and P. Miller (eds) *The Foucault Effect: Studies in Governmentality*. Chicago: University of Chicago Press.

Foucault, M. (1994) 'The Subject and Power', in J. Faubion (ed.) *Michel Foucault: Power: Essential Works of Foucault 1954–1984, Vol. 3*. London: Penguin.

Foucault, M. (1997) *Society Must be Defended: Lectures at the Collège de France 1975–6*. London: Penguin.

Foucault, M. (2002) 'What Is Critique?', in D. Ingram (ed.) *The Political*. Oxford: Blackwell.
Foucault, M. (2008) *The Birth of Biopolitics: Lectures at the Collège de France 1978–9*. Basingstoke: Palgrave Macmillan.
Fraser, N. (1997) 'After the Family Wage: A PostIndustrial Thought Experiment', in *Justice Interruptus: Critical Reflections on the 'Postsocialist' Condition*. London: Routledge.
Fraser, N. (2001) 'Recognition without Ethics?', *Theory, Culture and Society* 18 (2–3), 21–42.
Fraser, N. (2008) 'Prioritizing Justice as Participatory Parity: A Reply to Kompridis and Forst', in K. Olson (ed.) *Adding Insult to Injury: Nancy Fraser Debates Her Critics*. London: Verso.
Fraser, N. (2009) 'Feminism, Capitalism and the Cunning of History', *New Left Review* 56 (March/April), 97–117.
Fraser, N. (2013) *The Fortunes of Feminism: From Women's Liberation, to Identity Politics, to Anti-Capitalism*. London: Verso.
Fraser, N. and Bedford, K. (2008) 'Social Rights and Gender Justice in the Neoliberal Moment: A Conversation about Welfare and Transnational Politics', *Feminist Theory* 9 (2), 225–45.
Fraser, N. and Honneth, A. (2003) *Redistribution or Recognition? A Political-Philosophical Exchange*. London: Verso.
Fraser, N. and Naple, N.A. (2004) 'To Interpret the World and To Change it: An Interview with Nancy Fraser', *Signs* 29 (4), 1103–24.
Freeman, C. (2000) *High Tech and High Heels in the Global Economy: Women, Work and Pink-Collar Identities in the Caribbean*. Durham, NC: Duke University Press.
Frost, L. and Hoggett, P. (2008) 'Human Agency and Social Suffering', *Critical Social Policy* 28 (4), 438–60.
Fung, A. (2007) 'Democratic Theory and Political Science: A Pragmatic Method of Constructive Engagement', *American Political Science Review* 101, 443–58.
Garber, M., Hanssen, B. and Walkowitz, R.L. (eds) (2000) *The Turn to Ethics*. London: Routledge.
Gaventa, J. (1982) *Power and Powerlessness: Quiescence and Rebellion in an Appalachian Valley*. Oxford: Clarendon Press.
Geras, N. (1987) 'Post-Marxism?', *New Left Review* 163 (May/June), 40–82.
Geras, N. (1999) *The Contract of Mutual Indifference: Political Philosophy after the Holocaust*. London: Verso.
Glover, R.W. (2012) 'Games Without Frontiers? Democratic Engagement, Agonistic Pluralism and the Question of Exclusion', *Philosophy and Social Criticism* 38 (1), 81–104.

Guess, R. (2008) *Philosophy and Real Politics*. Princeton: Princeton University Press.
Guess, R. (2009) *Politics and the Imagination*. Princeton: Princeton University Press.
Habermas, J. (1985) *The Philosophical Discourse of Modernity*. Cambridge: Polity.
Habermas, J. (1992) *Postmetaphysical Thinking: Philosophical Essays*. Cambridge: Polity.
Habermas, J. (1998) *The Inclusion of the Other: Studies in Political Theory*. Cambridge: Polity.
Hall, Cheryl (2005) *The Trouble with Passion: Political Theory beyond the Reign of Reason*. London: Routledge.
Hallward, P. (2009) 'Staging Equality: Rancière's Theatrocracy and the Limits of Anarchic Equality', in G. Rockhill and P. Watts (eds) *Jacques Rancière: History, Politics, Aesthetics*. Durham, NC: Duke University Press.
Heath, J. (2008) 'Resource Egalitarianism and the Politics of Recognition', in K. Olson (ed.) *Adding Insult to Injury: Nancy Fraser Debates Her Critics*. London: Verso.
The Hedgehog Review: Critical Reflections on Contemporary Culture (2005) Special Issue on Weak Ontologies. Charlottesville: University of Virginia.
Heller, A. (1991) 'The Concept of the Political', in D. Held (ed.) *Political Theory Today*. Cambridge: Polity.
Hewlett, N. (2007) *Badiou, Balibar, Rancière: Rethinking Emancipation*. London: Continuum.
Heyes, C. (2003) *The Grammar of Politics: Wittgenstein and Political Philosophy*. Ithaca, NY: Cornell University Press.
Hochschild, A.R. (2000) 'Global Care Chains and Emotional Surplus Value', in W. Hutton and A. Giddens (eds) *On the Edge: Living with Global Capitalism*. London: Jonathan Cape.
Honig, B. (1995) 'Towards an Agonistic Feminism: Hannah Arendt and the Politics of Identity', in B. Honig (ed.) *Feminist Interpretations of Hannah Arendt*. University Park: Pennsylvania State University Press.
Honig, B. and Stears, M. (2011) 'The New Realism: From Modus Vivendi to Justice', in J. Floyd and M. Stears (eds) *Political Philosophy versus History: Contextualism and Real Politics in Contemporary Political Thought*. Cambridge: Cambridge University Press.
Honneth, A. (1995) *The Struggle for Recognition: The Moral Grammar of Social Conflicts*. Cambridge: Polity.
Honneth, A. (1999) 'Postmodern Identity and Object-Relations

Theory: On the Seeming Obsolescence of Psychoanalysis', *Philosophical Explorations* 3, 225–42.
Honneth, A. (2004) 'A Social Pathology of Reason: On the Intellectual Legacy of Critical Theory', in F. Rush (ed.) *The Cambridge Companion to Critical Theory*. Cambridge: Cambridge University Press.
Honneth, A. (2007a) *Disrespect: The Normative Foundations of Critical Theory*. Cambridge: Polity.
Honneth, A. (2007b) 'Recognition as Ideology', in B. Van Den Brink and D. Owen (eds) *Recognition and Power: Axel Honneth and the Tradition of Critical Social Theory*. Cambridge: Cambridge University Press.
Honneth, A. (2008) *Reification: A New Look at an Old Idea*. Oxford: Oxford University Press.
Honneth, A. (2012a) 'Interview on "The Relevance of Contemporary French Philosophy for a Theory of Recognition"', in M. Bankovsky and A. Le Goff (eds) *Recognition Theory and Contemporary French Moral and Political Philosophy: Reopening the Dialogue*. Manchester: Manchester University Press.
Honneth, A. (2012b) *The I in We: Studies in the Theory of Recognition*. Cambridge: Polity.
Howarth, D.R. (2008) 'Ethos, Agonism and Populism: William Connolly and the Case for Radical Democracy', *British Journal of Politics and International Relations* 10, 171–93.
Hoy, D.C. (2005) *Critical Resistance: From Poststructuralism to Post-Critique*. Cambridge, MA: MIT Press.
Kioupkiolis, A. (2011) 'Keeping It Open: Ontology, Ethics, Knowledge and Radical Democracy', *Philosophy and Social Criticism* 37 (6), 691–708.
Kittay, E.F. (1999) *Love's Labour*. New York: Routledge.
Kleinman, A., Das, V. and Lock, M. (1996) 'Introduction', *Daedalus* 125 (1), Social Suffering, xi–xx.
Kogler, H.H. (1996) *The Power of Dialogue: Critical Hermeneutics after Gadamer and Foucault*. Cambridge, MA: MIT Press.
Kompridis, N. (2004) 'From Reason to Self-Realization? Axel Honneth and the "Ethical Turn" in Critical Theory', *Critical Horizons* 5, 323–60.
Kompridis, N. (2005) 'Normativizing Hybridity/Neutralizing Culture', *Political Theory* 33 (3), 318–43.
Laclau, E. (1994) 'Introduction', in E. Laclau (ed.) *The Making of Political Identities*. London: Verso.
Laclau, E. (1996) *Emancipations*. London: Verso.
Laclau, E. (2005) *On Populist Reason*. London: Verso.

Laclau, E. and Mouffe, C. (1985) *Hegemony and Socialist Strategy: Towards a Radical Democratic Politics*. London: Verso.

Lacoue-Labarthe, P. and Nancy, J.-L. (1997) *Retreating the Political*. London: Routledge.

Langer, L. (1996) 'The Alarmed Vision: Social Suffering and Holocaust Atrocity', *Daedelus* 125 (1), Social Suffering, 47–65.

Laplanche, J. (1999) *Essays on Otherness*. London: Routledge.

LaVaque-Manty, M. (2008) 'Finding Theoretical Concepts in the Real World: The Case of the Precariat', in B. de Bruin and C. Zurn (eds) *New Waves in Political Philosophy*. Basingstoke: Palgrave Macmillan.

Layton, L. (2004) *Who's that Girl? Who's that Boy?: Clinical Practice Meets Postmodern Gender Theory*. London: The Analytic Press.

Lazzeri, C. (2012) 'Confllicts of Recognition and Critical Sociology', in M. Bankovsky and A. Le Goff (eds) *Recognition Theory and Contemporary French Moral and Political Philosophy: Reopening the Dialogue*. Manchester: Manchester University Press.

Lear, J. (2008) 'The Slippery Middle', in A. Honneth (ed.) *Reification: A New Look at an Old Idea*. Oxford: Oxford University Press.

Lever, A. (2000) 'The Politics of Paradox: A Response to Wendy Brown', *Constellations* 7 (2), 242–54.

Lloyd, M. (2005) *Beyond Identity Politics: Feminism, Power and Politics*. London: Sage.

Lloyd, M. (2007a) 'Radical Democratic Activism and the Politics of Resignification', *Constellations* 14 (1), 129–46.

Lloyd, M (2007b) 'Review of Linda M. Zerilli, Feminism and the Abyss of Freedom', *Redescriptions: Yearbook of Political Thought and Conceptual History* 11, 237–42.

Luhrmann, T.M. (2006) 'Subjectivity', *Anthropological Theory* 6 (3), 345–61.

Lynch, K., Baker, J. and Lyons, M. (eds) (2009) *Affective Equality: Love, Care and Injustice*. Basingstoke: Palgrave Macmillan.

Macedo, S. and Williams, M. (2005) 'Introduction', in S. Macedo and M. Williams (eds) *Political Exclusion and Domination*. New York: New York University Press.

McNay, L. (2000) *Gender and Agency: Reconfiguring the Subject in Feminist and Social Theory*. Cambridge: Polity.

McNay, L. (2008a) *Against Recognition*. Cambridge: Polity.

McNay, L. (2008b) 'The Method of Critique', in D. Leopold and M. Stears (eds) *Political Theory: Methods and Approaches*. Oxford: Oxford University Press.

McNay, L. (2009) 'Self as Enterprise: Dilemmas of Control and Resistance in Foucault's *The Birth of Biopolitics*', *Theory, Culture and Society* 26 (6), 1–23.

McNay L. (2012) 'The Politics of Suffering: Foucault contra Honneth', in M. Bankovsky and A. Le Goff (eds) *Recognition Theory and Contemporary French Moral and Political Philosophy: Reopening the Dialogue*. Manchester: Manchester University Press.

McRobbie, A. (2002) 'A Mixed Bag of Misfortunes: Bourdieu's Weight of the World', *Theory, Culture and Society* 19 (3), 129–38.

McRobbie, A. (2008) *The Aftermath of Feminism: Gender, Culture and Social Change*. London: Sage.

Madhok, S. (2013) 'Action, Agency, Coercion: Reformatting Agency for Oppressive Contexts', in S. Madhok, A. Phillips and K. Wilson (eds) *Gender, Agency and Coercion*. London: Palgrave Macmillan.

Mahmood, S. (2001) 'Feminist Theory, Embodiment, and the Docile Agent: Some Reflections on the Egyptian Islamic Revival', *Cultural Anthropology* 16 (2), 202–36.

Mansbridge, J. (1991) 'Feminism and Democracy', *The American Prospect* 1 (1), 126-39.

Mansbridge, J. (1996) 'Using Power/Fighting Power: The Polity', in S. Benhabib (ed.) *Democracy and Difference: Contesting the Boundaries of the Political*. Princeton: Princeton University Press.

Mansbridge, J. (2001) 'Complicating Oppositional Consciousness', in J. Mansbridge and A. Morris (eds) *Oppositional Consciousness: The Subjective Roots of Social Protest*. Chicago: University of Chicago Press.

Marchart, O. (2007) *Post-Foundational Political Thought: Political Difference in Nancy, Lefort, Badiou and Laclau*. Edinburgh: Edinburgh University Press.

Markell, P. (2003) *Bound by Recognition*. Princeton: Princeton University Press.

Martineau, W. and Squires, J. (2012) 'Addressing the "Dismal Disconnection": Normative Theory, Empirical Inquiry and Dialogical Research', *Political Studies* 60, 523–38.

May, T. (2008) *The Political Thought of Jacques Rancière: Creating Equality*. Edinburgh: Edinburgh University Press.

Medearis, J. (2005) 'Social Movements and Deliberative Democratic Theory', *British Journal of Political Science* 35, 53–75.

Menke, C. (2010) 'Neither Rawls Nor Adorno: Raymond Guess' Programme for a "Realist" Political Philosophy', *European Journal of Philosophy* 18 (1), 139–47.

Mills, C.W. (2005) '"Ideal Theory" as Ideology', *Hypatia* 20 (3), 165–84.

Mills, C.W. (2007) 'Multiculturalism as/and/or Anti-Racism', in A.S. Laden and D. Owen (eds) *Multculturalism and Political Theory*. Cambridge: Cambridge University Press.
Mitchell, J. (1971) *Woman's Estate*. Harmondsworth: Penguin.
Mouffe, C. (ed.) (1992) *Dimensions of Radical Democracy: Pluralism, Citizenship, Community*. London: Verso.
Mouffe, C. (1993) *The Return of the Political*. London: Verso.
Mouffe, C. (1994) 'For a Politics of Nomadic Identity', in G. Robertson, J. Bird, B. Curtis, M. Mash, T. Putnam, G. Robertson and L. Tickner (eds) *Travellers' Tales: Narratives of Home and Displacement*. London: Routledge.
Mouffe, C. (2000) *The Democratic Paradox*. London: Verso.
Mouffe, C. (2005) *On the Political*. London: Routledge.
Myers, E. (2013) *Worldly Ethics: Democratic Politics and Care for the World*. Durham, NC: Duke University Press.
Nancy, J.-L. (2001) *Being Singular Plural*. Stanford: Stanford University Press.
Nash, K. (1998) 'Beyond Liberalism? Feminist Theories of Democracy', in V. Randall and G. Waylen (eds) *Gender, Politics and the State*. London: Routledge.
Newman, S. (2008) 'Connolly's Democratic Pluralism and the Question of State Sovereignty', *British Journal of Politics and International Relations* 10, 227–40.
Newman, S. (2011) *The Politics of Postanarchism*. Edinburgh: Edinburgh University Press.
Nielson, L.B. (2000) 'Situating Legal Consciousness: Experiences and Attitudes of Ordinary Citizens about Law and Street Harrassment', *Law and Society Review* 34, 201–36.
Norris, A. (2006) 'Ernesto Laclau and the Logic of the Political', *Philosophy and Social Criticism* 32 (1), 111–34.
Norval, A.J. (2007) *Aversive Democracy: Inheritance and Originality in the Democratic Tradition*. Cambridge: Cambridge University Press.
Nussbaum, M. (2000) *Women and Human Development: The Capabilities Approach*. Cambridge: Cambridge University Press.
Nussbaum, M. (2003) *Upheavals of Thought: The Intelligence of Emotions*. Cambridge: Cambridge University Press.
Oliver, K. (2001) *Witnessing: Beyond Recognition*. Minneapolis: University of Minnesota Press.
Olson, K. (2008) 'Participatory Parity and Democratic Justice', in K. Olson (ed.) *Adding Insult to Injury: Nancy Fraser Debates Her Critics*. London: Verso.
O'Neill, O. (1996) *Towards Justice and Virtue: A Constructivist Account of Practical Reasoning*. Cambridge: Cambridge University Press.

Owen, D. (1999) 'Political Philosophy in a Post-Imperial Voice: James Tully and the Cultural Politics of Recognition', *Economy and Society* 24 (4), 520–49.

Owen, D. (2011) '"Reality Lost. Reality Regained": Ethics, Politics and Wishful Thinking in the Imagination of Raymond Guess' (unpublished paper).

Passavant, P. and Dean, J. (2001) 'Laws and Societies', *Constellations* 8 (3), 376–89.

Pelletier, C. (2009) 'Emancipation, Equality and Education: Rancière's Critique of Bourdieu and the Question of Performativity', *Discourse: Studies in the Politics of Education* 30 (2), 137–50.

Phillips, A. (1991) *Engendering Democracy*. Cambridge: Polity.

Pitkin, H. (1988) *The Attack of the Blob: Hannah Arendt's Concept of the Social*. Chicago: University of Chicago Press.

Probyn, E. (2004) 'Shame in the Habitus', in L. Adkins and B. Skeggs (eds) *Feminism after Bourdieu*. Oxford: Blackwell.

Rancière, J. (1991) *The Ignorant Schoolmaster: Five Lessons in Intellectual Emancipation*. Stanford: Stanford University Press.

Rancière, J. (1999) *Disagreement: Politics and Philosophy*. Minneapolis: University of Minnesota Press.

Rancière, J. (2001) 'Ten Theses on Politics', *Theory and Event* 5 (3).

Rancière, J. (2003) *The Philosopher and His Poor*. Durham, NC: Duke University Press.

Rancière, J. (2004a) 'Who Is the Subject of the Rights of Man?', *The South Atlantic Quarterly* 103 (2/3), 297–310.

Rancière, J. (2004b) *The Politics of Aesthetics*. New York: Continuum.

Rancière, J. (2006) 'The Ethical Turn of Aesthetics and Politics', *Critical Horizons* 7 (1), 1–20.

Rancière, J. (2007) *The Future of the Image*. London: Verso.

Rancière, J. (2012) *Proletarian Nights: The Workers' Dream in Nineteenth-Century France*. London: Verso.

Renault, E. (2008) 'The Political Philosophy of Social Suffering', in B. de Bruin and C. Zurn (eds) *New Waves in Political Philosophy*. Basingstoke: Palgrave Macmillan.

Renault, E. (2010) 'A Critical Theory of Social Suffering', *Critical Horizons* 11 (2), 221–41.

Ricoeur, P. (1983) *Time and Narrative: Vol 1*. Chicago: University of Chicago Press.

Robinson, A. and Tormey S. (2008) 'Laclau, Mouffe and Social Movements', in A. Little and M. Lloyd (eds) *Politics of Radical Democracy*. Edinburgh: Edinburgh University Press.

Rose, N. (1999) *Powers of Freedom: Reframing Political Thought*. Cambridge: Cambridge University Press.

Sanders, L. (1997) 'Against Deliberation', *Political Theory* 25 (3), 347–76.
Schaap, A. (2011) 'Enacting the Right to Have Rights: Jacques Rancière's Critique of Hannah Arendt', *European Journal of Political Theory* 10 (1), 22–45.
Scheuerman, W.E. (1999) 'Between Radicalism and Resignation: Democratic Theory in Habermas's *Between Facts and Norms*', in P. Dews (ed.) *Habermas: A Critical Reader*. Oxford: Blackwell.
Scott, J.C. (1990) *Domination and the Arts of Resistance: Hidden Transcripts*. New Haven: Yale University Press.
Shapiro, I. (2007) *The Flight from Reality in the Human Sciences*. Princeton: Princeton University Press.
Shapiro, M. (2001) *For Moral Ambiguity: National Culture and the Politics of the Family*. Minneapolis: University of Minnesota Press.
Skeggs B. (2004) 'Exchange Value and Affect: Bourdieu and the "Self"', in L. Adkins and B. Skeggs (eds) *Feminism after Bourdieu*. Oxford: Blackwell.
Spivak, G.C. (1987) 'Can the Subaltern Speak?', in C. Nelson and L. Grossberg (eds) *Marxism and the Interpretation of Culture*. London: Macmillan.
Standing, G. (2011) *The Precariat: The New Dangerous Class*. London: Bloomsbury Academic.
Stears, M. (2005) 'The Vocation of Political Theory: Principles, Empirical Inquiry and the Politics of Opportunity', *European Journal of Political Theory* 4 (4), 325–50.
Stears, M. (2010) *Demanding Democracy: American Radicals in Search of a New Politics*. Princeton: Princeton University Press.
Steedman, C. (1986) *Landscape for a Good Woman: A Story of Two Lives*. London: Virago.
Swift, A. and White, S. (2008) 'Political Theory, Social Science and Real Politics', in D. Leopold and M. Stears (eds) *Political Theory: Methods and Approaches*. Oxford: Oxford University Press.
Tambakaki, P. (2009) 'When Does Politics Happen?', *Parallax* 15 (3), 102–13.
Thiele, L. (1992) 'Review: Identity/Difference', *American Political Science Review* 86 (3), 777–8.
Thistle, S. (2000) 'The Trouble with Modernity: Gender and the Remaking of Social Theory', *Sociological Theory* 18 (2), 275–88.
Thompson, E.P. (1996) *The Poverty of Theory: An Orrery of Errors*. London: Merlin Press.
Tønder, L. and Thomassen, L. (eds) (2006a) *Radical Democracy: Politics between Abundance and Lack*. Manchester: Manchester University Press.

Tønder, L. and Thomassen, L. (2006b) 'Introduction', in L. Tønder and L. Thomassen (eds) *Radical Democracy: Politics between Abundance and Lack*. Manchester: Manchester University Press.

Tully, J. (1995) *Strange Multiplicity: Constitutionalism in an Age of Diversity*. Cambridge; Cambridge University Press.

Tully, J. (2008a) *Public Philosophy in a New Key: Vol. 1, Democracy and Civic Freedom*. Cambridge: Cambridge University Press.

Tully, J. (2008b) *Public Philosophy in a New Key: Vol. 2. Imperialism and Civic Freedom*. Cambridge: Cambridge University Press.

Van Den Brink, B. and Owen, D. (eds) (2007) *Recognition and Power: Axel Honneth and the Tradition of Critical Social Theory*. Cambridge: Cambridge University Press.

Vazquez-Arroyo, A.Y. (2004) 'Agonized Liberalism: The Liberal Theory of William E. Connolly', *Radical Philosophy* 127 (Sept./Oct.), 8–19.

Wacquant, L. (2008) *Urban Outcasts: A Comparative Sociology of Advanced Marginality*. Cambridge: Polity.

Wei-ming, T. (1996) 'Destructive Will and Ideological Holocaust: Maoism as a Source of Social Suffering in China', *Daedalus* 125 (1), Social Suffering, 149–79.

Wenman, M. (2003) '"Agonistic Pluralism" and Three Archetypal Forms of Politics', *Contemporary Political Theory* 2 (2), 165–86.

Wenman, M. (2008) 'William E. Connolly: Pluralism without Transcendence', *British Journal of Politics and International Relations* 10, 156–70.

White, S.K. (2000) *Sustaining Affirmation: The Strengths of Weak Ontology in Political Theory*. Princeton: Princeton University Press.

White, S.K. (2001) 'Three Conceptions of the Political: The Real World of Late Modern Democracy', in A. Botwinick and W.E. Connolly (eds) *Democracy and Vision: Sheldon Wolin and the Vicissitudes of the Political*. Princeton: Princeton University Press.

White, S.K. (2005) 'Weak Ontology, Genealogy and Critical Issues', *The Hedgehog Review: Critical Reflections on Contemporary Culture* 7 (2), 11–25.

White, S. K. (2009) *The Ethos of a Late-Modern Citizen*. Cambridge, MA: Harvard University Press.

Wilkinson, I. (2011) 'Social Suffering and the New Politics of Sensibility', in G. Delanty and S. Turner (eds) *Routledge International Handbook of Contemporary Social and Political Theory*. London: Routledge.

Williams, M. (1998) *Voice, Trust and Memory: Marginalized Groups and the Failings of Liberal Representation*. Princeton: Princeton University Press.

Williams, R. (1977) *Marxism and Literature*. Oxford: Oxford University Press.
Wolin, S. (1994) 'Fugitive Democracy', *Constellations* 1 (1), 11–25.
Wolin, S. (2000) 'Political Theory: From Vocation to Invocation', in J. Frank and J. Tambornino (eds) *Vocations of Political Theory*. Minneapolis: University Minnesota Press.
Wright, E.O. (2010) *Envisioning Real Utopias*. London: Verso.
Young, I.M. (2000) *Inclusion and Democracy*. Oxford: Oxford University Press.
Young, I.M. (2007) 'Structural Injustice and the Politics of Difference', in A.S. Laden and D. Owen (eds) *Multiculturalism and Political Theory*.Cambridge: Cambridge University Press.
Zerilli, L. (2005) *Feminism and the Abyss of Freedom*. Chicago: University of Chicago Press.
Zerilli, L. (2006) 'Feminist Theory and the Canon of Political Thought', in J. Dryzek, B. Honig and A. Phillips (eds) *Oxford Handbook of Political Theory*. Oxford: Oxford University Press.
Zerilli, L. (2009) 'Toward a Feminist Theory of Judgement', *Signs* 34 (2), 295–317.
Ziarek, E.P. (2001) *An Ethics of Dissensus: Postmodernity, Feminism and the Politics of Radical Democracy*. Stanford: Stanford University Press.
Žižek, S. (1999) *The Ticklish Subject: The Absent Centre of Political Ontology*. London: Verso.

Index

abstraction, 8–16, 77, 215
abyss of freedom concept, 114
action and activism: and identity, 112–17; new social movements, 91–2; permissible sorts, 196, 197; Rancière on, 166; *see also* resistance
Actor Network Theory *see* vitalist (speculative) materialisms
Adorno, Theodor, 1, 22, 210, 211, 219, 221
adversaries, 73
advertising, 59
Agamben, Giorgio, 153
ageing, 50
agency: agonist, 6, 7, 18–19, 24–5, 66, 67–8, 94–5, 217; and coercion, 155; Connolly's and Tully's approaches, 169–72, 175, 178–206; counter-hegemonic, 22, 91; and embodiment, 20–1, 87–8, 216–17; and feminist post-identity concerns, 98–9, 103–5, 108–31; and habitus concept, 19–20, 36, 63, 81–2, 121, 160; and indeterminacy, 25–6, 111–12, 113–22; and oppression, 16–20; origins, 91; paradox of enablement, 38; and pluralism, 26–7; presumption of by political theorists, 17, 29; Rancière's approach, 134, 138, 159–66; and sexuality, 102; and social suffering, 28–9, 36–66, 207–8, 209–10; *see also* action and activism; agonism; depoliticization; resistance
agonism: ability to tolerate perpetual, 93–4; and agency, 6, 7, 18–19, 24–5, 66, 67–8, 94–5, 217; and antagonism and deliberation, 69–75; associative, 66, 92; Connolly's and Tully's brands, 168–206; and consensus, 66; on democratic identities, 79–84, 100; on embodiment, power and time, 180–5; on emotions and political life, 85–9; on equality, 135–7, 141–2, 146, 147, 159–66; and exclusion, 7, 71–3, 75–6, 83–4; feminist politics of, 107; and linguistic universalism, 18–19; Mouffe's brand, 24–5, 68–97; and the ontological and ontic, 70–2, 74, 94–5, 169, 171–2, 178–80, 205–6, 215; and oppression, 96; on politics–ethics relationship, 172–80, 188–92; on power, exclusion and practice, 75–9; Rancière's brand, 26, 132–67; on recognition, 140–6; and separation of the real from the

agonism (*cont.*)
　ideal, 6; on the social, political and ethical, 89–94
agreement, 72–3, 93–4
Alcoff, Linda, 115, 130
Allen, Amy, 114
Allen, Danielle, 112–13, 143, 224–5
antagonism: Connolly on, 185; Mouffe on, 70–4, 86–8, 89, 91–2, 93, 139, 177
anti-essentialism, 79–80, 82–6
anti-foundationalism, 13
anti-globalization protests, 91
Appiah, Anthony, 188
Arendt, Hannah: and agonism, 66, 92; on democracy, 1; on human rights, 149, 152–3; and Little Rock desegregation episode, 224–5; Pitkin on, 89; on politics of suffering, 103, 105–8; on primacy of the political, 2–3, 12–13, 91, 138–9, 195, 215; representative thought notion, 128; on social realm, 15, 159; on turning away from the given, 112
Aristotle, 141, 149
Armitage, David, 194, 197, 198
Aron, Raymond, 213

Bader, Veit, 53–6
Badiou, Alain, 140, 147, 158
Barbados, 101
Bauman, Zygmunt, 45
Bedford, Kate, 100
Benhabib, Seyla, 127
Benjamin, Walter, 1, 57
Bergson, Henri, 181
Berlant, Lauren, 102, 118
Bernstein, Jay, 23, 56–7
Bickford, Susan, 109
Bosteels, Bruno, 96, 111
Bourdieu, Pierre: on action and limitations, 116; on agency, 118, 160–1, 162; on embodiment, 59, 182–3; on fictitious universalism, 6, 39; habitus concept, 19–20, 36, 81–2, 160; on linguistic legitimacy, 49; as miserabilist, 53, 55; on neoliberal capitalism, 131, 163; ontology of complicity, 62; on the political, 143–4; on political judgement, 128–9, 130; on political relations, 142–3; Rancière on, 134; on social suffering, 20–1, 28–30, 33–7, 217; on social weightlessness, 4, 39, 40–5, 56, 65–6
Brazil, 217
Brown, Wendy: on agency and indeterminacy, 25, 99; on neoliberalism, 222; on politics of suffering, 104–5, 108–9; on resistance, 123–4; on rights discourse, 118–20
Bubeck, Diemut, 90
Butler, Judith: on breaking with the given, 110, 113; on disclosure, 50; Mouffe's critique, 224; and performativity, 107, 126, 221; on politics–ethics relationship, 173; on recognition, 59, 62, 93

capitalism *see* neoliberal capitalism and governance
care work, 80, 90–1, 101, 214
Castoriadis, Cornelius, 113, 115
Cavell, Stanley: influence on Honneth, 60; influence on Mouffe, 68–9, 76, 78–9, 87–8, 92, 94
Celikates, R., 202
Charlesworth, Simon, 49, 51, 63, 182–4, 200
Cheah, Pheng, 83, 93–4
children, 61–2
China, 34
Chodorow, Nancy, 88
choice, 8–9
citizenship, agonist view, 77–8, 79–84, 195–6, 199
civil rights *see* rights
civil unions, 125; *see also* same-sex marriage
class issues, 42, 51–2, 87

collective action *see* action and activism
colonialism, 186
colonization of the lifeworld thesis, 49–50
communicative ethics, 41–4, 49–50, 66, 221
compassion, 105–6
conflict *see* agonism
Connolly, William: on agency, 169–72, 175, 178–92; author's critique, 26–7, 168–92, 206–7; on capitalism, 185, 188–9; on embodiment, power and time, 180–5; on exclusion, 191; Mouffe on, 92; and ontology, 169, 171–2, 178–80, 205–6, 215; on pluralism and equality, 185–8; on politics–ethics relationship, 172–80, 188–92; on practice–theory relationship, 169; on suffering, 175, 192
consciousness: legal consciousness, 120–1; political consciousness, 121–2
consensus politics: agonist view, 67–73, 74–5, 78; author's view, 210; deliberative view, 73–4, 141–4; Rancière's view, 141–4
constructivism, 171
Coole, Diana, 117, 171
Cooper, Davina, 124–5
Correa, Sonia, 152
Critical Theory, 7, 47, 209
Crowder, George, 75, 223

Daedalus (journal), 30–1
Davis, Oliver, 157, 166
Day, Richard, 91, 92
Dean, Jodi, 164, 178
decision ethics, 92–3, 94
Deleuze, Gilles, 146, 162, 171
deliberative theory: and agonism, 72–5, 76, 85–6; on consensus politics, 73–4, 141–4; and social suffering, 24, 41–4, 49–50, 66; and Tully, 200–1

democracy: Arendt on, 1, 2–3, 12–13, 91, 138–9, 195, 215; fugitive democracy concept, 165; model overview, 1–2; Mouffe's definition, 92; Rancière on, 133–48, 156–9, 166–7; *see also* identity: political/democratic identity; the political
democratic proceduralism, 77–8
depoliticization: agonist view, 82; habitus concept, 19–20, 36, 63, 81–2, 121, 160; and lack of recognition, 46–52, 56–65; and linguistic universalism, 41–4; and neoliberal capitalism, 3, 131; and ontology, 178–80; and oppression, 28; as post-political phenomenon, 70; and social suffering, 37; *see also* agency; power relations
Deranty, Jean-Philippe, 18, 145
Derrida, Jacques, 224
Deveaux, Monique, 75
Dewey, John, 60
dialogue, 200–1; *see also* communicative ethics; deliberative theory
Dillon, Michael, 156
disagreement, 73, 141–2, 147
disclosing critique concept: author's advocation, 209–10, 212–13, 218; and Honneth, 24, 45–52, 65–6; and Rancière, 140–4, 147–54
discourse ethics *see* communicative ethics
disempowerment *see* agency; power relations
disharmony ethics, 93
domination *see* oppression
drag, 126
duration, 181–5

ecological issues, 100
education, 161
Ellison, Ralph, 224

embodiment: embodied experience, 20–1, 180–5, 216–17; somatization of injustice, 29–30, 50–1, 82, 87–8, 208
emotions: and political life, 85–9; as resistance, 123; and social hierarchy, 87
employment *see* work
enablement, paradox of, 38
enjoyment *see jouissance*
entrepreneurship, 59
environment, 100
equality and inequality: and agency, 16–20; and cultural vitalism, 190; and ethics, 191; and games of freedom concept, 195–205; and gender identity, 100; and neoliberal capitalism, 33, 189; and ontology, 9–16; paradox of enablement, 38; and pluralism, 185–8; problem-oriented approach, 214; Rancière on, 135–7, 141–2, 146, 147, 159–66; and recognition, 146; and social suffering, 20–4, 25, 28–66; *see also* justice and injustice; oppression; resistance
essentialism, 89–90; *see also* anti-essentialism
ethics: communicative ethics, 41–4, 49–50, 66, 221; decision ethics, 92–3, 94; disharmony ethics, 93; humanitarian ethics, 153; relationship with politics, 172–80, 188–92
ethos of generosity concept, 175–7, 188–92
exclusion and inclusion: and agonism, 7, 71–3, 75–6, 83–4; Arendt on, 224–5; Connolly on, 191; deliberative view, 76–7; and ethics, 173; and justice, 76; and lack of decisions, 92; and oppression, 83; Rancière on, 143, 163; and suffering, 109; Tully on, 198–9
experience *see* embodiment; social suffering

family life, 57, 61–2
Fanon, Frantz, 186
feminist political theory: and agency, 98–9, 103–5, 108–31; freedom-centred, 112–17; and indeterminacy, 113–25; and politics of suffering, 101–10, 114–15; post-identity, 25–6, 80–1, 90, 98–131; problem-oriented approaches, 214–15; on resistance, 122–5; rights-based approaches, 118–21; and universalism, 125–30
fictitious universalism, 6, 39
Flathman, Richard, 178
Forst, Rainer, 204, 211–12
Foucault, Michel: on citizenship, 195; on democracy, 1; on embodiment, 59; on ethical beliefs, 174; on governmentality and practices of the self, 195; on human rights, 151–2; on intellectuals, 192–3; on neoliberalism, 33, 131, 163, 189, 222; police concept, 151, 154–5; on politics of suffering, 103–4, 108, 109–10; on recognition, 58; on speaking for others, 146, 162; on turning away from the given, 110–12
fragmentation *see* individualization
Frankfurt School, 222
Fraser, Nancy: on Critical Theory, 7; on neoliberal capitalism, 131; on politicism, 96; on politics–ethics relationship, 173, 191; on recognition and misrecognition, 48, 105, 144, 145, 146, 197, 203, 205; on representation, 55; on second-wave cultural feminism, 100–1; on social suffering, 21
freedom: abyss of freedom concept, 114; and action, 112–17; games of freedom concept, 194–206; as indeterminacy, 110
Freeman, Carla, 101
French Revolution, 106
Frost, Samantha, 171

fugitive democracy concept, 165
fundamentalism, 100, 186

games of freedom concept, 194–206
Garber, Marjorie, 172
Gaventa, John, 37–8
Geertz, Clifford, 220
gender issues: care work, 80, 90–1, 101, 214; gender hierarchies, 221; gender identity, 25, 80–1, 90, 98–131, 145, 198; and human rights, 151; idealized premises of equality, 10–11, 32; and linguistic universalism, 42; and neoliberalism, 59; and recognition theory, 57; structural inequalities, 188; Tully on recent developments, 203; verbal harassment, 120–1; *see also* feminist political theory; women
generosity *see* ethos of generosity concept
Geras, Norman, 89
ghettoes, 34, 186–7
gift exchange, 220–1
Gilligan, Carole, 90
given, turning away from the, 110–13
globalization, 91, 100
Glover, Robert, 92–3, 192
Guess, Raymond, 6, 17, 39, 70, 173, 211

Habermas, Jürgen: Bourdieu's critique, 39, 41–4; colonization of the lifeworld thesis, 49–50; communicative ethics, 41–4, 66, 221; on democracy, 1, 141–2; Honneth's critique, 48–9; on identity politics, 100; on injustice and inequality, 24, 29; on political participation, 85; on politics–ethics relationship, 173, 174; Rancière's critique, 141–2; on rhetorical dimensions of language, 147; Tully's critique, 198

habitus concept, 19–20, 36, 63, 81–2, 121, 160
Hall, Cheryl, 86
Hallward, Peter, 140, 163
hegemonic political orders, legitimacy, 71–2
Heidegger, Martin, 60
Heller, Agnes, 2, 4
Hewlett, Nick, 164
Holocaust, 34, 182
homosexuality *see* queer politics
Honig, Bonnie, 92, 106–7, 201
Honneth, Axel: disclosing critique concept, 24, 45–52, 65–6, 147, 175, 212; and embodiment, 29–30; and interdisciplinary critique, 216; and ontology, 30, 56; and social theoretical negativism, 16; social theory of recognition, 46–52, 56–65, 144, 179, 197
Horkheimer, Max, 221
Hoy, David Couzens, 117
human rights *see* rights
humanitarian ethics, 153
hyper-ghettoes, 34

ideal vs real theory, 5–16, 210–12
identity: collective identity and the urban poor, 34; gender identity, 80–1, 90, 98–131, 145, 198; identity politics, 3, 99–131; Lacanian view, 86; personal identity and work, 51–2; political/democratic identity, 7, 79–84, 100; social identity, 86, 88; *see also* indeterminacy; recognition; social theory of recognition
imagination, 113–16
inclusion *see* exclusion and inclusion
independence, 8–9
indeterminacy: agency as, 25–6, 111–12, 113–22; problems with concept, 168, 208; and resistance, 122–5; as transgression, 110–22
India, 155
individualization, 33, 54–5, 59, 163, 186–7

inequality *see* equality and inequality
injustice *see* justice and injustice
intellectuals, role of, 132–3, 138, 160–2, 192–3
interdisciplinary critique, 215–16

Jacotot, Joseph, 161
jouissance, 86
judgement *see* political judgement
justice and injustice: agonist view, 78; and choice, 8–9; embodiment of injustice, 29–30, 50–1, 82, 87–8, 208; and ethics of care, 90; and exclusion, 76; Rawls's justice theory, 2, 76, 87–8, 222; and recognition, 144, 146; and the social, 23; Tully on, 194, 203; *see also* equality and inequality; resistance

Kant, Immanuel, 40
Kiopkiolis, Alexandros, 12, 179, 191
Kleinman, Arthur, 30–1
Kogler, Hans Herbert, 109–10
Kompridis, Nikolas, 64, 216

labour *see* work
Lacan, Jacques, 86–8, 115, 159
Laclau, Ernesto, 71, 89, 95, 164, 177
Lacoue-Labarthe, Philippe, 3
Langer, Lawrence, 34, 182
language *see* linguistics, and modelling democratic relations
Layton, Lynne, 87
Lear, Jonathan., 61
lector vs auctor fallacy, 40
legal consciousness, 120–1
Lever, Annabel, 118–20
Levinas, Emmanuel, 93, 224
linguistic dispropriation, 49
linguistic universalism, 18–19, 41–4
linguistics, and modelling democratic relations, 18–19
Little Rock desegregation incident, 112–13
Lloyd, Moya, 80–1, 95, 118
Luhrmann, Thomas, 183

Lukács, György, 60
Lyotard, Jean-François, 153

Macedo, Stephen, 83
McRobbie, Angela, 59
Madhok, Sumi, 155
Mahmood, Saba, 123, 125–6
Mansbridge, Jane, 37, 121–2
Marchart, Oliver, 69, 95
marginalization *see* equality and inequality; exclusion and inclusion
Marx, Karl, 118, 119, 148
Medearis, John, 43, 44
melancholia, 50
Menke, Christopher, 210
migrant labour, 55, 223
Mill, John Stuart, 223
Mills, Charles W., 9–11, 32, 215
miserabilism, 21–2, 53–6, 160, 162
misery *see* social suffering
misrecognition: and gender identity, 99, 103, 105, 108–9, 120–1, 198; *see also* recognition; social theory of recognition
Mitchell, Juliet, 114–15
modernity, 57
Mondragon cooperative, 217
Mouffe, Chantal: on aims of progressive democratic order, 177; on antagonism, agonism and deliberation, 69–75; author's critique, 24–5, 68–97; and consensus, 66; on democratic identities, 79–84, 100; on emotions and political life, 85–9; and exclusion, 7; and the ontological and ontic, 70–2, 74, 94–5, 215; on the political, 139; on power, exclusion and practice, 75–9; and practice, 179; on the social, political and ethical, 89–94
multiculturalism, 127, 187–8

Nancy, Jean-Luc, 3, 208
Nash, Kate, 81
nationalist movements, 85, 86

negative social critique *see* social theoretical negativism
neoliberal capitalism and governance: Connolly on, 185, 188–9; definitions, 222; and depoliticization, 3, 131; entrepreneurship discourse, 59; and individualization, 33, 54–5, 59, 163; and inequality, 189; irrationality, 212; and pluralization, 189; and second-wave cultural feminism, 100–1; and social control, 22, 28, 59–60; and social relations, 33; Tully on, 202; and women's work, 59, 101, 214–15
new social movements, 91–2
Nielson, Laura Beth, 120–1
non-identity *see* indeterminacy
Norval, Aletta, 80, 110
Nussbaum, Martha, 86, 127

object relations theory, 57, 60
Occupy movement, 91
Olson, Kevin, 37, 38
O'Neill, Onora, 8–9
the ontic, 94–5, 96
ontology: in Connolly's work, 169, 171–2, 178–80, 205–6, 215; and depoliticization, 178–80; to elaborate ideas of the political, 69–70; Foucault's critical ontology of the present notion, 110–11; in Honneth's work, 30, 56; in Mouffe's work, 70–2, 74, 94–5, 215; ontology of complicity, 56, 62; and oppression, 9–16; and power, 9–16, 178–80; problem with ontological approaches, 17, 19, 215, 219; Rancière's attack on political, 133–4, 137, 139–40; relationship with the ontic, 96; and social weightlessness, 208–9; strong ontology, 69; weak ontologies debate, 178
oppression: and agency, 16–20; agonist view, 96; and depoliticization, 28; embodiment, 29, 50–1, 82, 184; and exclusion and inclusion, 83; and indeterminacy, 111–12; and ontology, 9–16; and rights discourse, 118–21; senselessness of lived oppression, 87–8; and social suffering, 20–66, 104–5, 109–10; Tully on, 198–201; *see also* resistance
the Other, 7, 153
Owen, David, 214

pain *see* social suffering
paradox of enablement, 38
Parker, Richard, 152
Pascal, Blaise, 220
pathways *see* routinized pathways
performativity, 107, 126
Petchesky, Rosalind, 152
Pitkin, Hannah, 89
Plato, 141
pluralism: agonist, 26–7, 75–8, 177, 185–9, 202–3, 205; historical preoccupation, 3
Poland, 165
police concept, 135, 151, 154–60, 164
the political: Arendt on primacy of, 2–3, 12–13, 91, 138–9, 195, 215; Mouffe's view, 139; ontology to elaborate ideas of, 69–70; Rancière's view, 133–48, 156–9, 164–7, 217–18
political consciousness, 121–2
political fundamentalisms, 100
political judgement, 126–30
political movements, extreme, 85
politicism, 96
politics, relationship with ethics, 172–80, 188–92
Porto Alegre, 217
poverty: and individualization, 33, 54–5; living conditions and social solidarity, 163; and neoliberal capitalism, 33, 54–5; and social suffering, 35; World Bank social provisioning policies, 101

power, different approaches to critique of, 6–16
power relations: absence from Rancière's work, 155–6; agonist view, 75–6, 79–84, 93–4; and indeterminacy, 111–12; and ontology, 9–16, 178–80; paradox of enablement, 38; and perpetual agonism, 93–4; and recognition, 145; and resistance, 19–20, 37–44; and social suffering, 20–66; and subjects' lived experience, 109–10; and time, 183–5; Tully on, 199, 200, 202; *see also* agency; equality and inequality; justice and injustice
practice, 78–9, 179
practice–theory relationship, 79, 169, 192–205, 211
precariat concept, 54, 187, 189
prejudice, 42
proceduralism, 77–8, 177
protest *see* action and activism

queer politics, 59, 125, 156, 157

race issues: colonialism, 186; idealized premises of equality, 11, 32; and linguistic universalism, 42; Little Rock desegregation episode, 112–13; migrant labour, 55, 223; multiculturalism, 127, 187–8; suffering and agency, 104–5
radical democratic theory, author's suggested approaches, 207–19
Rancière, Jacques: on agency, 134, 138, 159–66; author's critique, 26, 132–67, 217–18; on consensus politics, 141–4; on disagreement, 141–2, 147; and disclosing critique, 140–4, 147–54; on equality, 135–7, 141–2, 146, 147, 159–66; on exclusion, 143, 163; on identity politics, 100; police concept, 135, 151, 154–60, 164; on the political, 133–48, 156–9, 164–7, 217–18; on politics–ethics relationship, 173; on recognition, 140–6; on rights discourse, 148–56; on the social, 135, 159
Rawls, John: analytical liberalism, 5; on democracy, 1; on identity politics, 100; justice theory, 2, 76, 87–8, 222; on political participation, 85; on politics–ethics relationship, 173, 174
Real Utopias project, 218
realism, ideal vs real theory, 5–16, 210–12
recognition, 140–6, 156–7, 173, 195–201, 205; *see also* misrecognition; social theory of recognition
reflexivity, 221
refugees, 149, 152–3
reification, 60–2
religious suffering, 175
Renault, Emmanuel, 18, 31
representation, 55
resistance: and indeterminacy, 122–5; reasons for lack of, 19–20, 37–44, 46–66, 87–8; slipperiness of concept, 54; viable strategies, 43–4; *see also* action and activism; agency; agonism
responsibility, for decisions, 92–3, 94
ressentiment, 109, 192
rhizome concept, 171
rights: civil rights, 112–13; rights discourse, 118–21, 148–56; sexual rights, 152
risk socialization, 100
Robespierre, Maximilien, 106
Robinson, Andrew, 89, 91–2
Rose, Nikolas, 60
routinized pathways, 124–5

same-sex marriage, 156, 157; *see also* civil unions
sans part concept, 162–3, 164, 165–6
sathins, 155
Schaap, Andrew, 149
Schmitt, Carl, 1, 2–3, 12–13, 71
scholastic epistemocentrism, 40

Scott, James, 53–5
self as enterprise concept, 222
self-sufficiency, 8–9
sexual rights *see* rights
Shapiro, Ian, 4, 74–5
the social: Arendt on, 15, 159; and justice, 23; origins and definitions of social weightlessness, 4, 39, 40–6, 56, 65–6; Rancière on, 135, 159; relationship with the political, 3–4
social control, 22, 28, 59–60; police concept, 135, 151, 154–60, 164
social fragmentation *see* individualization
social suffering: and agency, 28–9, 36–66, 207–8, 209–10; as collective experience, 35–6; Connolly on, 175, 192; and deliberative theory, 24, 41–4, 49–50, 66; emotional aspects, 35; importance to radical democratic theory, 20–4, 28–66, 207–8, 209–10, 212; and lack of recognition, 46–52, 56–66; mundane as opposed to traumatic, 34; and neoliberal capitalism, 33; reluctance to express, 87; social invisibility, 35; and time, 182–5; *see also* resistance; suffering, politics of
social theoretical negativism, 16, 20–4, 30, 45, 66, 213–14; *see also* social suffering
social theory of recognition, 46–52, 56–65, 144, 179, 197; epistemic recognition, 60–1; primordial/antecedent recognition, 60–3; reified modes, 60–2
social weightlessness concept, origins and definition, 4, 39, 40–6, 56, 65–6
society, agonist view, 71, 86, 88
Solidarity movement, 165
somatization *see* embodiment
Spain, 217
speculative materialisms *see* vitalist (speculative) materialisms
speech, legal regulation of, 120

Spivak, Gayatri Chakravorty, 42, 162
Standing, Guy, 51–2
the state: and human rights, 152–3; relation to the individual, 59; *see also* hegemonic political orders
statelessness, 149
Stears, Marc, 201, 211
Steedman, Carolyn, 62
strikes, 137
subaltern politics, 192–206
suffering, politics of, 101–10, 115–16, 217; *see also* social suffering
symbolic violence concept, 37

Taylor, Charles, 197
theory: theory–practice relationship, 79, 169, 192–205, 211; *see also* social theoretical negativism
Thiele, Leslie, 185
Thomassen, Lasse, 69, 171, 172
Thompson, E.P., 22
time, 181–5
Tønder, Lars, 69, 171, 172
Tormey, Simon, 89, 91–2
Tully, James: on agency, 169, 192–206; author's critique, 26–7, 168–9, 192–206; on critique of power, 7; on exclusion, 198–9; on experience, 84; on finalism, 218; games of freedom concept, 195–206; on justice, 194, 203; on neoliberal governance, 202; on oppression, 198–201; on power, 199–200, 202–3; on practice–theory relationship, 79, 169, 192–205, 211

the unconscious, 115–16
unemployment, 51, 182–4, 200
universalism: in feminist political theory, 125–30; fictitious universalism, 6, 39; linguistic universalism, 18–19, 41–4
USA, hyper-ghettoes, 34

Vazquez-Arroyo, A.Y., 191
victimhood, 31, 104–5, 107; *see also* suffering, politics of

vitalist (speculative) materialisms, 170–2

Wacquant, Loïc, 34, 186–7
weak ontologies debate, 178
wealth privatization, 100
Weber, Max, 9, 181
Wei-ming, Tu, 34
Wenman, Mark, 174, 186
White, Stephen K., 69–70, 96, 165, 172, 178
Wilkinson, Iain, 31
Williams, Bernard, 70
Williams, Melissa, 83
Williams, Raymond, 35
Winnicott, Donald, 57, 61
Wittgenstein, Ludwig, 68–9, 77–8, 78–9, 113, 128, 195
Wolin, Sheldon, 4, 165
women: female development workers in India, 155; homeless women, 184; suffragettes, 156; work in neoliberal era, 59, 101, 214–15; *see also* feminist political theory; gender issues
work: entrepreneurship, 59; importance of, 51–2; migrant labour, 55, 223; Mondragon cooperative, 217; strikes, 137; unemployment, 51, 182–4, 200; women's work in neoliberal era, 59, 101, 214–15
World Bank, 101
Wright, Erik Olin, 212, 216–17, 218

Young, Marion, 187–8

Zerilli, Linda, 25, 99, 107–8, 113–18, 123, 126–30
Ziarek, Ewa, 80, 110
Žižek, Slavoj, 140, 145, 151, 157–9